EIGHTEENTH-CENTURY FICTION
AND THE LAW OF PROPERTY

In *Eighteenth-Century Fiction and the Law of Property*, Wolfram Schmidgen draws on legal and economic writings to analyze the descriptions of houses, landscapes, and commodities in eighteenth-century fiction. His study argues that such descriptions are important to the British imagination of community. By making visible what it means to own something, they illuminate how competing concepts of property define the boundaries of the individual, of social community, and of political systems. In this way Schmidgen recovers description as a major feature of eighteenth-century prose, and he makes his case across a wide range of authors, including Daniel Defoe, Henry Fielding, William Blackstone, Adam Smith, and Ann Radcliffe. The book's most incisive theoretical contribution lies in its careful insistence on the unity of the human and the material: in Schmidgen's argument persons and things are inescapably entangled. This approach produces fresh insights into the relationship between law, literature, and economics.

WOLFRAM SCHMIDGEN is Assistant Professor at Washington University, St. Louis. His work has been published in *ELH*, *Eighteenth-Century Studies*, *Journal of British Studies*, and *Studies in the Novel*.

EIGHTEENTH-CENTURY FICTION AND THE LAW OF PROPERTY

WOLFRAM SCHMIDGEN

Washington University in St. Louis

CAMBRIDGE
UNIVERSITY PRESS

PUBLISHED BY THE PRESS SYNDICATE OF THE UNIVERSITY OF CAMBRIDGE
The Pitt Building, Trumpington Street, Cambridge, United Kingdom

CAMBRIDGE UNIVERSITY PRESS
The Edinburgh Building, Cambridge CB2 2RU, UK
40 West 20th Street, New York, NY 10011-4211, USA
477 Williamstown Road, Port Melbourne, VIC 3207, Australia
Ruiz de Alarcón 13, 28014 Madrid, Spain
Dock House, The Waterfront, Cape Town 8001, South Africa

http://www.cambridge.org

First published 2002

Printed in the United Kingdom at the University Press, Cambridge

Typeface Baskerville Monotype 11/12.5 pt   *System* LaTeX 2_ε [TB]

A catalogue record for this book is available from the British Library

ISBN 0 521 81702 1 hardback

Für meine Eltern

Contents

Acknowledgments

I would like to thank three outstanding scholars whose work and advice have been central to what this book is trying to do. Without Jim Chandler's patience and suggestiveness, Tom Mitchell's insistent clarity, and Paul Hunter's sense of what needed to be done next, much would have been written and argued, but without the same degree of critical reflexiveness. Reflecting the great institution they work for, all three have been impossibly demanding and impossibly generous. Jim's contribution deserves special emphasis. The things I've learnt from him are beyond counting or accounting.

Many friends and colleagues have provided additional support in this endeavor. I should like to thank the following for the sense of belonging they have given me along the way: John Bozaan, Fiona Becket, Ben Bönniger, Shoshannah Cohen, David Fairer, Christa Fischbach, Denis Flannery, Patricia DeMarco, Kristin Hammett, Tracy Hargreaves, Michele Healy, Bob Hellenga, Virginia Hellenga, Vivien Jones, Nance Klehm, Ethan Knapp, Tom Krise, Andrew McRae, Audrey Petty, Henning Schmidgen, John Whale, and David Wright.

Two anonymous readers for Cambridge University Press offered helpful comments on the script; thanks to both of them. Linda Bree, my editor, has been supportive throughout, and her attentive cooperation has eased the transition from manuscript to book. An earlier version of Chapter Six appeared in *Studies in the Novel*, and I would like to thank the editor for the permission to reprint. The first section of Chapter Four appeared, in slightly different shape, in *Eighteenth-Century Studies*, and two pages of material from Chapter Three have appeared in *ELH*.

The final stages in the writing of this book took place in St. Louis, in the company of Beth Landers. She has made everything new.

Introduction

This book examines how the eighteenth-century novel, along with legal, economic, and aesthetic texts, represents the relationship between persons and things. It contends that this relationship is dynamic and that its complexities have escaped commentators on eighteenth-century culture, too many of whom have relied on simplifying distinctions between the human and the material, mobility and immobility, body and space. A remarkable amount of cultural work has gone into linking persons and things, yet much of it has escaped critical scrutiny. In this book I argue that we can recover essential elements of such cultural work by focusing on an aspect of eighteenth-century fiction that has not received much attention: the description of material reality. My argument rests on the basic Marxist assumption that the social, political, and psychological structures of a community are shaped by the interaction between human and material spheres, but it insists that such interactions are not exclusively defined by the economic. They are molded as well by cultural forces, and I show that the descriptive association of persons and things plays a critical role in exploring and exposing the limits of communal forms abroad, in the far reaches of empire, and in the contested union of Great Britain itself. Eighteenth-century Britain is an important case for such an argument because it reveals the persistence and permutations of a communal imagination that closely aligns persons and things. For reasons that will gradually become clearer, the differentiation between human imagination and material causality that became pervasive in subsequent periods is still marginal at this time. Communities of persons and things in eighteenth-century Britain are on the whole characterized by permeable boundaries, by a sense of open traffic across human and material zones. Only very gradually, and against considerable resistance, are these boundaries delineated.

This book is about this process. Using community as an overarching concept, it wants to grasp the history of objectification as a more complex and varied process than it has traditionally been considered. While I subscribe to Georg Lukács's belief that "the history of the cease-less transformation of the forms of objectivity" is absolutely central to the understanding of human existence, I have always been puzzled by the reluctance of Marxist critics to consider in greater detail the struggles, twists, defeats, and regressions that shape the history of objectification.[1] Within traditional and nontraditional Marxist criticism, most energy has been spent on describing the total victory of capitalist commodification. This has promoted some questionable idealizations, which have blunted the historical specificity of categories such as "reification," "objectifica-tion," or "fetishism." Lukács himself (and after him Theodor Adorno, Lucien Goldmann, and Fredric Jameson) has tended to idealize the precapitalist commodity as an "organic-irrational, qualitatively condi-tioned unity" whose "*économie naturelle*" (to quote Goldmann) is vividly contradicted by the depraved capitalist commodity, a fragmented, alien structure deriving from a rationalist world of pure quantification.[2] Only slightly exaggerated here, such polarization tends to turn the history of objectification into a value-laden conflict between the good and the bad commodity, between humanist use value and dehumanizing exchange value.[3] Things, however, are not in reality that straightforward, and the readings I offer here try to be as responsive as possible to the dialectic complexities of what I see as a richly textured process of objectification that lacks obvious heroes or villains. I am assisted in this attempt by the transitional nature of Britain's development, its peculiar ability to foster complicated alliances between residual and emergent socio-economic forces. What eighteenth-century Britain allows us to see is the remark-able extent to which the forces of objectification are involved in a last-ing, deeply ambiguous struggle to alter the traditional communal forms embodied in landed property.

My argument reinforces J. G. A. Pocock's seminal work on property, community, and personality in two respects. Like Pocock, I do not think there is much evidence to diagnose a triumph of liberal individualism before the late eighteenth and early nineteenth centuries. And like him I recognize the endurance of landed property as a dominant paradigm of social and political community. I disagree, however, when Pocock insists that civic humanism (for him the central expression of land's moral and political superiority) is exempt from the conduct of "human relations . . . through the mediation of things."[4] Civic humanism cannot be rigorously distinguished, within the concrete context of eighteenth-century debate, from philosophically less self-conscious notions of landed property as a communal ground. It overlaps with actual, remaining feudal structures – and it has to if Pocock wants to validate his claim for civic humanism's wide significance.[5] What follows should be obvious: any act of grounding liberty and virtue in the possession of land relies on a materialist logic and can be studied within the legal framework of ownership as instituting a socially and psychologically formative link between persons and things. This is what Pocock denies and I strongly disagree with this denial.

Alongside this philosophical disagreement I wish to place another, more concretely historical point of differentiation. Pocock argues that the initial encounter between mobile and immobile forms of property in the late seventeenth and early eighteenth centuries quickly establishes opposite camps that henceforth engage in ideological battle. I can see how this may hold true for the arena of political debate, but the boundary between mobile and immobile forms of property is not that stable. In fact, it is in constant flux. If a differentiation eventually works itself out, it is only to be swallowed up again at the end of the century by a full reification of both mobile and immobile forms of property. In Pocock mobility and immobility tend to resemble disembodied discursive agents whose main concern is to win the debate. I hope to show not only a more fundamental interdependence of these two forces, but the existence of distinct hybrids that complicate the picture – forms of mobile property, for example, that behave in some respects like immobile property. These forces do not confine their activity to the sphere of discursive contest, and I will try to capture their participation in a transformative struggle with the communal forms of eighteenth-century society. To intervene in this way in Pocock's well-honed argument points to the difference between a history of political discourse and a literary criticism that is infused with a sense of literature's special figurative potential, a potential that allows it to go beyond the discursive statement of arguments and ideas. Discursive statement can, of course, draw on figurative language, but it is literature's – even eighteenth-century literature's – privilege to produce more integrated and more concrete representations of practice. In the following analyses I am interested in the constitution of ideas about community, but I am absorbed by the ways in which the novel figures the limits of community. It is through literature's extensive realm of figurative possibility that I will try to open a wider perspective on the problem of property, community, and objectification.

I have become increasingly conscious in recent years of how my recovery of more involved and unstable person-thing scenarios in eighteenth-century British culture speaks to our present cultural and historical moment. My study contributes to the growing recognition of a significant historical kinship between our freshly globalizing, late capitalist, postmodern world and the eighteenth century. Such recognition has manifested itself most clearly in the now undisputed claim that the eighteenth century marks the beginnings of our own consumer culture, as the starting point of the massive commodification and boundless circulation of things that we face under global capitalism. Since it emerged into wider visibility, in Neil McKendrick's *Birth of a Consumer Society: The Commercialization of Eighteenth-Century England* (1982), this argument has generated an impressive array of new scholarship.[6] Yet the success with which the case for an eighteenth-century consumer revolution has been made necessitates, I believe, even broader claims for basic connections between the eighteenth century's and our world. When, after most of the work for this book was finished, I revisited Fredric Jameson's *Postmodernism: or, the Cultural Logic of Late Capitalism* (1991), I was struck by how some of the central terms of his analysis – the "waning of affection," the "depthlessness" of cultural forms, the renewed cultural and economic centrality of space – resonated in significant ways with my emphasis on the porousness of persons and things and their shifting identities as they cross different geographic, social, and economic spaces.[7] For a moment it seemed as if a "long" nineteenth century had emerged whose structures of feeling – organized around notions of depth, interiority, and time – constituted an extensive cultural middle ground that separated two more closely related periods, the eighteenth century and the late twentieth/early twenty-first centuries.

For all its imprecisions, this insight was more than an optical illusion. While I am primarily concerned with the distinct characteristics of eighteenth-century literature and culture, I also hope to nourish the vision of the broader historical relationship I have invoked. The advances made in biotechnology over the past twenty years or so; the resultant commodification of the human body; and the growing power of the computer, digitalization, and miniaturization have made the distinction between persons and things once again an issue of burning political, economic, and legal significance. Science scholars such as Donna Haraway and Bruno Latour have prominently argued that we need to account for the mixtures of the human and the material that increasingly govern our lives.[8] I share with them a sense of urgency and the search for a language to represent these hybrid entities. It seems to me, however, that Haraway and Latour underestimate the conceptual and imaginative resources on offer in eighteenth-century Britain. When Latour suggests that the "enlightenment" separates the social from the natural and thereby excludes things from political representation while persons become its sole object, he overlooks how deeply things in eighteenth-century Britain were involved in processes of representation. As late as 1792 Thomas Paine, for example, could be seen to clarify the distinction between persons and things in matters of political representation. Only after drastic political reforms, he argued, would "the right of every man ... be the same, whether he lives in a city, a town or a village. The custom of attaching rights to *place*, or in other words, to inanimate matter, instead of to the *person*, independently of place, is too absurd to make any part of a rational argument."[9] In the British constitution, Paine emphasizes, things have rights, and it is the rights of things that limit and alter the rights of people. Paine's analysis points to a characteristic aspect of the construction of community in eighteenth-century Britain, and it forcibly reminds us that even in the so-called "enlightened" eighteenth century things have the power to occupy the position we are today used to reserving for human agents.

Latour contends that "we possess hundreds of myths describing the way subjects . . . construct the object," but lack accounts of "how objects construct subjects."[10] He is only half-right. In eighteenth-century Britain at least, the political and social functions of property and place indicate a rich mine for stories about how objects constitute subjects. This book wants to access this mine by probing fictional descriptions for the agency of nonhuman actors. It wants to show that Latour's slogan, "we have never been modern," has particular applicability to a community such as Britain, where modernization is mediated by premodern communal forms – by mixtures of persons and things.

If I hope to extend in this way the emergent kinship between our present and the eighteenth century, I also wish to correct a tendency that has appeared alongside this kinship. In the current excitement over a contemporary relevance that eighteenth-century literary scholars have not enjoyed for a while, the danger of erasing historical difference is acute. By emphasizing the intricate persistence of premodern communal forms in the eighteenth century, I wish to cultivate an appropriate sense of historical strangeness and secure a mediated relationship between the "then" and the "now." The appearance of nineteenth-century structures of feeling as a middle ground might make more immediate identifications tempting, but I wish to insist on a more explicit situatedness. We need the strangeness of the eighteenth century as much as its increasing familiarity. Needless to say, I cannot within the parameters of this book undertake the work of comparing past and present person-thing communities, but the following chapters will offer specific insights into how early modern cultures imagined those mixtures, hybridities, and marginal spaces that Haraway and Latour describe for today's technological culture.

CHAPTER ONE

Communal form and the transitional culture of the eighteenth-century novel

Landed property must be a central focus in any study of the construction of community in eighteenth-century Britain. Although the advances in domestic manufacture and foreign trade in the second half of the eighteenth century tend to stand out most in accounts of the rise of industrialism, these advances were more than matched by the significant growth of agricultural productivity in the period.[1] In addition to its crucial economic role, landed property remained, virtually undisputed until the end of the century, Britain's dominant social, political, and ideological paradigm.[2] The rapid expansion of movable forms of property in the eighteenth century – commodities, stocks, credit – challenged the real and ideological dominance of immovable property, but the rapidity with which movables spread did not result in a quick or fundamental transformation of the established world of immovables. Even Adam Smith, who considered the wide distribution of increasingly various and refined commodities a crucial measure of the difference between "civilized" and "savage" societies, in the end projected a national economy that historically emerged from the gains made on the landed estate and continued to be grounded in agriculture, which for Smith represented a privileged figure of productivity and secure wealth.[3] Landed property was too deeply entrenched, imaginatively and in fact, to be run over by what we have come to recognize, with good reason, as the "commercialization of eighteenth-century England."[4]

The combative language I have used here is, of course, questionable on a more fundamental level. While many eighteenth-century commentators painted conflictive scenarios in which movable and immovable forms of property face each other as opponents – the one corrupting and fleeting, the other virtuous and stable – a more flexible perspective which recognizes the essential connection between all forms of property makes greater conceptual and historical sense. This book investigates the relationship between persons and things under the assumption that "things" include movables as well as immovables, and that the boundary between "persons" and "things" is constantly redrawn. As the literature of the period reveals and as subsequent chapters will show, commodities can be immovable, land can be movable, persons can be viewed as things, things can assume human intentionality and, like human beings, they can have rights. I view the person-thing relationship as a complex tangle whose various forms and shapes emerge from distinct historical situations. I foreground property because the possessive is one of the essential modes by which we conceptualize and shape our relationship to things; in eighteenth-century Britain it vividly draws together social, cultural, political, and economic forces. To understand the depth of property's influence on British culture, however, one has to look first to landed property. It is here that the most sophisticated conceptual work was done – in law and political economy – and it is here that the most significant literary interventions took place, in that new popular medium, the novel. In the pages that follow, landed property will not feature as the curious remnant of an older world, but as the most characteristic figure of eighteenth-century Britain's long history of objectification. The evidence for its centrality is extensive, and I wish to touch here only on the areas of commerce, legislature, and constitution.

England's most prestigious and significant body of legal learning, the common law, was so exclusively concerned with the seemingly endless ways of holding and conveying property that a majority of the legal conflicts arising out of the eighteenth century's new commercial realities had to be adjudicated at the Court of Chancery, a court of equity that considered cases that could not be settled under common law.[5] It is symptomatic in this regard that one of the hallowed texts of the common law tradition, William Blackstone's *Commentaries on the Laws of England* (1765–69), had virtually nothing to say on the law of contract, the area of law whose fundamental commercial significance made it the dominant paradigm of nineteenth-century law.[6] Common lawyers and the environment of common law were not exactly congenial to the mental and cultural habits of the new commercial classes. While the predictive dimensions of trade and stockmarket fostered habits that were increasingly future-oriented, common lawyers continued to consider not the most recent but the oldest precedent as possessing the greatest authority.[7] If their procedures obliged them to look into the past to authorize present practice, common lawyers' relationship to the future was shaped by the stable transmission of current possessions. For them, the "mortemain," the "dead hand" of property conveyance, not the "invisible hand" of an interdependent market ensured future prosperity. Merchants and stockjobbers, meanwhile, dealt almost exclusively in a dynamic future whose profitable manipulation depended on the enforceability of contracts.

Even so, the authority of immovable property remained undisputed and the aristocracy and gentry were able to borrow large amounts of money on land that rarely functioned as a genuine security. As the equity of redemption illustrates, it was virtually impossible for moneylenders to recover money by forcing the sale of the land it was loaned on. Judges who felt that landed property had to be protected from the contractual obligations incurred by borrowing ruled overwhelmingly in favor of landowners, a pattern that was crucial in preserving and increasing the economic importance of land.[8] Protection was also forthcoming from the criminal law, which expanded exponentially between 1688 and 1820, adding more than 150 capital statutes to its books.[9] Almost all of these laws concerned offenses against property, including the notorious Black Act.[10] Their formulation and administration were largely in the hands of property owners who benefited from the fact that parliamentary representation and public office were tied to "the favourite safeguard of the age, the property qualification."[11] And because of primogeniture, coverture, and the restrictions that applied to their independent possession of things, women were automatically excluded from most of these aspects of public life.[12]

Cutting across the considerable ideological differences between common and natural law, concepts of property were central as well to defining the origins of society, the legitimacy of government, and the English constitution. This ideological function was strengthened by the successful Protestant settlement of 1689, which displaced strict genealogy and enthroned property rights. As the debate over the Bill of Rights shows, the limitation of the succession was argued largely in analogy to property law, and in the early eighteenth century even Tories began to be swayed by the argument that kings hold their crown by the same legal right as subjects their estate.[13] The developments of the seventeenth century sealed the final ascent of common law as the dominant national law and installed the language of property at the heart of politics. This heritage made it virtually impossible to talk about the legitimacy of government without mentioning property rights.[14] The first broad challenge to property's ideological dominance arrived somewhat belatedly in the heated political debates of the 1790s. But even in the nineteenth century, and notwithstanding successful parliamentary reforms, F. W. Maitland was forced to exclaim that "our whole constitutional law seems at times to be but an appendix to the law of real property."[15] While the ideological, social, and political force of landed property declined in the nineteenth century, the study of English law continued to depend on a firm knowledge of land law. It is safe to say that eighteenth-century Britain had not yet undergone the "social division of labour" by which Ernest Gellner characterizes the modern separation of state, culture, and society.[16] Despite attacks by political theorists such as Thomas Paine, eighteenth-century government and society were still intertwined, and it was landed property that kept them together by linking private right and public legitimacy, local and national government, and legislature, jurisdiction, and representation.[17] In Britain the eventual separation of state and society and the emergence of modern forms of national community are tied to the gradual removal of landed property from its social, political, and ideological functions, its demotion from its elevated position as a form of property with distinct civic capacities. If, for most of the eighteenth century, landed property is able to set the terms for the relationship of persons and things and thus for more comprehensive communal patterns, it finally loses that ability only when the distinction from movable property vanishes – at the point when both movable and immovable property have been fully reified.

The literary case studies I have assembled here show how vital the novel's contributions to this protracted, complex process of reification were. The selection of texts I present is limited – I offer extended readings of novels by Daniel Defoe, Henry Fielding, Ann Radcliffe, and Sir Walter Scott and briefer analyses of Samuel Richardson, Henry Mackenzie, and Laurence Sterne – but my approach should produce specific insights even over the long period that these texts inhabit. In offering selected vertical probes across this period, I wish to lay open the various practices – legal, aesthetic, economic – appropriated by these novels to fashion their textual worlds, and I hope to gain in cultural specificity what I may lose in literary-historical coverage. My goal is to provide as clear a sense as possible of how exactly these texts intervene in their cultural environment: what these novels make us see about property and community, and how. If performed at the right angle and in sufficient depth, these probes should also open up "horizontal" narrative connections between the different case studies they yield. Yet the concreteness of these connections will ultimately depend on the extent to which I shall be able to make good my claim that a profound, ongoing cultural dialogue about property is shaping the communal imagination of eighteenth-century Britain.

One of the larger claims I can make confidently even at this point is that the novels I have chosen – many of them safely within the now accepted canon – have not been appreciated enough for the intensity and persistence of their concern with the relation between persons and things. The reasons for this are numerous and I will address the reluctance of literary critics to examine the novel's preoccupations in this area in a moment. I simply wish to underline here that the eighteenth-century novel's continued and sometimes laborious rehearsal of plot lines that turn on issues of property – dramas of lost and found heirs, of the right succession, the propriety of ownership, and of the "proper" marriage abound – should not be seen as a failure to address vital social and political issues. Questions of property are at the center of eighteenth-century culture and they define the community of husband and wife as much as the national community represented in parliament and the social community that "places" people in distinct ranks. It is thus not surprising that the semantic link between "plot" (signifying "a series of events," "a small piece of ground," a "ground plan") and "property" should be especially visible in eighteenth-century narratives. The novel's engagement with "groundedness," in particular, will occupy this study in a number of ways.

The prominence of such concerns in the modern genre of the novel is really a sign of the extent to which the culture of property in eighteenth-century Britain managed to retain a vital tie to feudal institutions, institutions that helped foster the impression of a vast continuity linking the centuries and that influenced Britain's public and private life well into the Victorian period.[18] Immune to the twin forces of modern revolution and constitutionalism, eighteenth-century England was, in Tom Nairn's phrase, a "transitional" society whose negotiation of residual feudalism and emergent modernity reached no convulsive conclusion. Without a clear socio-cultural dominant, England's negotiation of residual and emergent forces, of older and more modern forms of property, was itself dominant. "More than any other society," Nairn writes, England "established the transition from the conditions of later feudalism to those of modernity . . . Neither feudal nor modern, it remained obstinately and successfully intermediate."[19] Nairn has not been alone in arguing for such transitionalism, and David McNally, R. S. Neale, and Raymond Williams have offered similar arguments (one has to wonder, indeed, whether Williams's influential distinction of emergent, dominant, and residual forces is not itself a specific response to British transitionalism).[20] Drawing on these historians and critics, I want to argue that the notion

of a transitional eighteenth century is crucial to understanding the pro-
file of possibilities exploited by the novel to articulate its communities of
persons and things. Such transitionalism should contribute something to
explaining, for example, why romance had such a powerful resurgence
in the second half of the eighteenth century, and why it could over-
throw what many critics saw as the cultural and literary gains made by
Defoe, Fielding, and Richardson. And it should contribute something
to the question of why the Gothic novel, with its cultivation of feudal
fear, should become, in an age of revolution and enlightenment, a genre
of delirious popularity. Generic atavisms such as these, it seems to me,
emerge from British culture's ingrained ability – fostered by the persistence of property – to see the present in close vicinity to the past, to
link even its turbulent commercialism to an always receding but never
disappearing feudal past. It would take, indeed, writers from Ireland or
Scotland such as Maria Edgeworth or Sir Walter Scott who were exposed
to more drastic historical changes and who possessed an acute sense of
cultural conflict, to produce novels that placed the feudal heritage beyond reach and enshrined it as a past that has come to an end. But even
then, the work of assigning the past to a distinct place in history activates
in someone like Scott a tremendous nostalgia for possessive modes of
community. Here, too, we see a continuous transformation rather than
abrupt departures: the communal function of landed property remains
a constant focus for the eighteenth-century novel, whose exploration of
new commercial and psychological possibilities is always in dialogue with
older conceptions of identity and wealth.

    Britain's expansive transitionalism raises some problems for the most
influential account of modern communal forms of the past twenty years,
Benedict Anderson's *Imagined Communities: Reflections on the Origin and Spread
of Nationalism* (1983). Anderson sees the appearance of modern communal
forms and the imaginative procedures that shape them as a sudden convergence, a "spontaneous distillation of a complex 'crossing' of discrete
historical forces."[21] As a general statement of the phenomenon under
study, Anderson's formulation would seem to be at odds with my observations on eighteenth-century culture. Incomplete though they have
been, these observations suggest that the emergence of modern communal forms in Britain must have been an indecisive and partial event.
The obdurate persistence of landed property as the ultimate ground of
social and political community indicates that the development of modern communal forms in Britain could hardly have been spontaneous.
This becomes even more obvious once we consider the novel, which is

given central place by Anderson for developing the imaginative procedures requisite for achieving a more abstract sense of community that
cuts across concretely localized regions. Anderson sees the novel as projecting the "'homogeneous empty time'" needed for the development
of modern communal forms, but his account of such projection implicitly discounts the eighteenth-century literary tradition.[22] For it is only in
the nineteenth century, after the period Anderson considers critical for
the birth of the modern nation, that the British novel begins to display
confidence in the modality of the "meanwhile" (the term Anderson uses
to characterize the complex multilevel plots he sees as essential in the
production of time as a contentless, neutral dimension). Consequently,
Anderson sounds as if it is only modern communal forms that require
the imaginative work of the novel and as if the rise of the novel coincides
with the rise of the modern nation state – which is patently not the case in
Britain. I want to argue that the novel in Britain, for a much longer time
than Anderson is willing to accept, figures and refigures traditionalist
communal forms, but without coming very close to producing a sense
of empty homogeneous time by the end of the eighteenth century. The
novel is certainly moving toward such a sense of time, but for most of
the century the more absorbing spectacle is not the literary construction
of the new, but the recomposition of the old communal model. And this
work of recomposition does not restrict itself to the domain of time alone.

However suggestive in many ways, Anderson's privileging of time in his
account of modern communal forms is finally limiting – especially when
we consider that for most of the eighteenth century the spatial figure of
the landed estate set the parameters for the communal imagination. In
fact, much may be said for emphasizing space rather than time in considering the eighteenth-century communal imagination, but it would be
a mistake simply to switch categories – no matter how tempting that
might be, given the recent resurgence of space as a term of historical and
cultural analysis.[23] We actually need a more comprehensive approach
to the communal imagination, an approach that moves us beyond the
problematic stress on homogeneous time and sudden convergence. If
the novel eventually begins to figure time as a neutral framework that
relativizes the locally grounded order of landed property, this development needs to be situated within the larger relational web of time, space,
and practice that I consider crucial to understanding communal forms.
Anthony Giddens has made much of such relationality in his account of
modernity, and some of his claims provide guideposts for my discussion.
In *The Consequences of Modernity* (1990) Giddens suggests that all social

community rests on a more or less complex, more or less mediated relation of time, space, and practice. The modernization of social relations in Western Europe begins, Giddens argues, in the seventeenth century and it involves three central mechanisms: the separation of time and space and their emergence as "contentless dimensions" that exist apart from social life; the development of what he calls "disembedding mechanisms" that " 'lift out' social activity from localized contexts"; and the "reflexive appropriation of knowledge," by which he means the "production of systematic knowledge about social life."[24] These three interlocking mechanisms present the process of modernization as a basic shift in the relationship between time, space, and practice.

While Giddens is not interested in questions of community as such, his model puts the emphasis where it should be: on relationships. It avoids the danger of isolating time or space and replicating what appears to be their current existence as separate spheres. Because it foregrounds flexible relationships, Giddens's model offers better access to what I see as the gradual establishment of more modern communal forms; it will enable a more attentive tracing of the subtle shifts, partial disturbances, and temporary realignments effected by the novel's imagined communities. But instead of considering these issues in the abstract, I would like to move on to a more concrete discussion of the type of immobile property that best represents the traditionalist communal form with which the novel interacts.

I

If there is one type of landed property that occupies, in one way or another, all the novels I examine in detail, it is the manorial estate. Recognized for some time as an idealizing trope of feudalism and baronial plenitude in seventeenth-century poetry, the manor also has an importance for the history of the novel that has not been registered.[25] In texts as diverse as *Robinson Crusoe* (1709), *Tom Jones* (1749), *A Sicilian Romance* (1790), and *Waverley* (1814), to name only the novels that concern me most closely here, the manor is central. In them the seventeenth-century manor becomes a deeply contested figure; it haunts these texts as inescapable ground, ideal state, delusive chimera, and sentimental image. The manor was not the dominant form of landholding in eighteenth-century Britain, and already in 1696 Samuel Carter estimated that only about a third of all British landed property was manorial.[26] Even if one adds E. P. Thompson's remark that one should not merely count the acres in

estimating the importance of the manor, but consider also the often considerable number of farmers who made a living on the basis of customary
tenures, manorial landholdings were not socio-economically dominant
in the eighteenth century.[27] But if the manor as an actual community was
on the decline in the seventeenth and eighteenth centuries, its ideological
and imaginative value continued to be extremely high throughout this
period.

Such value can be measured not only by the emerging tradition of the
country house poem in the seventeenth century, but also – as befits an age
increasingly self-conscious about the communal function of property – by
the growing legal visibility of the manor. The publication in 1641 of
Edward Coke's *The Compleate Copy-Holder, Wherein Is Contained a Learned
Discourse of the Antiquity and Nature of Manors and Copy-Holds*, is the central event in the legal recognition of the manor as a distinct communal
form.[28] Because of its general importance for what I shall be doing in the
following chapters, it is necessary to look at Coke's text in some detail.
To describe "the very forme of Manors, which is observed amongst us
at this present houre" is Coke's declared goal.[29] In a first allusion to the
political dimensions of his legal discourse, Coke presents the manor as a
"little common weale" (52) whose "essential parts" have been in continuous existence from Saxon times to the seventeenth century (8). The two
"material causes" of the manor are "Demesnes and Services," by which
Coke refers to the manorial integration of land and social practice. He
devotes a considerable part of his treatise to delineating what he prefers to
call the "jurisdictions" or "fruits of a Manor" (22), those practices that belong to or grow out of the manorial estate. Among these he lists the lord's
privilege of appointing a guardian for heirs who are too young to accept
responsibility for the lands they inherit, or the payment of "reliefe," a
certain sum of money that becomes due when a freeholder is at full age at
the death of his ancestor (24, 30). To understand the significance of these
and similar manorial practices, it is important to recognize what Coke's
preferred metaphor of the "fruits" of the manor tries to make clear: that
such practices are not rooted in the person of the owner, but in the land
and the kind of tenure by which it is held. A particularly striking illus-
tration of the way in which manorial land concretely embodies certain
powers and rights is provided by the regulations regarding forfeiture. "If
a Horse striketh his Keeper," Coke explains, "and killeth him: or if a man
driveth his Cart, and seeking to redresse it, falleth, and the Cart wheele
running over him, presseth him to death," "then immediately that thing
which is the cause of that untimely death, becometh forfeited unto the

Lord" (45). Though not every manor possesses such duties, the example Coke offers here makes tangible the sense in which the territory of the manor has itself distinct rights incorporated into it, rights that, in this case, secure certain movable possessions of the dead against the claims of their relatives. These rights are, indeed, self-activating. As Coke's stress on the moment of death indicates – "*then immediately*" forfeiture takes place – no legal action needs to be brought to ensure forfeiture of these goods. No human agency is necessary, and it is the land itself that seems to be capable of legal action, preempting all other claims. It is in contexts such as these that Blackstone's decision to call one of his four volumes on the laws of England *Of the Rights of Things* suddenly makes striking sense.

This complex unity of practice and land, of right and territory, however, does not come about without the intervention of a third factor that Coke distinguishes as "the efficient cause of a Manor," and that cause is time. In what must be the key passage of the entire text, Coke rises to the challenge of capturing this third factor as follows:

The efficient cause of a Manor is expressed in these words, of long continuance, for indeede time is the mother, or rather the nurse of manors; time is the soule that giveth life unto every Manor, without which a Manor decayeth and dyeth, for tis not the two materiall causes of a Manor, but the efficient cause (knitting and uniting together those two materiall causes) that maketh a Manor. Hence it is that the King himselfe cannot create a perfect Manor at this day, for such things as receive their perfection by the continuance of time, come not within the compasse of a Kings Prerogative. (52)

Time itself, a traditionalist time of "long continuance," joins the manor's two material causes, land and practice. It is the manor's venerable origin, dating back to the ancient liberties of Saxon England, that for Coke has made its union of practice and land as inextricable as it is irresistible. Coke's "little common weal" shows here its political face. In Coke's vision the manor reaches right back into England's ancient constitution, and it is such rootedness in a time before time that allows the manor to resist the prerogative of the king. And while manors can no longer be created, not even by the king himself, such temporal integrity is matched by considerable spatial fixity: manors cannot be enlarged (54–55), and can be divided only in a way that preserves the combination of demesne and service in each of the newly created units (61). The manor is thus a communal form in which the operation of a continuous, uninterrupted time has integrated land and practice to such an extent that they cannot be separated. So complex and gradual is this process, in fact, that it can never be recreated by deliberate human action. In this sense the manor is a self-sufficient, self-shaping entity whose political independence hinges on the extent to which time has "knitted together" a particular title to land with a recognizable set of practices. We are dealing with a communal form, then, in which time, space, and practice are closely interrelated. Certainly, time and space are not the "contentless dimensions" Giddens suggests they become in modern society. On the contrary: if manorial space concretely embodies specific practices and thus possesses distinct qualities, then manorial time is also a qualitative, not a quantitative, force. As Coke's invocation of time as "mother" and "nurse" suggests, time has powers of its own and, as the force that joins land and practice, it does not function as a neutral frame that measures human activity, but concretely participates in it.

Coke's exposition may so far have seemed to favor baronial power (even as he carefully locates such power in the manor, not the baron), but that is only one part of his agenda, and probably not the most important one. Coke's political strategy comes out clearly in his attempt to expand the ranks of privileged manorial tenants by suggesting that copyholders are *de facto* freeholders, and thus part of that important group of landholders who were seen to ensure British liberty because of their independence from baronial interference and their right to elect members of parliament.[30] This is a significant move because the title of copyhold – originally considered an inferior tenure because of the base services attached to it – rests on custom, and custom has a special relationship to time and to common law, and thus to the ancient rights and liberties of the English people Coke wants to defend against the encroaching Stuarts. Customs are, indeed, "defined to be a Law, or Right not written, which being established by long use, and the consent of our Ancestors, hath beene, and is daily practised" (68). This formulation recalls the emphasis Coke had laid on "long continuance of time" in defining the efficient cause of the manor, and he does, in fact, closely associate the manor with custom, even in the long central passage I have already begun to quote. He there goes on to state that the king cannot "create any new custome" and then argues that this untouchability of immemorial custom ultimately lies behind the king's inability to "create a perfect Manor at this day" (53). Custom bolsters both the independence of the manor from royal prerogative and the independence of copyholders from manorial lords, a balancing act that shows how Coke utilizes custom as a

protective shield to prevent hierarchical power relationships from becoming oppressive.

Customs can be an effective shield because they embody a particularly
close union between practice, land, and law. Antiquarian Thomas Blount
tells us, for example, that "by the Custom of Warham in the County of
Dorset, both Males and Females have a right equally in the partition of
Lands and Tenements . . . And is so unusuall a Custom, that perhaps it
may be hard to find the like elsewhere in England."[31] The local custom
has here the power to defeat rules of primogeniture that otherwise govern
all of England. It is with arrangements like this in mind that we need to
approach expressions such as Samuel Carter's that "custom lies upon the
land," that it "binds the land," or, to turn to Matthew Hale, that customs
are "fix'd to the Land."[32] Coke himself suggests such an irresistibly close
relationship between custom and land for the copyholder when he describes how "Costume . . . fixeth a Copyholder instantly in his land" (82).
I find all of these expressions symptomatic because they exhibit the tendency of manorial communities to blur the distinction between practice
and space, persons and things, human and material spheres.

In an already familiar pattern, custom's union with the land depends
on a specific relationship to time. Coke makes the essential point when he
states that "a Custome never extendeth to a thing newly created . . . what
things soever have their beginning, since the memory of man, Custome
maintains not" (75). The ultimate authority of custom lies in its immemorial nature, its source in a time before time. Blackstone draws out some
of the implications of Coke's statement when he addresses the validity of
custom at common law. To be legally valid, Blackstone argues, a custom
must "have been used so long, that the memory of man runneth not to
the contrary. So that if any one can shew the beginning of it, it is no good
custom . . . It must have been *continued.* Any interruption would cause a
temporary ceasing: the revival gives it a new beginning, which will be
within time of memory, and thereupon the custom will be void."[33] Quite
in keeping with the communal form of the manor outlined by Coke, custom "lies on the land" by virtue of being indistinguishable from the flow
of time. For a custom to be valid, time has to be unable to measure it. The
determination of the precise moment in which a certain custom began
immediately dispels its authority as a binding social pattern. We touch
here on the reflexivity of knowledge that Giddens notes as a modernizing mechanism. The inquiry into the precise circumstances that gave
rise to a certain custom would produce precisely the kind of systematic
knowledge of social life that customs have to elude in order to be binding.

A valid custom has to maintain a primary relationship with time; once it is separated from and appears within time, as a recognizable stage in an historical development, all validity is gone.[34]

The manor thus illuminates what it means to speak, with Giddens, of a premodern "embedding" of social relations in a localized context. Its integration of territory and social practice through length of time interrupts the reach of national customs and laws and disables the inquiry into precise origins. Social life in the manor remains tied to the present moment and the present location, both of which represent an unchanging, continuous existence. Such regionalism managed to survive into the eighteenth century in part because a genuine national legislation was still lacking. Parliament's growing power notwithstanding, statutes on poor relief, crime, and even taxation were largely reactive, tailored to particular regions, and quickly challenged when they contradicted local customs.[35] As the particularities of concrete places with their personalized power relations and distinctive social practices are not fully integrated into a more abstract, homogeneous national space and administrative apparatus, the differentiation between a generalized "space" and a particularized "place" remains incomplete. The issue of manorial jurisdictions, to which I turn now, underscores this. It has particular relevance for the construction of political community in eighteenth-century Britain.

In delineating his communal form, Coke finally adds one last essential ingredient, which he describes as the "causa sine qua non" of the manor: the baronial court or "Court Baron" (57). The owner of a manorial estate exercised, by virtue of his tenure, certain jurisdictional rights that could even include the power over the life and death of his tenants (an aspect of which novelists such as Radcliffe and Scott would make careful use, as we shall see). When Coke calls such jurisdictions the "chiefe prop and Pillar of a Manor" (57), he is broadening the manor's ability to resist intrusion from the outside, but he is also promoting the "feudal identification of government and property" that legal historians have recognized as a continuing influence on eighteenth-century ideas of right and government.[36] Even Daniel Defoe, typically viewed as the standard bearer of modern commerce and mobile property, was notably vocal when it came to this issue. In 1702 he compared feudal modes of government with present-day practices:

In former Days the Freehold gave a Right of Government to the Freeholder, and Vassalage and Villinage was deriv'd from this Right, that every Man who will live in my Land shall be my Servant; if he wont, let him go about his Business, and live somewhere else: And 'tis the same still in right reasoning. And I make no question that Property of Land is the best Title to Government in the World; and if the King was universal Landlord, he ought to be Universal Governour of Right, and the People so living on his Lands ought to obey him, or go off his Premises.[37]

Though the idea is several hundred years old, the possession of land continues to guarantee, in Defoe's eyes, governmental power. "There can be no Legal Power in England," he asserts in the same pamphlet, "but what has its Original in the Possessors; for Property is the Foundation of Power."[38] Although he suggests that the Commons "represent" the people, Defoe ultimately embraces the assumption, central to concepts of legitimacy at the time, that the assembled members of the two houses gain their powers because they literally represent the territory of Great Britain. That this legitimation of power originates in feudal systems of tenure is for Defoe no drawback; on the contrary, such continuity illustrates for him the general validity of the assumption that "Property of Land is the best Title to Government in the World." The "chiefe prop and Pillar" of the manor thus occupies a distinct place in eighteenth-century constitutional ideas. Obviously, the manor presents a less mediated version of the link between legal power and possession, but it ultimately draws on the same source of legitimacy that Defoe identifies for national government. Both rely on a primary association of land and law, the belief that the law originates in the possessive division of the soil. Noting the frequently spatial origin of legal concepts, Carl Schmitt has used the term "nomos" to refer to such a belief in the "groundedness" of social and political community.[39] The idea that the division of the soil produces and legitimizes a certain social and political order is central to the possessive imagination of community, and it is significant within not only a national but also a colonial context, as I will show in a sustained reading of *Robinson Crusoe*.

In emphasizing the manor's link to the culture of custom and regionalism, I have followed the lead of E. P. Thompson, whose *Customs in Common* (1993) highlights the same connection. Yet my intentions differ from his. Thompson is interested in the manor mainly because he wishes to document the resistance of "plebs" to "patricians," of a "rebellious traditional culture" to the gradual reification and homogenization of social life by the commercial and landed classes.[40] He pits common law as the instrument of these classes against custom, but he does not emphasize enough that the concept of custom itself is linked to the common law in a number of ways. As I have tried to argue, one of the reasons why the manor assumes fresh relevance in the eighteenth century is that, after the demise of the Stuarts and the constitutional rise of property as a paradigm of political community, it is able to embody basic constitutional realities of eighteenth-century Britain: the legitimation of legislative power through landed possession, the dominance of the local over the national, the importance of custom. These constitutional realities, however, fall under common law. Even if custom may challenge common law, it is common law that defines the validity of a custom. The conflict foregrounded by Thompson does not tell the whole story. Coke himself had already suggested that custom and common law were not at odds, and he appropriated their relationship to distribute power more evenly in a still hierarchical "common weale." I want to suggest that custom belongs to perhaps an equal extent to the culture of local, popular resistance and the ideology of the "culturally hegemonic" gentry, to use Thompson's term.[41] In many ways "plebs" and "patricians" both exploited the authority of established usage. This is illustrated rather strikingly for the patrician side when we consider that the common law's legitimacy was constructed through an appeal to its origins in customary culture, an appeal that became particularly urgent whenever common lawyers felt they had to defend their "unwritten" *lex non scripta* against competing systems, be they different national laws, civil law, statutory law, or utilitarian concepts of law.

Moreover, the reliance on precedent and case law, and the notion that common law is shaped by the actual decisions of judges, easily supported arguments that the common law itself was essentially customary in nature – not fixed in unchangeable forms but flexible and infinitely adaptable to circumstance and the changing practices of the nation. It is this line of argument that Hale made strong when he commented on the composite nature of English law later in the seventeenth century. Unlike Coke, who had a more developed sense of the purity of common law, Hale believed that it was characteristic of English law that "Use and Custom, and Judicial Decisions and Resolutions, and Acts of Parliament, tho' not now extant, might introduce some new Laws, and alter some Old, which we now take to be the very Common Law itself, tho' the Times and precise Periods of such Alterations are not explicitly or clearly known." This sense of a complex and untraceable intermixture of different aspects of law culminates in Hale's comparison of the common law to the "Argonauts Ship [that] was the same when it returned home, as it was when it went out, tho' in that long Voyage it had successive Amendments, and scarce came back with any of its former Materials."[42] As one of the oldest and most prestigious forms of tenure, the manorial estate with its accumulated usages and immemorial customs shares something with Hale's ship, a connection that Blackstone was to make more explicit when he decided to represent the common law by the figure of a manor house whose original shape had virtually disappeared under layers of continuous additions, alterations, and repairs. On the level of discursive practice, common law and custom are often impossible to separate, and I intend to put some pressure on the language of those who, like Blackstone, capitalized on the link between a fluid, localized social practice and the legitimacy of the law.

II

As actual communal reality, as historically specific expression of existent patterns of government, as concrete embodiment of traditionalist communal forms, and as ideological figure, the manor can thus be seen as a central *Gestalt* of Britain's propertied culture. The novel's interaction with this *Gestalt* includes an important thematic dimension, but its most intriguing work comes to bear on the manor's communal form – its grounding of social and political community in the division of the soil, its blurring of human and material spheres, and its overall integration of time with practice and space. This work on communal form finds a central focus in the novel's descriptive acts. It is in the description of landscapes, houses, and objects that I see the novel shift the relationship between persons and things, mobility and immobility, body and space, and it is here that it closely interacts with the groundedness and integration so characteristic of the manor's communal form. While eighteenth-century narratives turn almost inescapably on conflicts over property, descriptions bracket the distributive logic of plot (who gets what, when, why, how) and figure the relational patterns that link human and material spheres. They present a key to the novel's attempt at making visible the grounding of communal forms in possessive relationships.

My claim for the importance of description in the eighteenth-century novel goes against the grain of some well-established critical assumptions. In criticism of eighteenth-century literature, it is usually poetry and not fiction that is associated with description. The tradition of topographic poetry, graced by such prominent practitioners as John Denham, Ben Jonson, Andrew Marvell, Alexander Pope, and James Thomson, has always seemed more vital than prose description and has been the object of now classic studies by Earl Wasserman, John Barrell, James Turner, Anne Janowitz, and others.[43] The eighteenth-century novel has seemed by comparison firmly committed to narrative, with description as a negligible appendix.[44] Most critical thinking about prose description has instead focused on the nineteenth-century novel, whose so-called "realism" has been seen to go hand in hand with the rise of description. In Marxist criticism this distinction between eighteenth- and nineteenth-century fiction has been strengthened further by associating the descriptive with advanced modes of capitalist production. In his emotional "Narrate or Describe?" (1936) Georg Lukács, exercising the traditional Marxist suspicion of spatial structure, argues that the ascendance of descriptive over narrative modes in nineteenth-century fiction indicates "the domination of capitalist prose over the inner poetry of human experience."[45] For Lukács the reification of social relations by the industrial revolution is directly reflected in the dominance of description's immobilizing spatial monotony over the temporal, dynamic, and life-giving forces of narrative. In *History and Class Consciousness* (1923) he sketches the larger socio-economic context when he states that, under industrial capitalism, "time sheds its qualitative, variable, flowing character; it congeals into an exactly delimited, quantifiable continuum filled with quantifiable 'things' (the reified, mechanically objectified 'performance' of the worker, wholly separated from his total human personality); in short, it becomes space."[46] Lukács's critique of nineteenth-century fiction as promoting such spatialization of time by descriptively arresting narrative invokes a venerable prejudice of Western aesthetics according to which description always has to be held in check lest its pleasant, but empty, ornamental function undermine the quasi-organic unity of narrative. In this tradition narration and description relate to each other like "master and slave, leader and led, essential and accessory." As Michel Beaujour has shown, this hierarchical scenario in which description is always the illegitimate upstart has had a remarkable tendency to reproduce itself across different aesthetic and methodological contexts, from classicism to modernism, surrealism, and structuralism.[47]

Lukács's alarmist attitude, for example, can be rediscovered in Roland Barthes's important "The Reality Effect," which represents something of a structuralist companion piece to Lukács's Marxist account. In Barthes's analysis, Lukács's vitalist, anthropocentric vocabulary for narrative is replaced by a notion of structural traffic. "Description," Barthes observes, "is quite different [from narrative]: it has no predictive aspect; it is 'analogical', its structure being purely additive, and not incorporating that circuit of choices and alternatives which make a narration look like a vast traffic control center, provided with referential (and not merely discursive) temporality."[48] Barthes's contrast between narrative and description recognizes the former as a complex distributive center and limits the latter by granting it merely an additive, not a relational, function. In this way Barthes not only gives an impoverishing account of the descriptive function, but also seems to discount those heavily episodic, paratactic narratives that in the eighteenth century approximate to additive structures. The metaphor of the "traffic control center," at any rate, raises questions about its historical adequacy even for nineteenth-century narratives. Barthes's resistance to recognizing description as a relational mode finds its active fulfillment in his final explanation of the reality effect. The apparently "useless" or "superfluous" descriptive detail is redeemed by the creation of what Barthes calls "the referential illusion."[49] If the descriptive detail does not mean anything beyond its immediate reference, that is for Barthes precisely its most important function. For by seeming to denote directly the details of reality, without any further symbolic significance, descriptions create the appearance, in Fredric Jameson's words, of a "a sense of raw data existing objectively out there."[50] With this final twist the "scandalous" status of the useless descriptive detail – its apparent failure to participate in the work of signification – is resolved and description can now assume its limited function in the traffic center of narrative structure.

Barthes's take on description is one of the more extreme illustrations available for the impoverishing association of description with realism. The unfortunate concentration on realism and nineteenth-century fiction has made it difficult, indeed, to view prose description outside a referential paradigm. Even Jameson, whose brilliant analysis of description in Flaubert has influenced my own interpretive strategies, unblinkingly identifies the realistic novel with description and description with referentiality, an assumption presumably motivated by his enthusiastic reception of Lukács's "Describe or Narrate?"[51] While Jameson recognizes description as a relational medium, he nonetheless aligns it with reification, a sense of "the object so radically sundered from the subject that our language and symbolic systems can do no more than designate it from afar."[52] I do not dispute the validity of this reading (though I will argue that it needs to be moved back historically), but by presenting description as the characteristic feature of realism in the novel, Jameson reinforces the assumption that description is inherently tied to the referential illusion and arrives as a significant literary mode with the large-scale reification of social relations ushered in by the industrial revolution. In this way Jameson's attempt to combine structuralist and Marxist perspectives reproduces limiting parameters for the analysis of prose description.

I want to redraw this critical map by making the case that novelistic description is a crucial eighteenth-century mode because of the novel's profound engagement with Britain's culture of property and its distinctive modes of objectification. The descriptive is not automatically tied to a referential function that simply reifies social relations. Such a view ignores an entire landscape of variation and difference. The descriptive is instead a complex relational and predictive mode that intersects persons and things in different ways across historically varying legal, economic, epistemological, aesthetic, and political paradigms. From feudal, mercantile, and industrial modes of production, to the aesthetic of the visible, the invisible, the sublime, and the picturesque, to the modern nation and premodern communal forms, fictional descriptions engage the relation between the human and the material on a variety of fronts simultaneously. This variety can be grasped only by leaving behind description's association with realism and referentiality. Neither the actual correspondence of a "sign" with "reality" nor the illusion of such a correspondence will play a constitutive role in my analysis. Instead, I approach the descriptive in a constructivist spirit that recognizes it as a semi-independent medium with the ability to figure different versions of the world. My general assumption throughout this book will be that all forms of description, whether "realistic" or not, are privileged places for observing the literary figuration of social practice. They capture more immediately than other literary modes the relationship between human and material spheres, and in showing us this fundamental aspect of all social life they also reveal just how long and varied is the history of objectification.

I make such a strong case for description in part for strategic reasons. For even those critics who consider description a fictional mode that demands close critical attention frequently treat it as an epiphenomenon of narrative. Thus José Manuel Lopes, in his recent *Foregrounded Description in Prose Fiction: Five Cross-Literary Studies* (1995) sets out to redeem the descriptive act from its status as a "dispensable ornament of narration," but his opening move already indicates that description is bound to remain in the shadow of narrative. "I designate as background description," Lopes begins, "any descriptive material that does not seem to play a predominant narrative function; conversely, the term foregrounded description applies to all descriptive segments shown to have a more relevant

narrative role."[53] It should be clear at once that this does not at all redress the old claim about description's inferiority. It merely refines it by
distinguishing between worthy and unworthy descriptions on the basis
of the extent of their involvement with narrative (unsurprisingly, that
distinction is underwritten by Lopes's historical sense that descriptions
take on narrative importance only in the nineteenth century).[54]

One senses in Lopes's desire to classify description through narrative
the presence of Gerard Genette, whose influential argument on description as one of the "negative limits of narrative" is worth following in
some detail.[55] Genette makes clear right away that description is "quite
naturally *ancilla narrationis*, the ever-necessary, ever-submissive, never-
emancipated slave [of narrative]." Yet, curiously, he also suggests that
description is the more independent literary mode: "Description is more
indispensable than narration, since it is easier to describe without relating than it is to relate without describing."[56] Narrative cannot do without
description, but description can do without narrative. Or, to draw out
another implication, description is naturally the property of narrative,
but actually freely alienable. Genette exposes here why description has
traditionally been feared and kept under. Unless description is held in
check, we risk that it break free from the obligation to interact with the
human world of narrative. This danger may explain, in fact, Genette's
strange construction of slavery as something that comes "naturally" to
description. Why this should be the case remains unclear, and it seems
to me that Genette's unfortunate metaphor of "natural slavery" further
illustrates the apparently overwhelming need to control description, even
if that means casting narrative in the role of slaveholder. Genette cuts
short these disturbing and revelatory tensions by summing up: "the study
of the relations between the narrative and the descriptive amount . . . in
essence to a consideration of the diegetic functions of description, that
is to say, the role played by the descriptive passages or aspects in the
general economy of narrative."[57] After some rather anxious passages,
description is once again simply a property of narrative, an object of
human action.

I am not sure how keen I am to gain a reputation as the critic who
liberated description from narrative bondage, and I am not in any case
certain that this is a feasible undertaking. The difficulties Barthes, Lopes,
Genette, and others have encountered grow to some extent out of a
genuine problem concerning description's identity. As Genette points
out, in its opposition to narrative, description is "one of the major features of our literary consciousness," yet it is impossible to identify it as

a distinct mode of representation, for "to recount an event and to describe an object are two similar operations, which bring into play the same resources of language."[58] But even as these problems of identification persist – and they will make their presence felt in this study – they should not be taken as evidence that description is simply an aspect of narrative. Genette at least hints at a more differentiated picture in a brusque historical sketch according to which description left behind its "ornamental" role in the nineteenth century to become "explanatory and symbolic," a change Genette encapsulates by stating: "description has lost in terms of autonomy what it has gained in dramatic importance." With telling irony Genette proposes that description can become important only when it submits to the forces of narrative, under whose direction alone it can become "explanatory" and "symbolic." Conversely, as long as description was "ornamental," it could also retain its "autonomy" because it remained extraneous to narrative, an independence that is again ironically broken because a position outside of narrative is also inessential, providing merely convenient resting places for the otherwise narrative-hungry reader. The disturbing ambiguities of Genette's formal definition resurface here as the poles of an historical transformation in which description moves from frivolous autonomy in youth to a middle age of responsible service. Ultimately, even Genette's more differentiated historical account yields to the desire to control description. Granted a phase of historical autonomy only at the price of insignificance, and importance only at the price of dependence, description simply cannot win.

Such carefully calculated irony, combined with the bizarre metaphor of "natural slavery," indicates that Genette is a victim of what W. J. T. Mitchell has called "ekphrastic fear."[59] While he concedes the closeness of descriptive to narrative modes of representation, such a concession has to be quickly modified by the argument that description is always – or at least as long as it can claim any importance – dominated by narrative. Because of these distortions Genette's essay does not provide a useful model for doing work on description. In fact, since the domination of description by narrative remains a moral and aesthetic imperative for Genette, his position cannot be sharply distinguished from the debate over description in eighteenth-century Britain. Much of that debate, as Ralph Cohen's study of James Thomson's *The Seasons* has shown, evolved around the effect the descriptive had on the "unity" and "plan" of a sprawling composition such as Thomson's.[60] If Thomson had elevated the old rhetorical trope of description with its mainly ornamental function into the central principle of his composition, how could that composition resist turning into the disordered "heap of shining materials" Samuel Johnson would recognize in Richard Savage's imitation of Thomson's long poem?[61] Such worries about unity have to do with the classical concern over description as a poetic self-indulgence, more invested in displaying the poet's technical versatility than in genuinely furthering the coherence of the composition and thus repelling or – worse still – unduly absorbing the reader's attention and undermining the purpose of the poem. As Rene de Bossu phrased it, only those poets too preoccupied with their own "immortality ... will stuff a Poem with Descriptions either ill placed, or ill manag'd, with affected and useless Figures, with forc'd and insipid Sentences, with Similes more fine than just, and with other such like Ornaments: And by this means they destroy the Idea they ought to give of their Subject."[62] What is required "if in the middle of a great Action, anything is describ'd, that seems to interrupt and distract the Reader's Mind ... [is] that the Effect of these Descriptions declare the Reason and Necessity of them, and that by this means they be embody'd, if I may so say, in the Action."[63] De Bossu's insistence on embodying the "stuff" of description in narrative is closely related to Genette's essentially normative outlook. For both writers description has to be controlled by narrative because narrative is the locus of order and signification.

Such resemblance of structuralist analysis and normative aesthetics in the end goes back to a shared view of the literary artifact as a unified structure. Barthes's example shows with particular clarity that description is only "scandalous" because its seeming uselessness militates against the idea of a deeply interrelated structure in which no element can be without a discrete function. The desire to master this structure is challenged by description's alliance with what Barthes sees as "a kind of narrative *luxury*, profligate to the extent of throwing up 'useless' details and increasing the cost of narrative information."[64] Barthes's extraordinary vocabulary invokes the eighteenth-century debate, concerned as it was with presenting excessive description as a "heap of shining materials" whose pursuit equals "running after false Lights, and glittering Thoughts by an indiscreet Vanity."[65] Eluding the chaste demands of structural functionality, the luxuriating descriptive provokes Barthes to redouble his efforts. If structural analysis is to be "truly exhaustive," he persists, it has to "try to encompass the ultimate detail, the indivisible unit, the fleeting transition, in order to assign these a place in the structure."[66]

Both structuralism and neoclassicism fear a breakdown of structure, the one because it has staked its methodological success on the assumption of a structure whose dense functionality can be penetrated and rendered transparent down to the last indivisible element, the other because it desires to preserve what it defines, with similar stringency and moral overtones, as the regular order and directionality of literary artifacts. In a sense structuralism objectifies the prescriptive declarations of neoclassical aesthetics, which now emerge as actual historically and analytically ascertainable facts. The argument for controlling description is no longer made in defense of a normatively defined standard of beauty and moral purpose, but in response to a concept of structure whose protocols of internal cohesion cannot tolerate a "rogue" element like description. Simultaneously outside and inside, indefinable yet clearly present, dispensable and central, description escapes the grasp of structure.

Yet no matter how overwhelming this tradition of policing description may seem, there is an alternative classical tradition in which description was accepted as a regular inhabitant of more flexibly imagined compositions. Recent criticism of Homer's description of Achilles' shield in the *Iliad* – one of the central bones of contention in the eighteenth-century debate over the descriptive – has begun to establish the position that the image of the shield organizes and holds together the entire poem. The usefulness of such revisionism is questionable, since it threatens simply to invert the familiar hierarchy, with description on top. Indeed, this problem is highlighted by the description of the shield itself, which seems designed to "undermine," as Mitchell has pointed out, "the oppositions of movement and stasis, narrative action and descriptive scene."[67] Following a line of research more immediately helpful to my concerns, Shadi Bartsch has turned to the beginnings of Greek romance to argue that the descriptive was utilized for literary purposes that went far beyond rhetorical exercise.[68] This tradition was familiar in eighteenth-century Britain – if not through theoretical debate, then through the practice of writers such as Lucian – and is able to shed some fresh light on a passage that might easily seem the most patently ornamental setpiece description of eighteenth-century prose, Henry Fielding's view of the Allworthy manor. When seen within the context of possessive communal forms, however, Fielding's descriptive scene acquires a significance that rivals Homer's shield, and this alone should provide strong incentive to revise the traditional view that eighteenth-century prose "lack[s] . . . a descriptive rhetoric."[69] *Tom Jones*, indeed, loosens narrative's one-sided grip on description not only by showing that descriptions can shape narrative form (and can be predictive despite Barthes's censure), but also by indicating that narratives can have descriptive functions – a subversive suggestion, considering the primacy typically accorded to narrative. Fielding's interest in creating an equivalence between narrative and description should, moreover, go some way toward dispelling the view that this relationship is fated to be hierarchical. A key text in my argument, Fielding's novel thus gives significant weight to the conceptual revision I wish to propose.

A study of the actual practice of novelistic description in the eighteenth century shows that Genette's suggestion of a move of description from the outside of narrative form to its inside – ultimately envisioned as an enslavement that domesticates the alien and makes it the dutiful means of narrative exposition – is not only politically bizarre but historically inadequate. As my remarks on *Tom Jones* have already begun to indicate, the relationship between description and narrative is far more complex and variable. Like the boundary between persons and things, it is constantly under negotiation. While it may be "devilishly difficult," as Mitchell notes, to say anything definitive about the developing relationship between description and narrative, I believe that the more practical considerations of property and community that I pursue in this book will at least foster a growing sense of how a culture imbued with possessive ideas interrelates descriptive and narrative elements to represent different stages and modes of objectification.[70]

That a study concerned with the communal form of the manor should suggest such a revision is perhaps not surprising. If this communal form can be shown to integrate time, space, and practice, one should expect that its novelistic articulation brings the two literary modes most prominently associated with the figuration of time and space into productive contact. This interaction between narrative and description discloses the problems and tensions implicit in the long history of eighteenth-century objectification and communal imagination. While it is possible to begin by making description central to the analysis, such a move has to remain preliminary. The intricacy of the connection between the relational and the distributional depiction of persons and things makes it impossible to maintain an exclusive association of description with space and objects, and of narrative with time and action. We have to recognize instead that both modes are able to figure the relational web of time, space, and practice that shapes communal forms, albeit by foregrounding different aspects of the inescapable entanglement between human and material spheres. To grasp the history of these entanglements within the overall context of British transitionalism as a complex, multilayered process and not as something that begins abruptly in, say, 1778 or reaches "maturity" in the nineteenth century is one of the important aims of this study.

CHAPTER TWO

Terra nullius, *cannibalism, and the natural law of appropriation in* Robinson Crusoe

Alan Ryan once suggested that English law "discouraged" inquiry into the phenomenology and genesis of ownership. Unlike civil law, the basis of most European legal systems, common law is unable to answer questions such as " 'What is it to be the owner of something?' or 'How does a thing become mine?' "[1] This is so because common law treats the fact of possession as a fundamental social given. Its main concern is with describing the established ways in which property can be held and conveyed; the problem of how something can be appropriated that was not previously owned remains outside its conceptual boundaries. This treatment of possession as a *fait accompli* is most strikingly illuminated by the doctrine of universal possession, introduced by the Normans as *nulle terre sans seigneur.*[2] According to a fundamental fiction of common law, all English land originally belonged to the English crown. In all of England there is not one piece of land that is not possessed – either by the crown directly or by those who hold, through the system of English tenure, mediately or immediately from the crown. The only aspect of common law that deals with the problem of how something becomes property is known as "occupation" – a term that has central significance in natural law. In common law, however, occupation is marginal. "The laws of England," as William Blackstone points out, have "confined [occupation] within a very narrow compass."[3] So narrow, indeed, that Blackstone's extensive *Commentaries on the Laws of England* can dispense with this topic in five pages.[4]

The common law's blind spot with respect to appropriation made it a problematic candidate for justifying English colonial land claims. Indeed, the three central legal mechanisms for claiming foreign territories – conquest, cession, and occupation – were worked out in natural law, or, as it came to be called, the law of nations.[5] The increasing relevance of natural law in regulating questions of international sovereignty emerges in exemplary fashion for the English context in the seventeenth-century conflict over fishing rights with Holland. Evolving around the question of whether one can occupy the open sea and acquire proprietary rights in it, this debate helped one of its participants, Hugo Grotius, to launch his seminal *De Iure Belli ac Pacis* (1625). Grotius's famous work addressed the genesis and phenomenology of ownership on a broad philosophical level, but without leaving behind, as we shall see, the exigencies of empire.

Even though the common law was sidelined in the initial struggle for overseas sovereignty, it eventually regained some authority over questions of colonial land claims – after an extended period of domination by natural law.[6] Addressing realities that came into being in the second half of the eighteenth century, the 1992 decision of the Australian High Court to recognize native title to land and to reject the doctrine of *terra nullius* (*Mabo* v. *State of Queensland*) illuminates the shifting historical relations between natural and common law.[7] *Terra nullius* is the term that came to be linked with occupation, the natural law notion that proved to be central to the British justification of colonial land claims.[8] It literally means "no person's land," but in colonial practice this did not imply that such land was uninhabited. On the contrary, as developed by European nations, the doctrine of *terra nullius* made it possible to distinguish between the occupation of land and the mere presence of native peoples on land, and thus enabled an original claim to possession. When James Cook "discovered" Australia in 1770, he judged its inhabitants to be "in the pure state of nature" and treated the land as unoccupied.[9] Cook's judgment was based on a definition of occupation that was developed in sixteenth- and seventeenth-century natural law and was refined in the eighteenth century by Emeric de Vattel. Vattel's *Le Droit de Gens ou Principes de la Loi Naturelle* (1758) addressed the question of colonial land claims with unprecedented explicitness and moved the concept of occupation closer to becoming a recognized principle of international law.[10] Like others before him, Vattel considered any territory that did not show clear signs of cultivation and permanent settlement and that was not physically connected to a larger national unit to be vacant – unoccupied and hence unpossessed. Australia qualified as *terra nullius* because, in the eyes of the colonizer, its inhabitants had not reached a level of social and economic organization that would have introduced exclusive property rights. Property was an unfamiliar concept in Australia – or so Cook thought – and this assumption allowed the English to claim that they were the first owners of previously unpossessed Australian land. The crown established not only territorial, but proprietary, title – that is, actual possession of the land itself.[11] This claim was made good by effective occupation according to natural law, the mode of appropriation that England preferred and that involved the enclosing, fencing in, and cultivating of *terra nullius*.[12]

When the Australian High Court rejected *terra nullius* in 1992, it differentiated between natural and common law by emphasizing the latter's inherent respect for customary usage. Native title was recognized by the court because it "has its origin in and is given its content by the traditional laws acknowledged by and the traditional customs observed by the indigenous inhabitants of a territory."[13] It is precisely this customary order that the natural law concept of occupation had neutralized. More than 200 years after Cook's "discovery," such neutralization emerges in an Australian courtroom as a scandal that, in the words of Judge Toohey, is "at odds with basic values of the common law."[14] The natural law elements that had initially supplemented common law for the purposes of colonial appropriation are now rejected as alien to the common law's respect for customary usage.

I emphasize the Mabo case here not to present the reassertion of common law as a morality play for a postcolonial age. The High Court's decision was far from revolutionary and followed in large part the established common law precedent of the United States, Canada, and New Zealand.[15] I am interested rather in the historical tensions between natural and customary rights revealed by Mabo. I wish to draw on the history of these tensions to situate the discussion of a text that was published some time before *terra nullius* hardened, around the end of the eighteenth century, into a doctrine recognized by most European nations.[16] Daniel Defoe's *Robinson Crusoe* (1719) presents the conceptual assumptions that would congeal into the notion of *terra nullius* in a state of deep cultural and ideological uncertainty. Defoe's novel shows the extent to which "vacant" land could seem like an unnatural, frightening condition from the perspective of a culture that treated possession as an unproblematic social given. Alberico Gentili, the 1587 regius professor of civil law at Oxford and an important precursor of Grotius, points to the characteristic tension between "emptiness" and "fullness" in the British view of property. He justified the appropriation of *terra nullius* by pointing out that "the law of nature ... abhors a vacuum," and thus adapted the medieval notion of the *horror vacui* to the problematic of the "empty" spaces of the new world.[17] The absence of possessive ties, Gentili suggests, constitutes a void that interrupts and distorts the interconnected fullness ("plenum") of nature. To an English audience accustomed to the common law's assumption of universal ownership, Gentili's suggestion that such possessive plenitude constitutes a state of natural interconnect-edness must have made immediate sense.[18] Defoe's novel confirms this. It shows that, to an Englishman, the experience of land without owner can be extremely unsettling. With an urgency fully understandable only against the backdrop of the institution of *nulle terre sans seigneur, Robinson Crusoe* dramatizes the questions "what is it to be the owner of something?" and "how does a thing become mine?" English law has no ready answers to these questions, and the cultural shock that Crusoe experiences in the proprietary vacuum of his island goes deep.

I

When Robinson Crusoe discovers a footprint on his solitary island, his confined existence is ruptured. After fifteen years of complete isolation, without any reasonable prospect of reentering human society, Crusoe has to consider for the first time the possibility that the island he assumed to be vacant may be inhabited.[19] Appearing roughly midway through the novel, the footprint marks a turning point in Crusoe's life. "But now I come to a new scene of my life," he announces. "It happened one day about noon going towards my boat, I was exceedingly surprized with the print of a man's naked foot on the shore, which was very plain to be seen in the sand" (162). These initial phrases have a measured and factual tone, but this tone merely throws into relief Crusoe's frantic response to this discovery of a single footprint. "Like a man perfectly confused and out of my self," Crusoe is "terrify'd to the last degree" and unable "to describe how many various shapes affrighted imagination represented things to me in . . . and what strange unaccountable whimsies came into my thoughts" (162). Crusoe's "new scene of life" opens with a disproportionate fit of anxiety and an imagination spinning out of control.

In a moment of retrospective reflection, Crusoe himself marvels how it was possible that he "was ready to sink into the ground at but the shadow or silent appearance of a man's having set his foot in the island." To see one of his own species after fifteen lonely years should indeed have "seemed to me a raising from death to life, and the greatest blessing that Heaven it self . . . could bestow" (164). Not unaware of his extraordinary response, Crusoe fails to explain it adequately. When he claims that his shrinking from the prospect of human company "exemplified . . . in the most lively manner imaginable" the proverb that "to day we love what to morrow we hate," we are left to wonder how such a bland epithet can account for Crusoe's bizarre reaction.[20] What is behind his unreasonable fear?

Many readers of Defoe's novel have pondered this question, and they have correctly pointed to Crusoe's fear of cannibalism.[21] After dismissing the possibility that the footprint could belong to the devil, Crusoe concludes, hyperbolically, "that it must be some more dangerous creature, viz. that it must be some of the savages of the main-land over-against me" (163). The fear of being devoured that this conclusion activates is a dominant yet remarkably erratic character trait of Crusoe. As such, it creates substantial problems for interpretations that foreground the economic, theological, or developmental coherence of Crusoe's behavior. The nagging persistence of Crusoe's irrational fear through two-thirds of the novel undercuts arguments that stress economic rationality, religious improvement, or self-mastery as keys to understanding Crusoe's island life.[22] Readings that, on the other hand, have emphasized the centrality of Crusoe's strange fear have usually grown out of an explanatory framework in which psychological problems become final, irreducible causes. Critics such as Leo Braudy, Everett Zimmerman, Homer Obed Brown, and a number of psychoanalytic readers have been able to recover Crusoe's strangeness only at the expense of dislocating him from particular historical contexts.[23] Even Peter Hulme, who has arguably made the greatest strides in returning *Robinson Crusoe* to the Caribbean, struggles to translate the "parable of the self" he suspects behind Crusoe's cannibalistic fear into the political and social terms of his argument.[24] To present a convincing political and historical context for Crusoe's fear remains one of the important challenges in the criticism of Defoe's novel.

I approach this challenge by arguing that the volatility of Crusoe's response to the footprint and to cannibalism in general springs from the immense personal and cultural pressures of occupying unowned territory, an apparently vacant space that, according to the precepts of natural law, is open to appropriation. When seen in the context of property, Crusoe's fear does not manifest what Dianne Armstrong has analyzed as an underlying anxiety over paternal domination, nor does it represent, in John Richetti's phrase, "the turbulent world of experience," or simply "the rage within," as Everett Zimmerman has suggested.[25] My focus on property and *terra nullius* opens a more direct route to the meaning of Crusoe's behavior by linking cannibalistic revulsion to the history of colonial land claims, and by enabling a profoundly dialectic account of the relation between cannibal and colonizer.[26] In Defoe's novel, I want to argue, the question of property – the distinction of "mine" and "thine" – is intimately related to the issue of cannibalism.

The scene that immediately precedes Crusoe's footprint discovery presents a first clue to the relation of property and cannibalism in Defoe's text. Crusoe discloses what is at stake in his discovery in a curious act of summing up fifteen years on the island. It is worth excerpting this passage at some length:

You are to understand that now I had, as I may call it, two plantations in the island; one my little fortification or tent, with the wall about it under the rock, with the cave behind me, which by this time I had enlarged into several apartments or caves, one within another . . .

As for my wall, made, as before, with long stakes or piles, those piles grew all like trees, and were by this time grown so big, and spread so very much, that there was not the least appearance to anyone's view of any habitation behind them.

Near this dwelling of mine, but a little farther within the land, and upon lower ground, lay my two pieces of corn-ground, which I kept duly culti- vated and sowed, and which duly yielded me their harvest in its season; and whenever I had occasion for more corn, I had more land adjoyning as fit as that.

Besides this, I had my country seat, and I had now a tollerable plantation there also; for first, I had my little bower, as I called it, which I kept in repair; that is to say, I kept the hedge which circled it in constantly fitted up to its usual height, the ladder standing always on the inside; I kept the trees . . . always so cut, that they might spread and grow thick and wild . . . In the middle of this I had my tent always standing, being a piece of sail spread over poles for that purpose, and which never wanted any repair or renewing . . .

Adjoyning to this I had my enclosures for my cattle, that is to say, my goats. And as I had taken an inconceivable deal of pains to fence and enclose this ground, so I was uneasy to see it kept entire . . .

This will testify for me that I was not idle, and that I spared no pains to bring to pass whatever appeared necessary for my comfortable support . . . I used frequently to visit my boat, and I kept all things about or belonging to her in very good order; sometimes I went out in her to divert my self, but no more hazardous voyages would I go, nor scarce ever above a stone's cast or two from the shore. But now I come to a new scene of my life. (160–161)

This laborious, painstakingly detailed description of Crusoe's belong- ings is animated by the desire to present the joining of human and ma- terial spheres as a controlled, ongoing, and expanding activity. It shows

us a man who seeks to establish an indisputable sense of connection between himself and his surroundings. Crusoe's confident declaration "You
are to understand that now I had" indicates his desire to make known
what he considers to be properly "his." The extent of his belongings
("two plantations," a chief seat with "several apartments," a "country
seat" with a "bower," a boat), the unproblematic claim to "more land,"
and the habitual range of his occasional boat trips all announce someone who is in control of his insular environment. This control is made
conspicuous by the exhibition of visible signs of cultivation. Fortifica-
tions, walls, plantations, hedges, and enclosures: these elements present
the visible marks that Crusoe's labor has left on the island's surface.
To show such evidence of occupation is the inventory's basic possessive
strategy. The extent of his possessions, in fact, inspired Crusoe slightly
earlier in the novel to imagine, "with a secret kind of pleasure," "that
this was all my own, that I was king and lord of all this country in-
defeasibly, and had a right of possession; and if I could convey it, I
might have it in inheritance as compleatly as any lord of a mannor in
England" (114).

Such confidence notwithstanding, Crusoe's inventory also registers a
radical anxiety over the possibility of turning the island into property.
This anxiety is most strikingly evident in Crusoe's interest in concealment. The wall that marks the boundaries of his habitation, for instance,
simultaneously renders Crusoe's dwelling invisible. Yet paradoxically,
Crusoe's descriptive act makes both house and wall visible and declares
as private property what, in actuality, is not immediately recognizable
as such. The most vivid example of this paradox is "the ladder standing
always on the inside" of the hedge. Emblematic of the exclusive nature of private property, the hidden means of entering Crusoe's abode
is descriptively exposed, the invisible and the visible always remaining
confusingly close neighbors. Further contradictions surface in the repeated emphasis on constant upkeep and persistent use. Crusoe never
tires of telling us that things are "duly cultivated," "kept entire" or "in
very good order," and never want "any repair or renewing." "Keeping"
is, characteristically, the most frequent verb in the passage. In contrast
to his manorial fantasy, which turned on the idea of inheritance and
thus on a notion of property that is independent of actual possession,
Crusoe asserts property here through use only. Property coincides with
physical contact as Crusoe nervously suggests that only as long as he
remains in touch with the things that surround him, and produces
visible evidence of his continued intention to use, can he make any

legitimate claim to these things. David Hume pinpoints this fundamental insecurity:

What is meant by possession ... is not so easy [to define] as may at first sight be imagin'd. We are said to be in possession of any thing, not only when we immediately touch it, but also when we are so situated with respect to it, as to have it in our power to use it; and may move, alter, or destroy it, according to our present pleasure or advantage. This relation, then, is a species of cause and effect ... But here we may observe, that as the power of using any object becomes more or less certain, according as the interruptions we may meet with are more or less probable; and as this probability may increase by insensible degrees, 'tis in many cases impossible to determine when possession begins or ends; nor is there any certain standard, by which we can decide such controversies.[27]

The problem of when possession begins and ends if you rely on the probability of use alone is precisely what Crusoe exposes in his descriptive act – if that is what it is. I have so far assumed it is, but in considering Crusoe's nervous assertions of use, one cannot help but notice that his description is shot through with narrative elements. Crusoe's possessive anxiety produces an inventory that constantly slides into narrative in the attempt to secure a sense of belonging; the spatial scene is punctured by narrative moments that account for the activities that bring Crusoe into contact with his things. Of course, these narrative moments do not recount actual single events – they are almost without exception summary statements of what Crusoe always does or did. And what he always does, predominantly, is to "keep" things in exactly the same state. Needless to say, this is not an attempt to suggest possession through the long continuance of certain practices. The tone is too urgent for that and the activities too detailed and too interested in proving contact with all the possessions. No, these narrative elements actually express a desire to align the human with the material through the causal relationship Hume stresses. But by taking place with such repetitiveness and by keeping the appearance of things exactly the same, the acts narrated tend to annul themselves by blending into the scene. They articulate a desire not for transformation, but for stasis and continuity, a desire that approximates them, in all their recurring sameness, to the objects themselves. The zealous devotion they show to the maintenance of everything in exactly the same shape and form represents a wish for material permanence. Narrative, the domain of event and change, fights here against itself to join the descriptive scene, to blend with the material world and extinguish human time and changeability in the permanence of space. Under pressure to delimit and define ownership, causality fades into repetition and narrative aligns itself with the descriptive scene.

Crusoe's vacillation between claiming the island as private property and doubting whether this is possible at all, between the necessity of showing the signs of ownership and the wish for concealment, discloses how unstable is Crusoe's relation to his environment. The laboriousness of his inventory, its repetitive and enumerative strains, its anxious interrelation of human and material spheres, and its dissolution of narrative in the descriptive scene present a deeply conflicted possessive scenario. Crusoe's rationale for presenting the inventory only deepens this impression. When he notes that his description "will testify for me that I was not idle, and that I spared no pains to bring to pass whatever appeared necessary for my comfortable support," he does more than simply assert the moral value of an active life. Crusoe stresses that his activities on the island are confined to what is "necessary for my comfortable support" in order to legitimize his extensive possessions by tying them to the inherently modest enterprise of self-preservation, while forgetting that his inventory has already offered far more ambitious legitimations. Once again Crusoe presents contradictory claims. What on the one hand gives rise to manorial fantasies is on the other supposed merely to support life's basic requirements for food and shelter.

Even before the arrival of another human being, the impact of the footprint can be felt in the inventory's trembling search for a clear sense of belonging. It is no accident that Crusoe's unstable descriptive act immediately precedes the footprint discovery. Conjuring up a title from the vacant space of *terra nullius*, Crusoe's description attempts to preempt the challenge of the footprint by asserting dominion before rejoining the human community. Indeed, the footprint itself had already been connected to the question of property within sixteenth- and seventeenth-century natural law. Johann Wolfgang Textor, for instance, notes that "in obtaining possession of an estate there is no need for the party to walk over every particular bit of soil, it being enough that he should enter on some part of it with intent to possess." And Cornelius van Bynkershoek stresses that "even that which has not been touched all round by our hands and feet is conceived of as occupied." Speaking of conquest, Gentili remarks that "the conqueror acquires the whole of the conquered, and not merely the things which the victor presses with his foot or holds in his hand."[28] These passages refer to the footprint to stress that even a very partial contact of feet with soil could suffice to indicate "intent to possess," and it is this possibility that Crusoe's extravagant response registers. Both textually and contextually, then, Defoe's iconic footprint episode reveals itself to be a specific allusion to the problem of dominion in the "new world."

II

In establishing dominion Crusoe is without the support of British institutions. Although he is an English subject and as such owes allegiance to the crown, Crusoe lacks royal authorization and has to acquire property alone.[29] This, in fact, is his declared preference. In Defoe's sequel, *The Farther Adventures of Robinson Crusoe* (1719), Crusoe – at a point when his possessive rights have been freshly confirmed – is openly hostile to the idea that his property should be associated with any nation: "I never so much as pretended to plant in the Name of any Government or Nation, or to acknowledge any Prince, or to call my People Subjects to any one Nation more than another."[30] This statement reflects on the nature of English colonial practice in the mid-seventeenth century, the time of Crusoe's arrival on the island. English colonial practice at this time was not yet shaped by government policy and was "to a far greater degree . . . decided by individual merchants and skippers, operating in the broad legal penumbra between trade and piracy, and impelled by self-interest rather than patriotism."[31] Defoe's account of Crusoe's adventures is thus not an unusually individualistic vision of empire making; it simply affirms that in the seventeenth century English colonialism and international law were not integrated with government policy. Indeed, despite the disclaimer about national affiliation, Crusoe's activities on the island are actually representative of the "English way" in colonial landtakings. Defoe's narrative fits precisely with what scholars such as Anthony Pagden and Patricia Seed have described as the English reliance on enclosure, fencing, and cultivation in establishing overseas title.[32] Crusoe's rejection of national affiliation is thus not a critique of English colonial practice. Defoe's ultimate aim, I suggest, is rejecting institutions and practices at home. This becomes apparent in Defoe's decision to place Crusoe's fantasy of manorial title within the context of *terra nullius*. In doing this Defoe offers a direct challenge to English common law.

As his twelve-book poem *Jure Divino* (1706) demonstrates, Defoe was highly critical of England's national law. *Jure Divino* presents a sustained natural law attack on the divine right of kings whose ideological centerpiece – the assertion of a natural right to self-defense that precedes all government and civil compacts – is closely related to John Locke's critique of Robert Filmer in *Two Treatises of Government* (1689).[33] Defoe's attack on divine right also activates a passionate rejection of all claims to legitimacy based on custom and prescription. "Length of Time, or Continuation of Possession," Defoe argues, "can make no Title good, that was not so in itself . . . All those People therefore that would build Titles upon Length of Time in Possession, build them upon a wrong Foundation; since no Prescription will serve in this case."[34] The simple endurance of certain social practices, or, as Defoe mimics (and mocks) the language of common law, "usage beyond the memory of time," is thus roundly dismissed as the basis for law and legitimate title.[35] In keeping with Defoe's political orientation, Crusoe makes not the slightest pretension to a title based on length of possession. Not only after fifteen years, but even after twenty-eight, Crusoe seeks no refuge in length of occupation.[36] In thus discounting customary authority – the "Bastard of Antiquity" as Defoe brashly called it – *Robinson Crusoe* makes room for the fiction of original possession.[37] It is through this fiction – and the account of the origins of property it necessitates – that Defoe offers his critique of English institutions. Crusoe's possessive claim presents the taunting spectacle of an Englishman who gains landed property outside the realm of English customs, independent of the traditional apparatus of tenure and inheritance.

At no point is this spectacle more taunting than when Crusoe, "with a secret kind of pleasure," fantasizes that he might have his island "in inheritance as completely as any lord of a mannor in England." This later repeated reference (139) to manorial landholdings is highly relevant, for the English manor was the type of landed property most closely associated with land claims based on customary authority. This holds true, as we have seen, not only for the manor itself, considered "an ancient Royalty or Lordship" that "must be Time out of Mind," but also for the most common title to land within the manor, the copyhold estate.[38] In fact, the manor's origins in the impenetrable mists of immemorial time, its union of land and practice, and its immunity to becoming the object of human intervention or reproduction render it almost interchangeable with the notion of custom. That much is indeed suggested by Edward Coke when he not just compares, but causally connects the impossibility of creating a new manor with the impossibility of creating a new custom.[39] From the perspective of common law, a new manor is oxymoronic in exactly the same way as a new custom. In this sense, then, Crusoe's manorial fantasy is not only an appropriation of one of the oldest and most prestigious English titles, but of customary authority itself – of a whole way of thinking about law and legitimacy. Whether we regard the "secret kind of pleasure" Crusoe feels in imagining himself to be lord of the manor as a self-consciously seditious moment or not, his fantasy of a *new* manor – the very thing that, according to Coke, no one, not even the king, can create – challenges fundamental assumptions of common law.

That challenge is all the more pointed because one of the prominent possessive strategies of Crusoe's inventory, the exhibition of visible signs of cultivation, draws on natural law, Defoe's ideological weapon of choice in *Jure Divino*. Natural law's emergence into philosophical prominence in the sixteenth and seventeenth centuries was fueled by the exigencies of the increasingly worldwide engagement of Western Europe's colonial powers. Prominent natural law thinkers such as Francisco de Vitoria, Francisco Suarez, Alberico Gentili, Hugo Grotius, John Selden, Samuel Pufendorf, and John Locke, to name only a few, all responded, in one way or another, to the problems of legitimate use and possession that asserted themselves so powerfully with the discovery of the supposedly open spaces of the western hemisphere and the increasing volume of international trade.[40] Mediated in part by seventeenth-century dissenters, natural law was a familiar mode of thought for Defoe and we have direct evidence of his familiarity with Grotius, Pufendorf, and Locke.[41]

Under natural law the visible signs of cultivation in Crusoe's inventory constitute evidence of successful occupation. Natural law's central possessive mode, occupation "is the only natural and primary mode of acquisition" according to Grotius. He makes special mention in this respect of "hitherto uncultivated islands in the sea," an example to which he frequently resorts.[42] The island is a privileged case in Grotius's work not only because it has great practical relevance for the colonial enterprise, but also because the island's physical features ideally embody Grotius's condition of possibility for ownership: definite limits. The following passage explains this in detail:

Occupation takes place only in the case of a thing which has definite limits. For this reason Thucydides calls unoccupied land "devoid of boundaries," and Isocrates characterized the land taken over by the Athenians as "having boundaries fixed by us." Liquids, on the contrary, have no limits in themselves. "Water," says Aristotle, "is not bounded by a boundary of its own substance." Liquids therefore cannot be taken possession of unless they are contained in something else; as being thus contained, lakes and ponds have been taken possession of.[43]

A cultivated island surrounded by what Crusoe calls the "boundless ocean" (164) constitutes a particularly striking example of the creation of private ownership through the introduction of limits and boundaries. Initially distinguished from the sea mainly by its outline, the vacant island, once occupied, gradually realizes its potential for a more thorough differentiation from the boundless realm. Crusoe's inventory provides evidence of such segmentation in great detail, and his practice of surveying the island from his boat confirms the island's status as an eminently possessible, because naturally limited, object. Not incidentally, Grotius's identification of possession with spatial segmentation goes hand in hand with a rejection of all claims founded on temporal duration. Pursuing a point closely related to Defoe's rejection of "Length of Time, or Continuation of Possession," Grotius explains that "time ... in its own nature has no effective force; nothing is done by time, though everything is done in time."[44] The qualitative, transformative time that common law recognized is here discounted. For Grotius time itself is powerless and he dissociates the two entities that the common law notion of immemorial custom fuses together: time serves as a generalized, unspecified framework for social practice, not as its undifferentiated partner. What Grotius and Defoe both insist on is the disembedding of practice from time, and such disembedding cuts directly against the legitimizing logic of common law, dependent as it is on the fact of continuance beyond memory. The island's construction as *terra nullius* annuls established usage and the forces of the past, and Crusoe attempts to enact a new relation between persons and things, unmediated by custom.

Not surprisingly, that new relation also involves a differentiation of practice from space. As *terra nullius* the island is a negative space – a boundless vacuum, to take up Gentili's point, in search of a possessive content. As such, the island's space does not embody any rights or practices, and Crusoe's labor has to attempt to transform emptiness into structured fullness. But as we have already begun to see, this transformation fails to stabilize the relationship between practice and space. Even as Crusoe's labor leaves its signature on the land, no reliable link to the environment is established. On the contrary, Crusoe's constant, compulsory renewal of physical engagement with his material surroundings indicates that the original dissociation of practice and space – which was one of the conditions for appropriating the island – persists even after fifteen years, even after Crusoe fancies himself lord of the manor.

The colonial context of Crusoe's adventures thus serves Defoe as a vehicle for exploring fundamental differences between natural and common law. The English manor is the most concrete (and seductive) figure in Defoe's novel for a configuration of persons and things that relies entirely on the traditional social mechanisms of tenure and established usage. Crusoe's manorial fantasy is subversive because, by imagining a new manor on a natural law basis, it rejects the embedded relations of time, space, and practice characteristic of customary law and manorial community. Transplanted into the colonial context, the traditional communal form of Britain's propertied culture is removed from its conceptual foundations, but whether natural law can provide an alternative grounding remains open to question. The assertion of private possession independent of all established communal practice is fraught with insecurities and a title by occupation alone fails to put Crusoe at ease. In appealing to the legitimizing limits of "necessary and comfortable support," Crusoe attempts to reconcile the extent of his appropriation with the natural limits of self-preservation, but this appeal also activates a claim more fundamental than occupation. The following passage from Locke's second treatise of government indicates in what sense:

God commanded, and his Wants forced [Man] to labour. That was his Property which could not be taken from him where-ever he had fixed it. And hence subduing and cultivating the Earth, and having dominion, we see are joyned together. The one gave Title to the other. So that God, by commanding to subdue, gave Authority so far to appropriate. And the Condition of Humane Life, which requires Labour and Materials to work on, necessarily introduces private Possessions. The measure of Property, Nature has well set, by the Extent of Men's Labour and the Conveniency of Life: No Mans Labour could subdue, or appropriate all.[45]

Locke's central claim in this passage is that the "Condition of Humane Life ... necessarily introduces private Possessions." Taken in its strict sense, what Locke is saying here is that private property is the natural effect of human survival.[46] It is this claim for private property as a fundamental condition of human life that creates the legitimizing effect of the appeal to "necessary and comfortable support." In suggesting that his establishment of dominion is linked to his survival, Crusoe points to human nature as the origin of property. These origins are asserted in an extended attempt to make narrative the master of description, an attempt that discloses what Crusoe's act of appropriation has to do with his fear of the cannibal.

III

At the beginning of Crusoe's history on the island stands the experience of shipwreck. Shortly before he is stranded on the island, Crusoe reports that his ship encountered a violent storm. It rolls helplessly toward the island when "a raging wave, mountain-like, came rowling a-stern of us, and ... took us with such a fury that it overset the boat at once ... we were all swallowed up in a moment." In his hazardous approach to the island, Crusoe is washed over by an incoming wave, "buried ... at once 20 or 30 feet deep in its own body," then "covered ... with water" and again "swallowed up," until finally he exults in having been "saved, as I may say, out of the very grave." During this dramatic scene the threat of being swallowed alternates with an interior violation of bodily boundaries. Crusoe is, at various points, "half-dead with the water" he has to swallow, "ready to burst with holding my breath," and feels his breath to be "quite out of my body" (64-65).

We have here a vivid image of a boundless relation between self and environment that represents a precise antidote to the bounded state Crusoe tries to display in his possessive inventory. The transition from a boundless to a bounded state, however, is markedly gradual and Crusoe's arrival on the island signals only a relative change of his situation. In fact, when Crusoe first sees the island during the storm, he remarks that the "land looked more frightful than the sea" (64). One reason why this remark is not as puzzling as it might seem emerges from Grotius's distinction between land and sea. In Grotius's view of property, the critical difference between land and sea is their potential for possession. As long as land is unenclosed and unoccupied, it remains common – "boundless" like the sea, if endowed with the potential of becoming property. Considering this similarity between *terra nullius* and the sea, it is rather fitting that, once Crusoe reaches the beach, the fear of being "swallowed" is almost immediately replaced by the fear of being "devoured":

After I got to the shore and had escaped drowning, instead of being thankful to God for my deliverance, having first vomited with the great quantity of salt water which was gotten in my stomach, and recovering my self a little, I ran about the shore, wringing my hand and beating my head and face . . . till tyred and faint I was forced to lye down on the ground to repose, but durst not sleep for fear of being devoured. (86)

Though the local point of this passage is to expose Crusoe's irrational behavior as a result of his religious ignorance, the fear of being "devoured" turns out to be the more enduring theme. It stays with Crusoe even after his conversion. In the early stages of his island life, "security from ravenous creatures, whether men or beasts" (76) is Crusoe's driving concern, even though the island seems uninhabited and without any threatening animals (71). His earliest project to defend himself against such assumed threats is the construction of a dwelling. Crusoe's thoughts at this point are "wholly employed about securing my self against either savages, if any should appear, or wild beasts, if any were in the island; and I had many thoughts of the method how to do this, and what kind of dwelling to make" (76). Crusoe's habitation is thus the direct result of an attempt at self-preservation. As the descriptions of his ever-expanding enclosures indicate, the fear of being devoured is the central motivation of such building activities.

Protected on one side by a hill, Crusoe's initial habitation is surrounded, in a "half-circle" by "two rows of stakes." Pleased with this arrangement, Crusoe notes that he was "completely fenced in, and fortify'd, as I thought, from all the world" (77). Nonetheless, he soon expands his "strong pale of posts" further by raising "a kind of wall up against it of turfs, about two feet thick on the outside" (84). Ten months later, still citing the purpose of "defence," he plants "a hedge . . . in a semicircle around my wall" by placing "trees or stakes in a double row, at about eight yards distance from my first fence" (119). The climax of these efforts comes with the discovery of the footprint and the concrete expectation of cannibals after fifteen years of continuous anxieties. Crusoe creates yet another fortification around his dwelling and increases the thickness of his wall "to above ten feet" (168). When he concludes his narrative of multiple enclosures by emphasizing that "human prudence" alone guided him, Crusoe really exposes the gap between his excessive enclosing habit and the goal of prudent self-preservation. As he himself concedes at this point, "meer fear" has produced the rapid multiplication of enclosures (169).

Crusoe's compulsive habit has a wide symbolic reference, but its most immediate meaning refers us to the origin of property. The creation of private property, Defoe's narrative linking of several described sites suggests, is natural because it results directly from the fundamental human right to self-defense. Exposed to the legal and social vacuum of *terra nullius*, Crusoe's acquisition of original title is not only possible, it is absolutely necessary. Yet as Crusoe's enclosures multiply around his dwelling, self-preservation becomes a less and less credible legitimation. Indeed, the continual spread of his personal area around him comes to represent synecdochically the cultivation and possession of the entire island, an enterprise that, though it exceeds the limits of self-preservation, is simultaneously connected back to property's origin in human necessity. Defoe's text here displays a certain awareness concerning this ideological legitimation of property in human survival. I have already commented on the paradoxical combination of visibility and invisibility that marks Crusoe's spatial segmentation of the island. What we confront now is the imposition of a narrative trajectory on such doubleness. Crusoe expands his possessive grasp by creating wider and wider enclosures around him, but with each expansion a higher degree of invisibility is claimed. Paradoxically joining territorial expansion and increasingly effective concealment, Defoe's invisible, growing enclosure discloses that the grounding of property in self-preservation, as the only effective response to the *horror vacui* of *terra nullius*, constitutes an ideological camouflage for limitless expansion. The insecurity I noted initially in Crusoe's inventory modulates here into a sly assertiveness that extends to the relationship between narrative and description. If possessive insecurity had earlier led to narrative's disappearance into the descriptive assertion of material continuity, narrative can now envelop and direct the descriptive into a movement of material expansion.

I should like to recall at this point that self-preservation is only the generic name for Crusoe's rather particular motivation in creating property. The centrifugal dynamic of Crusoe's activities – culminating in his attempt "to view the circumference of my little kingdom" from his boat (147) – is really propelled by his fear of being devoured by cannibals. The initial creation of enclosures around him served to shield Crusoe's body from being devoured, and in this sense these enclosures are extensions of the self that counteract the penetration of the body by the sea and its imagined ingestion by cannibals. The creation of property, then, is presented as a necessary defense against the cannibals, whose devouring habits now appear to express concretely the island's *horror vacui*. In order to grasp the full significance of this connection between cannibalism and property, we need to determine the precise place occupied by the term "devour" in Defoe's political imagination.

IV

Defoe uses the term "devour" in a variety of contexts, from a general characterization of human depravity ("Mankind delights his Neighbour to devour") to the specific condemnation of stockjobbers as "the worst sort of devourers: ... true Canibals."[47] And yet, while Defoe associates "devour" with different subjects, his political beliefs give its prominent use in *Robinson Crusoe* a particular significance. In *Jure Divino* the conjunction of "devour" and "power" is the most frequently heard rhyme and Defoe creates a profusion of couplets that describe the abuse of political power as an act of devouring.[48] In one instance Defoe explains a reference to Saturn by noting that "the Antients represent him eating his own children, which I understand to mean Tyrannizing over his Subjects in a bloody devouring manner."[49] But the metaphor reveals its most specific political dimension in Defoe's view of property.

While he explicitly rejects the idea of a commonwealth, Defoe views the possession of land as the origin and ultimate legitimizing ground of all legal and political rights.[50] The "Original Right of all Men to the Government of themselves" is in Defoe's view universal, but is in itself insufficient for participation in civic processes. Political rights for Defoe derive directly from landed property and he argues this case so vehemently that he relegates all those who do not possess land to the status of rightless temporary residents. "I do not place this Right [of jurisdiction] upon the Inhabitants," Defoe differentiates, "but upon the Freeholders; the Freeholders are the proper Owners of the Country; it is their own, and the other Inhabitants are but Sojourners, like Lodgers in a House, and ought to be subject to such Laws as the Freeholders impose upon them, or else they must remove." A little later Defoe amplifies his point even further: "No Person has any Right to live in England, but they to whom England belongs; the freeholders of England have it in possession; England is their own, and no Body has any thing to do here but themselves."[51] This seems like an extreme position for someone whose dominant ideological framework is seventeenth-century natural law. For one thing, even as Defoe alludes, like Coke, to the freeholder's ability to resist monarchical intrusion, is he not also endorsing the system of English tenures as defined by common law? And does not the constitutional literalism of equating legislative authority with proprietary right recall a basic feudal pattern? (Defoe confirms this link when he claims that the homages and services paid under the manorial system present a just "Acknowledgment that the Right of the Land gave a certain Right of Government to the Possessor."[52]) How does all of this fit the context of natural law?

Defoe's *The Original Power of the Collective Body of the People of England Examined and Asserted* (1702), from which these quotations are taken, is far from embracing common law. Despite his acceptance of manorial homage, Defoe makes unmistakably clear – in a move that anticipates Crusoe's desire to base manorial title on natural law – that the origin of all title lies not in feudal grants, but in a natural right to possession. "The Rights to Lands, Mannors, and Lordships," Defoe argues, "was not Originally a Right granted by Patents from Kings or Acts of Parliament, but a natural Right of Possession handed down by Custom and ancient Usage."[53] As in *Robinson Crusoe*, Defoe suggests here that natural law grounds common law, the latter merely "handing down" what was begun in nature. This "natural Right of Possession" is ultimately identical with the "original right of self-government." Even though its practical political significance is diminished by the uneven distribution of property over the course of history, this natural right nonetheless stands at the beginning of all private possession.

Grounding property in nature, before social compacts and the particular arrangements of the common law, but acknowledging the validity of these arrangements, Defoe is able to argue in two directions at once and neutralize the conflict between natural and common law. On the one hand, he can claim that there is no contradiction but rather a continuity between "the Original Right of all Men to the Government of themselves" and the "Sovereign Judicature" enjoyed by English landowners.[54] Both natural and common law ultimately confirm that right and property go together. On the other hand, and under the additional proviso that the House of Commons is "the representative Body of the People," Defoe is able to exploit the suggested continuity between original right and status quo and speak sweepingly of "the Original Right of the People of England" as an active element in the political process. Only eventually does he concede that these "People" are really England's freeholders. In this backhanded manner Defoe is able to speak of the "people's right" within the limits of a society whose political structure still rests on feudal institutions. Such strategic maneuverings notwithstanding, he insists that possession "explains" government because "Property is the Foundation of Power."[55] Similarly, the compatibility of natural and common law as respects the foundation of right in property is not a ploy to win over the landed establishment. The intricate course that Defoe's political rhetoric steers ultimately follows the desire to discover natural law at the bottom of English institutions.

Especially significant for a consideration of *Robinson Crusoe*'s metaphorics is Defoe's insistence that, even if the possession of land is the only source of right, this possession finds its ultimate legitimizing ground in a natural right of property that originates in the individual's self-government. Though presumably no verifiable historical link survives, self-government is the ultimate source for the possession of landed property, while landed property gives rights to civil government. Property in this scenario is never merely the right to one's self or the right to one's belongings, and Defoe evokes Locke's extended sense of one's own as "Life, Liberty, and Estate."[56] According to this model rights are treated as property, and Defoe's possessive sense of right is evident in his use of spatial metaphors when he describes right violations as "invasions," "encroachments," or a "breaking in upon."[57] Our own continuing familiarity with an expression such as "an invasion of liberty" shows that the possessive rights tradition still has its verbal echoes.[58] This conception of rights as property and, inversely, of property as the source of right, illuminates Defoe's poetic practice. The following lines from *Jure Divino* take on a distinct meaning when considered in this light:

> The Voice of Bondage, and Destruction's known,
> And summons all men to defend their own:
> Freedom's the native Right of all Mankind,
> And they that slight it, leave their Sense behind.
> No Laws of God our Property expose,
> Kings were the People's Guards, their Freedom to inclose;
> And they who what they should defend invade,
> Forfeit their Office, have their Trust betray'd.[59]

This is by no means graceful poetry, but these lines show forcefully the deep reciprocity of right and property in Defoe's political thought. With no hesitation and virtually no attempt at poetic mediation, this stanza stitches together the "defense of our own" with the "native right to freedom," and "property" with "enclosed freedom." As the stanza progresses, Defoe's typical guardedness about any assertion of radical right surfaces, and what is initially presented as an unconditional "native" right is more and more identified with landed property. But while right is presented in possessive terms – as exposed *property* and *inclosed* right – Defoe also alludes to the origin of rights in the possession of property. The term "trust" in the final line of the stanza is central in Defoe's political vocabulary, and it calls to mind Locke's notion of the strictly fiduciary relation between governors and governed. The fundamental purpose of "entrusting" the governors with certain duties, however, is the "preservation of property" and it is only the propertied, as we have seen, who enjoy any political rights.[60]

Defoe's reciprocal sense of the relation between right and property inextricably connects interior and exterior possession, making it impossible to reduce the sphere of one's own to either person or thing. This irreducible sense of one's own is a crucial feature of Grotius's and Locke's accounts of natural law and it is highlighted in Defoe's resourceful figural use of the term "devour." The logic of Defoe's political beliefs makes "devour" a fitting metaphor for a political cannibalism of the civil subject – "Then view the small Extent of Native Power,/And how unqualify'd their Subjects to devour" – but also enables an extension of that metaphor into a cannibalism of property. Tyranny, in Defoe's favorite rhyme, "Can ravage Countries, Property devour,/And trample Law beneath the Feet of Power."[61] As property is a natural extension of the possessive self, the metaphorical uses of "devour" can expand with the sphere of one's own to encompass both person and thing. So when Crusoe states that he wishes "to keep [the cannibals] from devouring me and all I had" (186), his use of zeugma is not accidental. It precisely captures the irreducibility of one's own in which "me" and "all I had" can be subject to exactly the same threat.

Defoe's political imagination thus underscores how Crusoe's excessive fear of being devoured is directly related to the question of property. It is a specific response to the disruption of the intimate tie he has established between himself and his possessions, and it reveals the spherical sense of one's own that I have shown to be crucial to Defoe's construction of a political subject. Countering centrifugal extension with centripetal invasion, the cannibal figures a fundamental threat to the community between person and thing sponsored by natural law. This function of cannibalism as the figural "other" of natural law is literalized in the model of appropriation that underwrites Crusoe's widening enclosures.

v

Locke assumes, as we have seen, that "subduing and cultivating the Earth, and having dominion ... are joyned together." How, concretely, do we get from cultivation to dominion? Locke's famous answer is that man has "in himself the great Foundation of Property."[62] What Locke refers to here is the notion of the possessive self that he derived from the basic natural law concept of the *suum*: the sphere of one's own that we found to be basic to Defoe's political imagination.[63] Locke explains this sphere and its function in the process of creating property as follows:

Though the Earth, and all inferior Creatures be common to all Men, yet every Man has a Property in his own Person. This no Body has any Right to but himself. The Labour of his Body and the Work of his Hands, we may say, are properly his. Whatsoever then he removes out of the State that Nature hath provided, and left it in, he hath mixed his Labour with, and joyned to it something that is his own, and thereby makes it his Property.[64]

The absolute exclusive right one has to one's body founds here the claim to property in exterior things. The "mixing" of two bodies through the medium of labor can result in property only because the possessive self is able to add something to the thing it appropriates. This addition differentiates the thing from its unappropriated environment. Property is thus an extension of the self in a very specific sense; the act of appropriation does not introduce a new relation into the world, but communicates to a wider field what already exists in the property we have in our bodies. I contend that this process is behind the centrifugal extension of Crusoe's property and its continuity with the project of self-defense.[65]

The implications of Locke's account for the construction of social and political communities are momentous. To grasp them it is useful to consider briefly Pufendorf's account of property. Unlike Locke, Pufendorf insists on the fundamental conventionality of private property and presents a completely different community of persons and things:

When, indeed, certain things came under ownership, and the rest were still free from ownership, no new qualities should be understood to have been imposed on such things; but rather, upon the beginning of ownership in things, a certain moral quality arose among men, of which the men were the subjects, and the things only the terms ... so, when ownership had once been established, each man was given the right to dispose of his own property, and among the non-owners there arose the obligation to keep hands off such property. The things themselves, however, obtained therefrom only an extrinsic denomination, inasmuch as they form the object of such a right or obligation.[66]

The most obvious difference from Locke's account of the origin of property is that the authority of possession depends on the obligation to respect that which is another's. Ownership does not arise naturally out of an interaction between person and thing, but rather has to be "established." "The right to dispose of his own property" is "given," it needs to be imposed by convention because no one has it naturally. Before the agreement on a right to property, Pufendorf argues, no property can exist. The consequence of such conventionality is that ownership founds a community between "men" and not between "men" and "things." The thing itself does not change; whether it is free from ownership or owned by someone, its intrinsic nature remains the same. What does change with my acquisition of something is the relation I have to other members of the community, who, provided that the community has agreed to respect private property, are now under the moral obligation to abstain from what is mine.

Pufendorf's statement throws light on an aspect of Locke's definition of property that has not been sufficiently emphasized in Locke criticism, but becomes accessible through Defoe's novel.[67] In sharp contrast to Pufendorf's account of the origin of property, Locke's presupposes a primary intimacy between person and thing, an intimacy whose consummation changes the intrinsic nature of the thing. "Mixing" is not a metaphor in Locke's account because it captures Locke's literalist conception of the appropriating act as a transfer of something human to the thing appropriated. As his use of the term "mixture" in the context of human and cross-species reproduction indicates, Locke sees "mixing" as a fundamental mode of life (more fundamental than "separateness") and uses it to emphasize an inextricable union in which two sides are "jumbled together."[68] It is in this sense, I want to argue, that Locke uses "mixing" in the famous passage on property. Property is created when something that is "our own" is "joyned" to the thing that we are appropriating. The origin of property is natural in this scenario because it does not require the prior consent of a community. Property can be created in complete isolation, independent of all social convention, because it is produced in the transfer of a fundamental human quality to an exterior object. It may seem that this conception of property as a union of two bodies carries medieval overtones, along the lines of Sir John Fortescue's notion that "property takes the place of the man's bodily integrity . . . and so thenceforth accompanies his blood."[69] But Locke's emphasis on property as a tangible corporal phenomenon, it seems to me, grows out of the pressures of his intellectual project: to assert private property as preceding the conventions of social community.

From a political perspective Pufendorf makes no provision for a radical right of resistance; the sphere of one's own exists, strictly speaking, only by virtue of the community's agreement to respect it. But while Locke successfully carves out an uninvadable, independent realm of private property that remains fundamental even under the arrangements of civil society, he has achieved this by making property more than a right. In Locke's account property is essentialized; the difference between a possessed and an unpossessed thing is not nominal but substantive, the thing itself bearing the imprint of possession. It is only thus that private property and exclusive possession can successfully be claimed to preexist social conventions. But there is another important consequence. In basing the appropriative process on a physical traffic between person and thing, Locke also reinforces his construction of the self as possessive matter that can be joined to material objects. The boundary between human and material spheres is permeable in Locke, and as things become human-material hybrids through appropriation, private property becomes a very private thing indeed. Crusoe's terror after the footprint discovery makes this perfectly clear. Unprotected by communal practice and agreement, Crusoe's property is exclusive only by virtue of the fact that it bears the imprint of his extended self. When the footprint appears on the beach, it is not only Crusoe's property that is invaded, but a part of himself. Even though it appears in an area remote from his usual haunts and habitation, the footprint goes to the heart of Crusoe's possessive claim. It is more than a challenge to his dream of originary possession because it threatens the radically individualistic foundation of Crusoe's property in a naturally conceived self-extension. If the transformation of the island into property rests concretely on the bodily extensions of the possessive self, then the footprint presents a highly charged physical event that merits all the excitement Crusoe shows.

Cannibalism haunts *Robinson Crusoe* in such profound ways because it represents a radical threat to what natural law proponents like Grotius, Locke, or Defoe consider the nucleus of all property, right, and social order: the possessive self or *suum*. It is cannibalism's blatant contradiction of natural law's foundational category that leads Grotius, for instance, to single it out when he makes his case for punishment as a just cause of war. In sharp contrast to Pufendorf (who could attack Grotius on this score because he was less invested in the category of the possessive self), Grotius argued that to "feed on human flesh" was so egregious a violation of natural law that it demanded punishment. Cannibalism justified war, even if the party undertaking it had suffered no injury.[70] In considering violations of natural law a just cause of war, Grotius offers, as Barbara Arneil notes, a powerful legitimation for the colonial enterprise.[71] Grotius echoes, indeed, earlier arguments by Gentili and Juan Ginés de Sepúlveda for the legitimacy of dispossessing American natives.[72] Anthony Pagden has shown how, in a treatise dating from 1550, Sepúlveda argued that the consistent violations of natural law by Indians constituted "grounds for a just war in which the vanquished might be deprived of all their rights, including their liberty, their *dominium corporis suis*." Not even use rights could be claimed by the Indians, Sepúlveda contended, because the practice of cannibalism and human sacrifice constituted the "most grisly violations of those limited use rights which men have over their own bodies." As national customs, cannibalism and human sacrifice demonstrated that Indian societies ignored God's gift of property, even in its limited form as use right. Such hostility toward the divine grant justified the taking of all Indian goods.[73]

In a longstanding European tradition that predates the colonization of America, the cannibal's lack of private property translates into the absence of social, legal, and familial distinctions. The caption of an early woodcut (1505) illustrating Columbus's first voyage to the new world, for instance, describes American natives as follows:

No one owns anything but all things are in common. And the men have as wives those that please them, be they mothers, sisters or friends, therein they make no difference. They also fight with each other. They also eat each other even those who are slain, and hang the flesh of them in the smoke. They live one hundred and fifty years. And have no government.[74]

The absence of a boundary between "mine" and "thine" is here the first characteristic of a society that knows no limits. Incest, war, and cannibalism are the horrifying manifestations of a precivil state in which all things, including people, are truly common. "Every man," as Hobbes describes the state of nature, "has a right to everything; even to one another's body."[75] Exclusive property, the caption implies, is fundamental to right, government, and moral order. Without the ordered association of persons and things provided by private property, social and sexual anarchy breaks out, and cannibalism is its most terrible, but also most symptomatic consequence. "Regarding such barbarians," Grotius concludes his discussion of cannibalism, war is "sanctioned by nature." While "the most just war is against savage beasts, the next [is] against men who are like beasts."[76] Locke essentially shares this position when he embraces the "strange Doctrine . . . that *in the State of Nature, every one has the Executive Power* of the Law of Nature" (Locke's italics). An offender, he argues, has "by the unjust Violence and Slaughter he hath committed upon one, declared War against all Mankind, and therefore may be destroyed as a Lyon or a Tyger, one of those wild Savage Beasts, with whom Men can have no Society nor Security."[77] In a later passage that repeats these lines, Locke contends that such "revolting from his own kind to that of Beasts" effects a "forfeiture" of that otherwise inviolable property in the person and its goods.[78]

When Crusoe confronts the question of cannibalism directly, he frequently attests to his "abhorrence" of the cannibals' "unnatural custom." In Crusoe's view these savages have been "suffered by Providence to have no other guide than that of their own abominable and vitiated passions; and consequently were left, and perhaps had been so for some ages, to act such horrid things and receive such dreadful customs" (177). While Defoe sounds here a familiar theme – the depravity that results from customs unchecked by a higher standard – and effectively states that cannibalism violates natural law, his protagonist hesitates as to whether such violations constitute just grounds for war. Despite his abhorrence of man-eating, Crusoe's desire "to kill them all" is frequently interrupted by doubts over why he should "attack people who had neither done, or intended me any wrong" (232).

Defoe's novel maintains Crusoe's oscillation between the fervent wish for destruction and uncertainty regarding its justice until the very moment of actual attack. Defoe manages this so carefully that Crusoe, wrestling with last-minute doubts over the justice of attacking, decides to wait in hiding and "act then as God would direct" (233). Letting Crusoe fire at the cannibals "in the name of God" (234), the novel diffuses the driving forces behind Crusoe's slaughter of twenty-one savages. Yet they surface nonetheless shortly before the one-sided confrontation between Crusoe and the "naked unarmed wretches" (232). Referring to the cannibals who had just landed on the shore, Crusoe reports:

I observed also that they were landed not where they had done when Friday made his escape, but nearer to my creek, where the shore was low, and where a thick wood came close almost down to the sea. This, with the abhorrence of the inhumane errand these wretches came about, filled me with such indignation that I came down again to Friday, and told him I was resolved to go down to them, and kill them all. (232)

In keeping with what I have argued about the relation between cannibalism and property in Defoe's novel, Crusoe's indignation is fueled as
much by the challenge to his dominion as by the practice of man-eating.
In the topography Crusoe delineates, the cannibals arrive in a spot where
the distance between land and sea is painfully short. The "thick wood"
that comes "almost down to the sea" and the closeness of "my creek" –
figure of the transition from sea to land – symbolize a precarious vicinity between bounded and boundless, proper and common realms that
is threatened with collapse by the devourers' pushing in from the sea.
Not incidentally, it is immediately after the killing of the cannibals – and
shortly before increased company "put us out of fear of the savages"
(246) – that Crusoe makes his first straightforward claim to absolute possession of the entire island.[79] Only after the cannibals have been defeated
and expelled from the island does Crusoe feel that his possessive claim
is fully vindicated.

In the final analysis there is no difference between Crusoe's anxiety
over property and his fear of being devoured: these reactions are responses to the same threat, the fundamental challenge of the cannibal to
the sphere of one's own. Both figuratively and literally, the cannibal disrupts the possessive intimacy between Crusoe and his surroundings and
disturbs the independent construction of private property. Natural law's
nexus of self, property, and right confronts in the cannibal its "other" in
the precise sense that the cannibal stands for an inversion of the centrifugal extensions of the possessive self. Such precision points to cannibalism's
ideological function. *Robinson Crusoe*'s disclosure of cannibalism's link to
the conceptual world of natural law confirms those anthropologists who
have argued for cannibalism as a colonial imaginary.[80] Yet Crusoe's constant fear of being devoured does not represent a loss of contact with
reality. It is a specific response to the pressures exerted by the emergence
of what European eyes were eager to view as the "vacant" spaces of
America. Crusoe's *horror vacui* grows out of the European attempt to assert dominion over the *terra nullius* of the "New World" according to the
supposedly universal rules of natural law, rules whose reformulation in
the sixteenth and seventeenth centuries was itself deeply implicated in
Western Europe's colonial enterprise.

Robinson Crusoe's most radical achievement, however, is not to present
cannibalism as a precise counterforce to Crusoe's appropriative self-
extension, but to suggest that Locke's model of appropriation itself
constitutes an inverted cannibalism. This startling approximation of
cannibal and colonizer finds its most arresting expression when Crusoe

suspects that the footprint he has discovered is really his own, and not the cannibal's:

In the middle of these cogitations, apprehensions, and reflections, it came into my thought one day, that all this might be a meer chimera of my own, and that this foot might be the print of my own foot, when I came on shore from my boat . . . Again I considered also that I could by no means tell for certain where I had trod, and where I had not; and that if at last this was only the print of my own foot, I had played the part of those fools who strive to make stories of spectres and apparitions, and then are frighted at them more than any body. (165–166)

Given the significance of cannibalism in *Robinson Crusoe*, it is difficult not to see this passage as a highly self-conscious moment that invites us to look beyond the "chimera" of the footprint to the "chimera" of cannibalism itself. Defoe's text indicates here that Crusoe's fear of cannibalism may indeed be caused by something imaginary and that Crusoe, as he later reflects, "might be truly said to start at my own shadow" (166). The momentarily suspended distinction between cannibal and colonizer calls our attention to the thin line that separates Locke's appropriative act from the cannibalistic act.

I have already shown how Locke's attempt to found private property in nature, as a positive right that cannot be reduced to a community's duties, led him to essentialize property. To assert exclusive property on this individualist plan, Locke resorted to the critical metaphor of "mixing," which described the creation of private property as a transferal of bodily substance to the thing appropriated. "He that . . . subdued, tilled and sowed any part of [the Earth], thereby annexed to it something that was his Property, which another had no Title to, nor could without injury take from him."[81] Possession, as Locke underscores here, originates in the physical union of two bodies. This means, however, that Crusoe's centrifugal self-extension can also be viewed as an act of incorporation, of making his surroundings part of his body. The only difference from cannibalism is that, instead of making things part of the body by taking them in and collapsing boundaries, Crusoe exteriorizes such internal "mixing" and makes things part of himself by distributing his body's property across the island in ever wider circles, thus creating boundaries. Locke himself appears to have sensed this relation between appropriative and ingestive acts. Note, for instance, how the meaning of "injury" in the passage just quoted threatens to narrow to "bodily harm" in the context of an appropriative model in which something of the body is "annexed" to something outside the body. The cannibal, it would seem, specializes in this kind of "injury."

Even more significant, however, is Locke's rhetorical preparation for his "mixing" metaphor. At this critical point of his argument, Locke introduces an example that comes close on the heels of his programmatic declaration that he "shall endeavour to shew, how Men might come to have Property in several Parts of that which God gave to Mankind in common, and that without any express Compact of all the Commoners."[82] Musing on the "Necessity" of such a means of appropriation, Locke turns to his example: "The Fruit, or Venison, which nourishes the wild Indian, who knows no Inclosure, and is still a Tenant in common, must be his, and so his, i.e. a part of him, that another can no longer have any right to it, before it can do him any good for the support of his Life." One important feature of this passage is the care Locke takes to make clear that the "wild Indian," unfamiliar with enclosure, has no landed rights to "the vacant places of America."[83] Despite this restriction, however, the Indian can serve as a persuasive example for the naturalness of exclusive property. To be sure, Locke believes that, technically, the act of collecting and not the act of ingestion creates title to movables. Yet the notion of "nourishment" as "a part of him" draws on the ingestive act as a vivid figure for a property that is inalienable because it is physically tied to the body. For Locke eating is a pertinent metaphor for demonstrating the natural basis of exclusive possession.

The cannibal in *Robinson Crusoe*, then, not only threatens to resist the centrifugal dynamic of the possessive self, but represents the colonizer's "other" in a far more disturbing, dialectical sense. As the colonizer's shadow, the man-eater shows that there is no universally valid, natural foundation of private property. Every appropriative act that occurs in a social vacuum is ultimately an act of devouring. It is his reliance on the centrifugal extensions of the self that makes Crusoe recognize himself in the cannibal's step. For while these extensions sublimate cannibalism by exteriorizing the process of ingestion, their genealogy is still unmistakable. The chimera of the cannibal as the radically "other" is conjured up to veil this genealogy, but Crusoe's exaggerated fear indicates that the displacement and refinement of "devouring" is not yet complete. Cannibal and colonizer are still too close to each other; the appropriation of *terra nullius* remains connected to the primary ingestion that is projected on to the savage. Crusoe's uncertainty over who left the footprint in the sand, he or the cannibal, is temporary, but his doubts present a vivid memento of the intimate relationship between *terra nullius,* cannibalism, and property that I have pursued from the outset.

Defoe's fictional experiment of a lone individual on a desert island establishes maximal distance from the dominant property paradigm of English culture, but it ultimately cannot leave behind the communal ideology of common law according to which property is the preestablished and hence legitimate ground of community. No matter how much Defoe wishes to suggest that a natural law claim may originate a common law claim – that Crusoe's vacant island may become a "new" manorial estate – the neutralization of time and space on the island is not conducive to the creation of a stable community. Grotius may well say that nothing is created *by* time and everything *within* it; the restlessness of Crusoe's anxious exertions seems to belie their creative efficacy. In the end Crusoe fails to produce a sense of groundedness, a settled fit between practice and space. What we get instead is a volatile intimacy, easily disturbed and interrupted. *Robinson Crusoe* struggles to break through and replace the integrated communal model of the manor, but it ultimately reveals that this communal model is too deeply ingrained to be quickly replaced by a radically individualistic, originary, and socially unconditioned possessive act.

While Defoe's elaborate descriptive-narrative acts attempt to articulate the phenomenology and genesis of property, they are successful mainly in disclosing the contradictions inherent in the natural law of appropriation. Defoe's descriptions show how, under this law, property cannot be established as a right but only as a thing, tied to the person with a painful concreteness that undermines the recognition of any title unless you, the owner, are present – both as actual part of the object and as its incessant user. It is this impossibility of identifying property as yours when you are physically absent that lies behind the irresolvable contradiction between visibility and invisibility – between the need to show and declare your property by drawing boundaries and the anxiety over exposing yourself that prompts the concealment of those boundaries. It is not possible for Crusoe, in other words, to rest content with a simple descriptive scene that would show the lines that connect human and material spheres. Because of its inherent volatility, the meeting of the proprietary vacuum of the island and the possessive matter of the self demands that narrative moments permeate the description to connect the latter's parts, to declare and secure the possessive character of the scene. And it also demands that such declarations are as often retracted, sometimes within the same movement – as when Crusoe's expanding enclosures promise ever better concealment even as they establish con-stantly growing possession. The absorption of narrative moments into the descriptive scene and the narrative production of descriptive scenes are both attempts at "mixture" in the Lockean sense. In such "jumbling together" of description and narrative, *Robinson Crusoe* finds one way to express formally the contradictory structure of possession in natural law. As Defoe's novel reveals, Locke's possessive individualism can only assert itself by creating hybrids of persons and things, by enmeshing human and material spheres to such an extent that the very notion of individualism becomes questionable.

CHAPTER THREE

Henry Fielding and the common law of plenitude

In the third book of *Joseph Andrews* (1742), Henry Fielding engages in a characteristic act of generic differentiation. He criticizes "those romance-writers, who intitle their books, the History of England, the History of France, of Spain, &c." because they only succeed in "describ[ing] countries and cities." Though such histories attempt to give an account of the "actions and characters of men," they are largely unsuccessful in this regard, producing "eternal contradictions." Fielding proposes that these writers should be given a name that better accords with their area of greatest accomplishment: he suggests calling them "topographers or chorographers." By distinction Fielding aligns his own writing practice with biography. His interest, he claims, lies in "actions and characters," not "countries and cities." Unlike the topographies of romance (which for Fielding included texts such as *Robinson Crusoe*[1]), biography delivers a "narrative of facts" that "may be relied on, tho we often mistake the age and country wherein they happened."[2]

But while *The History of the Adventures of Joseph Andrews* focuses our attention on a person and not a place, it also indicates the instability of the generic distinctions Fielding invokes. It is, after all, a "history of adventures" and not a "biography" that Fielding's title announces. Nor does Fielding, as the term "adventures" already suggests, reject the genre of romance entirely. In the preface to his book, he recommends the category of "comic romance" to characterize his "kind of writing."[3] Far from being disturbed by such instabilities, Fielding's novelistic practice promotes them. The generic turbulence thus generated sponsors, as Michael McKeon has shown, a "complicated dance of double negation" whereby simple romance and its opposites (history/biography) are criticized and transformed, yielding a self-conscious compound in which "comic romance" merges with "true history."[4] Such a complex merger, it follows from Fielding's generic maneuverings, must also characterize the relationship between description (aligned with romance, topography, place) and narrative (aligned with biography, action, character). *Joseph Andrews* does not go far in developing such a merger, but Fielding's next novel, *Tom Jones* (1749), because of its deep investment in questions of property and place, moves to a new level of interrelation. It makes the descriptive, as we shall see, central to the articulation of narrative form. Fielding's self-conscious combination of these modes brings *Tom Jones* into a detailed relationship with the communal forms available in *Robinson Crusoe*.

Critics interested in the "rise" of the novel have always struggled to find a place for Fielding within a historical scenario that recognizes Defoe's and Richardson's novels as crucial generic prototypes. This problem persists from Ian Watt to John Bender and Nancy Armstrong because they and others have tended to identify the novel as an essentially modern genre. As such, the novel has been seen to demote identities that depend on their position within a concretely localized social and geographical space, and to promote modern forms of self-enclosed, mobile individuality. It hardly matters whether these forms are seen as positive, according to the precepts of liberal individualism, or negative, according to the disciplined self envisioned by someone like Michel Foucault. What is important is that a majority of critics have found the temptation to look for modern institutions in the eighteenth-century novel irresistible. In the exciting rush of this search, many commentators on the eighteenth century have failed to acknowledge that even those texts by Richardson and Defoe that have been most persistently linked with economic, psychological, and sexual modernization exhibit hybrid structures and meanings that testify to the depth of the novel's engagement with premodern realities.

Even McKeon, who has insisted that the presence of traditional social and cultural forms needs to be recognized as an essential aspect of the eighteenth-century novel, in the end reinscribes such forms into a comprehensive process of modernization that, with the significant help of the novel, establishes terms such as "virtue" or "romance" as distinct categories that are abstracted from their previous embedded position within the concrete texture of social and cultural life. While McKeon can thus explain the premodern aspects of Fielding's novels, these aspects are no longer vital. Fielding's belief in institutions such as "social deference, custom, the law" is too self-conscious, and the deliberate instrumentality of these institutions within Fielding's work indicates, according to McKeon, an actual disenchantment that concedes their inefficacy.[5] To my mind this argument seriously underestimates the actual force of institutions such as social deference, custom, and law within the transitional culture of the British novel. On this level at least, McKeon replaces an argument that would be sensitive to the real power of traditionalist forces within eighteenth-century Britain (and the contradictions and discontinuities they cause) with an account that privileges the novel as a revolutionary modern genre capable of transmuting and neutralizing premodern communal forms.[6] But as the later eighteenth century shows, nothing happens decisively, in literary history or elsewhere, in a country that so effectively protected the core of its established institutions, so successfully demonstrated the power of gradualism.

In some ways Deidre Lynch's *The Economy of Character: Novels, Market Culture, and the Business of Inner Meaning* (1998) is more successful than McKeon's book in recognizing the eighteenth-century novel's difficult status as a modern genre. But even as it retrieves the premodern shape of individuality in eighteenth-century texts, Lynch's work validates the outdated distinction between "flat" and "round" characters as a fitting guide for the novel's journey from the eighteenth into the nineteenth century. Lynch's resourceful work of retrieval is invaluable, but while it effectively highlights the cultural constructedness of both "flat" and "round" characters, it does not go far enough in revising our perception of the novelistic construction of identity. The conceptually confused contrast between "flat" and "round" characters finds an historically sensitive exploration in Lynch, yet that exploration finally cannot disentangle itself from the old narrative line according to which the eighteenth-century novel constitutes a kind of overture to the "business of inner meaning," a business that is taken on by the nineteenth-century novel.

I should like to draw more decisively and more broadly on the eighteenth-century novel as a theoretical guide to the whole question of identity and its cultural construction. What the eighteenth-century novel suggests – and what my discussion of *Robinson Crusoe* has already begun to show – is that questions of identity need to be addressed by highlighting their communal aspect. The concept of "communal form," it seems to me, offers a more productive way of approaching *all* cultural articulations of identity. Even *Robinson Crusoe*, a text that has rarely escaped teleological patterns of interpretation emphasizing a solidification of the self, forcefully demonstrates the extent to which Crusoe's possessive individualism can be maintained only at the price of a claustrophobic intimacy between person and thing. Crusoe's painful oscillation between gaining and losing a bounded identity signals the shortcomings of all readings that wish to make Defoe's text central to a progressive rise of the novel that issues in modern forms of identity. Even more importantly, however, *Robinson Crusoe* forces us to acknowledge that communal forms underlie even the most potent ideologies of liberal individualism.

My point here is that all forms of identity are hybrid: mixtures of different elements, bundles of relationships. Fielding's *Tom Jones* underlines this by presenting the most profound celebration available in eighteenth-century British fiction of unbounded communal forms, of a tangible, possessive continuity between human and material spheres. From this perspective *Robinson Crusoe* and *Tom Jones* are not the mysteriously distant cousins of literary history whose elusive relationship can be grasped only through the extensive dialectic mediations to which critics like McKeon resort. These two books are closely related through their indepth exploration of the communal functions of the possessive and their recognition that the relationship between narrative and description is crucial to those functions. The most intriguing thing about their relationship, in fact, is the comprehensive precision with which their possessive worlds exclude each other. *Robinson Crusoe* is the only eighteenth-century novel to make the phenomenology and genesis of property a fundamental problem, but Defoe's novel is closely related to *Tom Jones* because Fielding, by representing possession as a fundamental social given, desires to neutralize the problems Defoe raises. If Defoe is eager to undermine the tacit communal consent of customary law by revealing its ultimate dependence on the possessive individualism of natural law, Fielding wishes to preserve established relationships. Their disturbance by the possessive individualism of the Blifils, indeed, is the origin of narrative movement in *Tom Jones*, and Fielding makes clear that such disturbances can be linked to natural law, the doctrine instinctively adopted by young Blifil.[7] "Pox of your Laws of Nature," (162) is Squire Western's line, but it resonates more widely within a fictional world that finds its starting and end points in the possessive fullness of the common law's *nulle terre sans seigneur* – a fullness, of course, that is the spectacular antagonist of the possessive void of *terra nullius*.

These differences even play themselves out on the level of religion. Considering his pronounced belief that "all the Sons of Man are Sons of Crime," Defoe's dismissal of usage and custom is not surprising. In Defoe's view custom is nothing but popular practice and, since it was "born of the Mob, and in the Crowd begun," could not serve as a standard for the required correction of human error.[8] It may well be, as Christopher Hill has pointed out, that the Protestant view of sin as ineluctable inheritance is "well suited to a society based on inherited status," but for Defoe such depravity also undercuts the common law's ultimate legitimizing ground, the quasi-spontaneous emanations of social practice.⁹ The dissenting tradition of the seventeenth century emphasized instead the universal standard of natural law, which it interpreted not as innately given, but as discoverable by reason.¹⁰ Defoe clearly participates in this tradition. Fielding's latitudinarian belief in man's fundamental goodness, on the other hand, is far more compatible with the common law's respect for established human practice.

Rather than dividing Defoe's and Fielding's novels, these ideological differences are so detailed as to bring them closer to each other. Considering them within a single interpretive framework is compelling not because literary history somehow has to account for two texts that have always seemed rather different, even as they both demanded a place within the history of the novel. Rather, *Robinson Crusoe* and *Tom Jones* must be analyzed together because they present two historically specific ways of making worlds out of possessive relations. In this way they both reveal the tremendous significance that concepts of property have in eighteenth-century Britain in articulating the social, legal, epistemological, and psychological limits of community. They both underline in equally forceful ways the need to look at communal forms rather than individuals, and at relationships rather than objects.

I

When Tom and Partridge, far away from Allworthy's Paradise Hall, lose their way in Worcester, they are suddenly enveloped by darkness and reach a very steep hill. Tom's sadness over having been forced to leave his love and his guardian makes him sigh: "Partridge, I wish I was at the Top of this Hill; it must certainly afford a most charming Prospect, especially by this Light: for the solemn Gloom which the Moon casts on all Objects, is beyond Expression beautiful" (443). Although it is bitterly cold, Tom is determined to have his view and ascends the hill with the reluctant Partridge. Yet our expectations are disappointed: the couple never reach the summit because Partridge – urging considerations more material than the pleasures of prospect – convinces Tom to pursue a light he sees on their way up. And so they abandon their ascent and find shelter in the house of the Man of the Hill.

After the Man has told his personal history (the relation takes up four chapters) he proposes to entertain Tom "with the Sight of some very fine Prospects" (486), the contemplation of which is one of the main consolations of his old age. The sun has just risen and it seems that, now, the pleasures of prospect will finally be indulged. But we are again disappointed, this time by a direct authorial intervention. Once Tom and his new acquaintance have mounted Mazard Hill:

one of the most noble Prospects in the World presented itself to their View, and which we would likewise present to the Reader; but for two Reasons. First, We despair of making those who have seen this Prospect, admire our Description. Secondly, We very much doubt whether those, who have not seen it, would understand it. (495)

On one level this is, of course, a fantastic joke. Fielding's use of two denied descriptions to frame the story of the Man of the Hill is meant to laugh us out of our readerly expectations. The perverse withholding of one of the most consciously cultivated enjoyments of the age, the pleasure of prospect, and the mock-seriousness with which Fielding justifies himself, together constitute one of the more ostentatious examples of Fielding's stress on the fictionality of fiction, and he disabuses us of any notion we may have of seeking aesthetic release in identifying with Tom's romantic mood through the medium of a beautiful description. That such strong demonstration of narratorial selectiveness takes as its object an expected description highlights the important status descriptive acts have in Fielding's novelistic practice. Just what that status is, however, is difficult to decide when Fielding declares description at one point to be an indispensable "Refresh[ment]" and at another a "Labour" that is to be shunned (151, 627). His evasiveness is all the more unnerving because, at the beginning of his sprawling novel, Fielding offers a magisterial description of the landscape surrounding *Tom Jones's* other man of the hill, Squire Allworthy. Granted, Fielding is even at this earlier moment remarkably self-deprecating about his descriptive act – he claims not to know how to get the reader down "from as high a Hill as Mr. Allworthy's ... without breaking thy Neck" (44) – but once these two hill scenes are placed side by side, Fielding's laughter takes on a more complex tone.[11] The humor of Fielding's refusal to describe actually depends on a rather specific aspect of contemporary aesthetic and philosophic debates.

The most perplexing and amusing aspect of Fielding's mock-apology is certainly his suggestion that the description of an unfamiliar scene – a scene of which no previous idea exists in the reader – might somehow be incomprehensible. Fielding's facetiousness invokes here the general issue of the relation of words and ideas, a relation prominently discussed in John Locke's *An Essay Concerning Human Understanding* (1689). For Locke the dissociation of words from ideas causes a breakdown of communication. "But so far as Words are of Use and Signification," he writes, "so far is there a constant connexion between the Sound and the Idea; and a Designation, that the one stand for the other: without which Application of them, they are nothing but so much insignificant Noise."[12] Locke's concern with the relationship between words and ideas is shown here by his insistence on the need for a "constant connexion" and a "Designation" that firmly and obviously link word and idea. The "insignificant Noise" that otherwise results figures in Fielding's joke as the intelligibility risk incurred by a description that paints an unknown scene.

Fielding's close friend James Harris addressed this risk within a more immediate literary context when he stated that:

being understood to others, either Hearers or Spectators, seems to be a common Requisite to all Mimetic Arts whatever ... it follows that Perspicuity must be Essential to them all; and that no prudent Artist would neglect, if it were possible, any just Advantage to attain this End. Now there can be no Advantage greater, than the Notoriety of the Subject imitated.[13]

But however clearly Fielding recognized the jocular potential of such a position, a wider survey of his writings reveals that he cared deeply about the proper relationship between words and ideas, and that his thinking followed Locke's in this respect.[14] Fielding's joke in the end points to a genuine worry that descriptive signifiers (understood as individual words as well as entire passages) can become isolated objects whose lack of grounding in their respective environments undermines textual unity and meaning. This is evident even in his confession that he does not know how to get the reader down from "as high a hill as" Allworthy's. That the reader may get stuck with the descriptive scene, up on the hill, rather than coming down into the concrete arena of human action points to the fear that descriptive passages can "disembed" themselves from their textual environment.

This potential for disembedding, in fact, is also behind the first part of Fielding's joke, his seeming anxiety that those who are familiar with the prospect may come to admire the description. Fielding alludes here to the strong pictorialism advocated by someone like Joseph Addison, who suggested that a verbal representation of a landscape may outstrip in vividness and enjoyment the actual scene. Such potential ascent of the copy over the original is worrying to Fielding. His critique of *Pamela* identifies Richardson's as a dangerous book because its "images" of seduction, in "resembling Life, out-glow it."[15] This concern over the pictorial powers of language finds its perhaps sharpest expression later in *Tom Jones* when Fielding repeats his refusal to give a detailed account of a scene. This time he defends himself by claiming that only those readers "whose Devotion to the Fair Sex, like that of the Papists to their Saints, wants to be raised by the Help of Pictures" (722) could insist on such an account. This aggressive comparison between pornographic images and religious icons shows that Fielding's bathetic withdrawal of description is related to a significant iconophobic undercurrent. While he believes in the primacy of sight as the most noble sense, Fielding stresses, like his friend Harris and his much-admired Rene de Bossu, the hierarchy of original and copy, the difference between visual and textual media, and the semantic and intratextual grounding of the descriptive signifier.[16] The danger of reading the description of a familiar or unfamiliar landscape, then, is that the description could turn into an appearance without reference beyond itself, and could be contemplated at the expense of the signified, in isolation from it, or in isolation from surrounding textual materials. In all three cases language threatens to become an object in its own right that no longer serves to support an overall communicative design rooted in a transparent relationality, but takes on an independent life, unattached, outside the sphere of obvious "Designation" and "constant connexion." Fielding's complicated stance toward description, then, has to do with the descriptive's possible independence from a clearly ordered hierarchical relationality, and its consequent potential for reification and fetishization. All of this, however, still does not explain why Fielding refuses description to *Tom Jones*'s second man of the hill and lavishly grants it to the first, Squire Allworthy. To resolve this question the politics of Fielding's descriptive acts need to be considered.

II

Fielding the topographer places Mazard Hill in Worcester, but the story of the Man takes us back to the landscape of the Allworthy estate in Somerset. The Man of the Hill grew up close by, in a "Village of Somersetshire, called Mark" (451). His story begins there, but his studies take him to Oxford and his moral failings eventually to London. The Man's story is one of gradual decline, and London figures as the place that completes his moral corruption. Only a tearful chance meeting with his father recalls the Man to his better instincts and allows him to return to Somerset. At this point the history of the Man of the Hill takes an intriguing turn. Another chance meeting gives the Man the opportunity to

save the life of his closest London gambling companion. Just as the Man
is exhorting this friend to reform his life of abandon, the two suddenly
hear of the Duke of Monmouth's arrival on the shores of England. It is
1685 and the revolt to replace the legitimate Catholic James Stuart with
the illegitimate Protestant James Scott is beginning.

Monmouth's arrival in this part of England is not accidental. It was
well known that Somerset promised substantial support at this time for
the cause of a Protestant crown. The region around Taunton, Bridgwater,
and Glastonbury was not only known as "Paradise" – a detail that may
have inspired Fielding to name the Allworthy estate Paradise Hall –
but also as the "nursery of rebellion."[17] Somerset had a strong history
of popular resistance that asserted itself during the years of the Civil
War and continued after the Restoration. In returning us to Somerset,
Fielding not only brings England's history of civil unrest into contact
with the Jacobite rising of 1745 – unfolding as the Man tells his story – he
also strengthens the association between the two men of the hill. Paradise
Hall, Fielding's archetypal English manor, is located in an area deeply
marked by England's long struggle against the Stuarts, Catholicism, and
absolutism.

The rebellion of 1685 is the first political event that figures in the
Man's account, which, up to this point, has exhibited all the trappings
of a moral tale of private vice. The casual manner in which the effect
of this news is registered is surprising: "Events of this Nature in the
Public," the Man allows, "are generally apt to eclipse all private concerns. Our Discourse, therefore, now became entirely political" (477).
What for a long time has had the appearance of a moral tale void
of any reference to public events shifts here – abruptly – into a story
about revolutionary politics in which the Man and his dissolute gambling friend risk their lives for the cause of a Protestant crown. They join
Monmouth at Bridgwater, are wounded during the battle at Sedgemoor,
captured by royal forces and imprisoned in "Taunton Gaol" (478–479).
We should be mistaken, I believe, to attribute this breathtaking shift to
overly digressive storytelling. The swiftness with which the moral tale
leaps here into political history needs to be seen instead as the narrative sign of a fluid relation between private and public that at this point
has force over the Man's life. The simple fact that this narrative shift
takes place is full of significance, for it points to a model of virtue in
which the private and the public, as well as the moral and the political, cannot be kept apart. Our surprise over the shift, indeed, tells us
more about the extent to which the heritage of liberal individualism has

taught us to keep these spheres apart than about any inconsistency in the narrative.

The impulse toward abrupt transition in the Man's story, however, does not end here. Just as abruptly – namely, as soon as the Revolution settlement of 1689 has removed the "Danger to which the Protestant Religion was . . . exposed under a Popish Prince" (477) – the Man, now thirty-one, retires from active life. After 1689, he concedes, his "History is little better than a Blank" (480). So complete is his seclusion that he remains ignorant of the Jacobite rebellions of 1715 and the present one of 1745. And so completely has the Man succeeded in dividing the public from the private, politics from morality, that his response to the current rebellion is a "loud Thanksgiving Prayer" for his deliverance from "all society with Human Nature" (478). Tom is exasperated. His own response to news of the rebellion still adhered to the model the Man had abandoned in 1689. All private concerns were immediately "eclipsed" and Tom rallied to the defense of the Hanoverian government and the Protestant succession (368). Given that Fielding presents the illegitimate Monmouth's attempt to fight for a Protestant crown as a foreshadowing of 1689 (477), Tom's own status as a bastard, along with his willingness to defend the Protestant settlement, develops an association between illegitimacy and the Glorious Revolution to which I shall return.

The Man's contrary responses to the Catholic threat to English liberty in 1685 and 1745 are central to understanding the significance of this episode. The point of the contrast between expedience and apathy is to expose the latter as a hopelessly inappropriate reaction to the national crisis that Fielding recognized in the Jacobite rebellion.[18] The Glorious Revolution, the story of the Man suggests, did not obviate an ideal of civic virtue in which the private and the public constitute a single continuous sphere. On the contrary, in Fielding's view, as we shall see, the revolution reinstituted a close link between public and private, and the Jacobite rebellion serves as a powerful reminder that this ideal of virtue remains integral to English liberty. In this context the man's retirement in Worcester, away from the revolutionary traditions of Somerset, assumes additional political significance. If Fielding notes that his novel presents "Scenes of private Life" (402), the story of the Man reminds us that, in *Tom Jones*, private life is a category that overlaps with public history and a politically charged topography. Once it ceases to engage the public, the private turns into the "blank" of the Man's postrevolutionary existence and is not worth our attention.

A "blank," of course, is also what Fielding presents us with descriptively, and we can now begin to discern the political motivation behind his refusal to describe the landscape around Mazard Hill. Fielding's censure of the Man's postrevolutionary retirement needs to be recognized, I believe, as an early critique of liberal individualism. The Man's retirement is criticized for its mistaken division of the private from the public, the political from the moral, and even the theological from social practice (after all, the Man piously celebrates a divine nature, but rejects all involvement with human beings). The ultimate object of criticism in the story of the Man is a conception of the individual as a fundamentally private being who is habitually estranged from the spheres of politics, government, and community, and perceives of any obligation issuing from these spheres as a bothersome duty at best and an intolerable intrusion at worst.[19] Fielding presents the Man's contemplation of prospects as an expression of such withdrawal, and he does not leave the Man of the Hill before he can reinforce this sense.

In a final scene that privileges the social immediacy of hearing over the distancing and separating powers of the eye, Fielding has Tom blindly race downhill to assist someone calling for help while the Man, true to his name, remains placidly on top of the hill, sticking to his initial resolution to enjoy "some very fine Prospects."[20] Agent and spectator, the famous two sides of Bernard Mandeville's and Adam Smith's divided self, are kept strictly apart, attached to two different characters.[21] The Man's position on the hill, his stubborn devotion to the prospect and the separating powers of the eye (all symbolic of his protoliberal individualism) further explain Fielding's refusal to describe: the potential disembedding effects of description, themselves allied with the eye, would reinforce the political and epistemological separations embodied by the Man. Like a signifier without a signified, the Man fails to be properly embedded and contextualized, and Fielding gives this failure its most concrete and theoretically most established expression in the Man's material relationship to "his" landscape. The Man does not own the land around Mazard Hill and, most significantly, expresses relief over having "no Estate" and not being "plagued with . . . Tenants and Stewards" (483). The nexus of obligations that comes with landed property is absent, and this constitutes the concrete precondition for the Man's enjoyment of landscape as a zone emptied of all social bonds and political meanings. Without property, the Man does not partake of the business of the nation and contradicts the classical ideal according to which civic virtue is grounded in the constant connection to independent landed possessions. The refusals, blanks, and absences with which Fielding surrounds his Man of the Hill thus link aesthetic and political preferences that appear to converge on the issue of property – the "proper" relationship between persons and things, readers and descriptions, viewers and landscape, dwellers and land, subjects and country.

III

Exactly what place property occupies in Fielding's thinking becomes clearer in a pamphlet he wrote in June 1747. Though the immediate occasion for *A Dialogue between a Gentleman of London ... and an Honest Alderman* is the 1747 election, Fielding uses the recently defeated Jacobite rebellion to offer more particular statements on the "Bill for abolishing Heretable Jurisdictions in Scotland" and the legitimacy of the Protestant succession. The bill, introduced to break the remaining feudal powers of Scottish landowners and to reduce the likelihood of another Jacobite uprising, had occupied Parliament between 7 April and 17 June 1747, when it received royal assent.[22] Major contributors to the debate included Lord Hardwicke, who introduced the bill, and Fielding's patron, George Lyttleton, to whom *Tom Jones* is dedicated. While Fielding's comments on the bill itself are limited, the contentious parliamentary debate merits closer consideration.

Judging from the evidence in William Cobbett's *The Parliamentary History of England*, the central conflict in the debate over the abolition of Scotland's heritable jurisdictions raged over the interpretation of Articles 18 and 20 of the Treaty of Union between England and Scotland. These articles, as Hardwicke pointed out, differentiate between "laws which concern public policy, and those which concern private right."[23] This distinction is crucial in the debate because, according to another of the treaty's provisions, regional, heritable jurisdictions were strictly incidental to the territory to which they were annexed. They were protected by the treaty as "reserved to the owners thereof as rights of property" (6 Anne, c.11), which places them in the area of "private right" and, as such, under stricter protection than matters of "public policy."[24] Of course, as both Hardwicke and Fielding argue, it is evident that the Scottish jurisdictions, while they might be considered inviolable property rights, at the same time affect public policy. Since they nurture a system of regional law, these jurisdictions stand in the way, in the words of the Gentleman of Fielding's *Dialogue*, of "diffusing the Justice of the Crown over all Parts of the Kingdom."[25] They rest on an inextricable integration of possession, place, and right that concretely intertwines, on this local level, private and public, property and government. It is this union of territory and jurisdiction that allows local custom and local law to resist "the Justice of the Crown," and it is this ability to resist that proponents of the law felt they had to break through.

The problem with this attempt, as the parliamentary debate shows, was the closeness with which these jurisdictions were attached to privately owned territory. They were, in effect, private property and could not simply be taken away without raising fundamental questions about the status of property in the British constitution in general. If "we compel any man in Scotland to sell his property," one opposition voice asserted, "we not only commit an evident breach of the Articles of the Union, but we shall render the property of every man, both in England and Scotland, precarious."[26] The fear of a destabilization of property by the government and thus of a split between private and public clearly emerges in the first article of the "Protest against committing the Heretable Jurisdiction Bill." That article succinctly states that the monetary compensation of those families who would lose their jurisdictional rights effectively means that "their ancient rights and inheritances [are] to be purchased by the public."[27] Improper proceedings indeed, given that the link between property and liberty in English political thought is so basic as to cut across the substantial rift, pointed up by J. G. A. Pocock, between Lockean and republican traditions.[28]

Still, the excitement over the threat to private property may seem exaggerated. After all, the Scottish jurisdictions were remnants of a feudal system that would seem to be long outdated in a polite and commercial society. Yet the identification of property and government in these local jurisdictions has significance for the eighteenth-century constitution as a whole. Apart from the tangible issue of government intrusion into private property, the fervour of the parliamentary debate is also indebted to the fact that the heritable jurisdictions confronted parliament with a concrete survivor of a full-blown feudal system whose union of property and government continues to haunt and influence eighteenth-century conceptions of social and political community (as can be seen, for instance, in the property qualifications required for most public offices). In this sense the distance between the conjunction of property and government in the heritable jurisdictions and in the eighteenth-century constitution is not that great. Broadly speaking, property legitimizes government in both cases. The main difference is that the heritable jurisdictions sponsor an immediate and literal identification of these two functions, whereas the eighteenth-century constitution relies on a variety of mechanisms that carefully mediate between them, allowing for a greater degree of centralization without dissolving local governance organized around landed property. Reforming this supposed feudal remnant of territorial jurisdiction, then, is not simply redressing an anachronism; it involves tampering with a structure that is recognizably connected to the present.

In Fielding's pamphlet the Gentleman responds to the purchasability of ancient rights and properties rather flatly, asserting that "private Justice" has to be reconciled with "public Good." The problematic nature of the government's seizure of private property is not directly addressed and Fielding appears to evade the critical issue. But this does not mean that he did not care about it. Indeed, in a different context, the Gentleman comes out with a significantly less controlled statement. Asserting that property rights affect, as a matter of course, "Public Right, Policy, and Civil Government," the Gentleman denies private rights a separate status and in effect supports the feudal elements of the eighteenth-century constitution.[29] And if we glance for a moment at *Tom Jones*, the Allworthy estate itself turns out to be one of those ancient English manors whose characteristic union of landed possession and court baron closely resembles the integration of territory and jurisdiction found in the Scottish estates.

To be sure, Fielding identifies Allworthy as a Justice of the Peace and, as such, he is associated with the increasing centralization of English law and the rapid decline of the court baron in the seventeenth and eighteenth centuries.[30] Justices of the Peace were appointed by the crown or the lord chancellor and their main function was to implement a continually increasing load of statutes. Though they were required to own independent property (as Fielding himself was to learn when he became a judge), their jurisdictional powers did not issue from the possession of a certain piece of land. They were thus linked to the national machinery of government – to the extent that such a thing existed in the eighteenth century – and were not part of an independent local government as embodied in manorial and heritable jurisdictions. Nonetheless, the role of the Justices in the eighteenth century cannot simply be summed up by the distinction between statute and custom, national government and local estate. As unambiguous as Fielding is in identifying Allworthy as a Justice of the Peace, he is equally interested in emphasizing the coincidence of territorial and judicial functions at Paradise Hall.

In two legal cases in *Tom Jones*, for example, Allworthy makes solitary judicial decisions in cases that by law require "double justice" – the agreement of at least two justices.[31] Allworthy's discretion is all the more striking because his close neighbor Squire Western also holds a commission of the peace and could easily be called upon to assist Allworthy in these cases. But Fielding prefers to present Allworthy in a position in which he can be seen to regulate the business of his estate alone. This association of landed possession and judicial function is underlined further by the fact that Western is also a manorial lord, and thus represents the same alignment of judicial function and unit of possession. Similarly, Fielding deliberately represents Squire Allworthy's "Hall" as the seat of justice and thus, harking back to the tradition in which the hall operated as a court of justice, aligns residential with judicial functions.[32] Paradise Hall also carries with it the offices of gamekeeper and constable, both of which were filled and invested with particular powers by the manorial lord.[33] Though shirked by some because of the unremunerated work it involved, the office of Justice of the Peace was attractive to many landowners because it allowed them to dominate affairs on the estate and in the parish.[34] Fielding contrasts his two justices Allworthy and Western, but in both cases he aligns territorial extent with judicial function in such a way as to present these two squires as patriarchal rulers of local affairs. In a pattern that corresponds to the historical development of local government in eighteenth-century Britain, Paradise Hall intertwines more modern forms of jurisdiction that are based on a more mediated relationship between property and government with older, local forms of justice that associate property and government directly.[35]

It is thus not surprising that the manor had special significance for Fielding's view of political economy; for him it stood at the heart of England's ancient constitution. His *An Enquiry into the Causes of the Late Increase of Robbers* (1751) argues that the manor founds the English polity, and he uses it as his point of departure for a discussion of the dangers posed to the eighteenth-century constitution by trade and luxury. While he criticizes the excessive powers the manorial lord held in ancient times, Fielding insists on the centrality of the manor as the communal form against which all subsequent change has to be measured. Using extensive references to Coke and Littleton, Fielding offers an account of modernization that is organized around the rise and fall of the copyhold estate, the most common tenure on the manorial estate, and the one most closely associated with local custom. For him the increasing independence of the copyhold tenant from the manorial lord is central to a continuous process of modernization that culminates in the "Introduction of Trade," which "hath indeed given a new Face to the whole Nation, hath in a great Measure subverted the former State of Affairs, and hath almost totally changed the Manners, Customs, and Habits of the People."[36] The central manifestation of this changed constitution – already underway in the dissociation of the copyhold from the manor – is the increased mobility of persons and things, the dominant concern of Fielding's treatise.[37]

One of Fielding's most symptomatic responses to such mobility is to advocate a return, in some form, to the ancient custom of "frankpledge" that ensured an unambiguous and permanent association between individual and neighborhood, thus averting what he saw as a representative evil of the eighteenth-century constitution: the unsupervised "wandering from Place to Place" of "idle Persons."[38] For Fielding the crucial point about frankpledge was that it ensured the confinement of "Subjects ... to the Places where they were ... incorporated."[39] In this sense frankpledge recalls the manorial economy and also underscores Fielding's reliance on embedded forms when it comes to imagining social community. His use of the manor in *Tom Jones* has to be seen in the light of his perception that it can represent a modernizing process that has ruinously resulted in an increasing mobility of persons and things, a mobility that undercuts the "incorporating" dynamic of the manorial community. With Paradise Hall, I want to suggest, Fielding tests the extent to which ancient communal forms still resist and absorb the increasing mobility of persons and things.

The embedding powers of the manor are, of course, also evident in the figure of the squire himself. Allworthy's close involvement with local affairs, his fatherly dispensation of charity, his tempering of justice with mercy, his generous hospitality, and his possession of "one of the largest Estates in the County" (34) make him one of those Justices of the Peace who were recognizable as the "familiar patriarchs of the neighborhood."[40] Fielding's depiction of Paradise Hall as a community that coheres around the possessive, judiciary, familial, and economic functions of the squire appeals to the communal pattern of the manor with its "informal, intimate, and diffuse regulation" and its elevation of the local and customary over the national and statutory.[41] In celebrating the intermixture of these different capacities in the single figure of the squire, Fielding draws a clear line between Allworthy and the Man of the Hill. He contradicts Locke, who, in criticizing Filmer's absolutist identification of familial and governmental authority, had insisted:

> That the Power of a Magistrate over a Subject, may be distinguished from that of a Father over his Children, a Master over his Servant, a Husband over his Wife, and a Lord over his Slave. All which distinct Powers happening sometimes together in the same Man, if he be considered under these different Relations, it may help us to distinguish these Powers from one another, and shew the Difference betwixt a Ruler of a Common-wealth, a Father of a Family, and a Captain of a Galley.[42]

The distinction of such functions in Squire Allworthy is never an issue in *Tom Jones*. Fielding is certainly no Filmerian, but even though judicial office is not inherently linked to landed possession, and even though paternal authority is not directly identified with governmental authority, Fielding's presentation of the Justice of the Peace recalls to life an older, patriarchal communal order whose basis in landed property effaces the differentiation of social and political, public and private capacities stressed by Locke.

Fielding contributes in this way to a pattern described by Sidney and Beatrice Webb in the early twentieth century. Despite the fact that, in legal and constitutional theory, the rise of the Justice of the Peace signals an ascent of statute over custom, of central government over local autonomy, in practice the period between 1689 and 1835 saw an extension of the autonomy of local rulers. Fielding's creation of a benevolent patriarch whose power rests on closely aligned territorial and judicial functions is less nostalgic than it may seem. It exploits the feudal residues contained within the eighteenth century's more mediated relationship between government and property to project a communal pattern in which these two aspects seem to belong together naturally, even while they are no longer organically linked. What Fielding's novel reveals is that the distance between the feudal past and eighteenth-century institutions is eminently bridgeable, a situation that must have been especially obvious to someone who studied law in the eighteenth century. As Fielding's *Enquiry* abundantly demonstrates, eighteenth-century lawyers did not consider the past a reservoir of long-lost traditions whose excavation excites a predominantly aesthetic sense. On the contrary, the lawyer's research into the remote legal past could produce guidelines for contemporary problems. Fielding did not demand new laws to cure the social ill of "wandering," but advocated the strict enforcement of old laws. He recognized a fundamental familiarity between past and present, and this awareness affects his treatment of the Justice of the Peace in *Tom Jones*.[43] The manorial court, though in decline, continued to exist in the eighteenth century and, as a judgment from 1822 found, its privileges could not be dissolved by a mere "non-user."[44] In the same way the manorial identification of possessive with judicial functions remains alive in the alignment of these functions in Fielding's portrayal of Squire Allworthy. The boundaries between the ancient and the modern are not clearly visible and the national still has not penetrated the local.

Given these preferences, the measured response that Fielding's Gentleman gives with regard to the abolition of Scotland's heritable jurisdiction has to be attributed to Fielding's pronounced anti-Jacobitism, if it can be attributed to Fielding at all. Property and government cannot be disentangled at Paradise Hall, and even if it is presided over by a nationally appointed Justice of the Peace, it maintains a local order: the old feudal patterns are preserved in the modern relationship. But if the state does not control the world of the estate, Fielding also avoids going too far in the opposite direction and turning the estate into the entity that controls the state. He rejects Defoe's argument that the legitimacy of national government originates in the estate, and instead develops a characteristically mediated relationship. This becomes clear when the pamphlet addresses the real target of the Jacobite rebellion: the legitimacy of the Protestant succession.

After a reference to the recent rebellion, the Gentleman undertakes to persuade his friend the Alderman that the "Right to the Crown" rests on "a clear and uncontestable Right." He asks: "What Right have you to your House, Mr. Alderman, for I think it is your own? . . . Doth not your Right consist in its being conveyed to you from those who had the absolute Property?" While the Alderman wonders how such a "plain" fact could even deserve inquiry, the Gentleman draws the crucial analogy: "is not the King's Right to his Crown as plain?"[45] This casual comparison between the right to property and the right to the crown is subsequently deepened beyond analogy. Referring again to the Alderman's absolute property in his house, the Gentleman continues his barrage:

G: Surely you would think it highly unjust in the Person who sold you your House . . . wantonly and of his own will to turn you out.
A: I think I should.
G: Have not then a Body of Men, or a whole People, the same Power of disposing

of what they possess; and are not they, their Heirs and Successors equally bound by their Grant?

A: There is a great Difference between the delegation of Power by a whole People, and the Disposition of Property by Individuals.[46]

This is the center of the debate over the legitimacy of the Protestant succession: while the Gentleman suggests that the legal right to private property is not merely analogous, but identical to the legal right to the crown, the Alderman rejects such an equation of private with public law. The delegation of state power has, in his view, little to do with the private conveyance of property. Yet the Gentleman does not leave matters here. He refines his equation, using real estate terms, in a detailed description of the Glorious Revolution: "For if the Sovereign Power devolved to the People by the Forfeiture and Abdication of King James the Second, the People have most certainly entailed the crown on the House of Hanover, and his Majesty enjoys it in the Right of that Entail."[47] The interruption of the direct line of descent in 1689 is here endowed with legal respectability through the term "entail," which provides that a proprietor may alter the line of succession and determine the path along which his property is to descend. The legitimacy of the succession, then, is defended against the genealogical challenge of the Jacobites by presenting it as a property transaction in which parliament is in the position of donor.

Fielding's reliance on the notion of an "entail" in defending the legitimacy of the Protestant crown means that he constructs the succession through common law. Echoing the debate over the Bill of Rights, which had foregrounded the advantages of the term "entail" by pointing to its place in the English common law tradition, Fielding considered the Act of Settlement an "Affirmance of Common Law."[48] The language of property, in his view, had been extended in 1689 from the private sphere of property conveyance into the public sphere of state legitimacy. This assumption implicitly discounts the fiduciary construction of political community advocated by Locke. Locke's use of the term "trust" to describe the relationship between the "people" and government, as Fielding must have realized, was problematic because it was not part of the language of common law and thus not part of the established language of property.[49] Trusts could be enforced only through equity, at the Court of Chancery, and to a common lawyer such as Fielding the uncertainties of equity must have appeared to provide a rather shaky foundation for state legitimacy. He preferred the language of common law because it represented a tried and tested

idiom – but it also allowed for the construction of political community through the more tangible and concretely binding terms of possession, terms that escaped the legal vagaries of the trust as much
as the abstractions of the language of contract, which was equally
underrepresented in common law.[50] This preference emerges in the following passage from *An Address to the Electors of Great Britain* (1740), in
which Fielding articulates the nature of the relationship that, at bottom,
legitimizes political community. Fielding discusses the location of power
in the constitution and notes that, after James II vacated the throne, the
people:

disposed the same to the Prince of Orange and the Princess Mary jointly for
Life, with successive Remainders in Tail to the Princess Mary, the Princess
Anne, and the Prince of Orange. Now that the whole Power is originally in the
People . . . will appear first from the Answer to this short Question: "Inasmuch
as every Limitation in Tail supposes a Reversion; and as that Reversion must be
in the Donor, in whom is the Reversion, after the said Limitation expires?" If,
as I conceive, it must be answered in the People, it follows they are the Donors,
and, consequently, the Power was originally in the People.[51]

Though slightly circular in its argument, this passage demonstrates
the extent to which Fielding considered the substance of private property law foundational for the definition of public legitimacy and power.
Fielding's reasons for adhering so closely to property law have to do,
I believe, with the pronounced tangibility of what he calls a "Limitation in Tail." Such tangibility comes into focus with the legal concept
of "reversion" that Fielding employs. As one of his closely studied legal textbooks, Thomas Wood's *An Institute of the Laws of England* (1720),
explains:

An Estate in Reversion . . . is the Residue of the Estate left in the Grantor, after
some particular Estate granted away, always Continuing in Him that granted
the particular Estate; or where the particular Estate is derived out of his Estate.
As in a Gift in Tail, the Reversion of the Fee-simple is in the Donor; in a Lease
for Life, or for Years, the Reversion is in the Lessor.[52]

In Wood's definition "reversion" does not designate the *process* of an estate
reverting to its original owner, but signifies a certain type of property:
that portion of a granted estate that remains in the original owner. This
legal fiction emphasizes the indivisibility of the original estate, which,
even though a piece of it is entailed and hence in possession of the donee
or donees, always remains tied to the actual possession of the donor or
donors. In fact, Wood's language, emphasizing a "Residue of the Estate

left in the Grantor," collapses the boundary between persons and things, suggesting that a part of the thing lodges "in" its original possessor. Invoking an incorporative relationship allows the reversion to be more than an abstract right to future possession, as Wood makes clear when he explains that "Reversions . . . are not Things Incorporeal in their own Nature." The implication is that, like corporeal estates, reversions "may be touched or handled" and hence constitute tangible possessions.[53] They belong to that class of contradictory objects that the common law calls "incorporeal things," and whose persistence from the Middle Ages into the eighteenth century, as William Holdsworth has noted, is both reason for and effect of the underdeveloped state of contract law within common law.[54]

Wood's definition helps us to see that Fielding's preference of entailment over trust and contract is motivated by the more tangible tie it establishes between donor and donee, governor and governed. The concept of reversion designates an actual, continued possession – an "estate in *praesenti*, though taking effect in *futuro*," as William Blackstone would capture this paradox.[55] If one accepts the logic of the common law on this point, it becomes quite literally impossible for the governors to be remote from the governed – an impossibility ensured by the incorruptible corporal bond that ties the original owner to his or her possessions and that resists the finality of the contract. The governors are always tangibly connected to the governed and it is this strict unifying quality that prompts Fielding to such detailed use of common law. Once again Fielding privileges a construction that effaces the boundaries between two entities, but stops short of connecting them organically. He thus resists the relationship between landed property and legitimate government advocated by Defoe and instead uses the conceptual tools of common law – a legal fiction, in effect – to construct a relationship that resembles a concretely binding relationship, but falls short of actually creating such a literal bond.

The work done by this one term "reversion" is deeply characteristic of the way in which Fielding's political imagination uses landed property. "Reversion" manages to efface several boundaries at once. By rendering a right to future possession an incorporating possession, the reversion cuts across boundaries of present and future, of the corporeal and the incorporeal, of person and thing, and is able to construct the absent as the present and the separate as the insolubly connected. All of this is done, of course, without actually identifying these different concepts. As with the combination of familial, charitable, economic, and judicial functions in the squire, Fielding resists an organic relationality. By effacing boundaries he avoids the absolutist language of organic unity according to which someone like Filmer could base the ruler's authority on the authority of the father. But Fielding equally avoids the differentiation of social and political functions advocated by Locke. Exploiting the survival of feudal forms in the language of real property, Fielding is able to hold on to the old immediacy of the manorial community, the integrated relationship between property and government, and the intermixture of functions in the patriarchal squire. This return to the manor is saved from anachronism and nostalgia by the reassertion in 1689 of landed property as the key concept in the construction of social and political community. Fielding takes advantage of this qualified reestablishment of the estate as a communal figure. In his legal-political vision of England's postrevolutionary order, the properly possessed estate reflects an ideal social community, but it is neither a symbol for the state nor a private thing merely contiguous to the civic domain, nor the literal constituent of state power. Fielding's manor escapes the alternatives of absolutism, capitalism, and republicanism by inhabiting the space of legal equation opened up to property after the Glorious Revolution, a space that sustains fertile continuities with older kinds of localized, traditionalist community.

What I have been arguing here about Fielding's uses of the estate discloses an additional set of pressures through which he perceived descriptive acts. Description is such a loaded issue for Fielding precisely because he relies on the possessive relation to construct social and political community. Description is the place where that relation becomes explicit, it is that area of literary representation where the link between human and material spheres is actively constructed. When Fielding sets out to describe his archetypal English manor in the early pages of his novel, the possessive relation and the function of the estate are very much on his mind. The problem is, as we have seen, that description is easily associated with the disembedding forces of modernity, and Fielding signaled his understanding of this by associating the postrevolutionary isolation of the Man of the Hill with an appreciation of landscape as a depoliticized zone, as a visual object emptied of social obligation and political meaning. The Man's protoliberal individualism was symbolized by the separating powers of the eye, and Fielding's refusal to describe was also a refusal to humor that eye. But if property is for Fielding fundamentally a phenomenon of a preestablished, inclusive relationality that stretches in a variety of directions, the description of property would seem to pose a particular challenge: how can a literary mode with a reputation for separation, disjunction, and even reification contribute to the concealing of boundaries and enact the integration that Fielding saw embodied in the manorial community? How, in short, could description capture the embedded world of the manor?

These questions identify a tension between Fielding's legal-political vision of community and a neoclassical aesthetic whose emphasis on unity promoted the critique of the descriptive that I addressed earlier. From an aesthetic outlook that stressed unity and cohesion, the descriptive appeared as an interruption, as a useless and extraneous embellishment that belonged to the era of figurative and ornamental excess that Restoration writers began to locate in the Renaissance.[56] We have seen how Fielding himself shared this outlook when his joke about description unearthed more serious concerns about the "constant connexion" that is supposed to ensure the durable embedding of the descriptive signifier in its semantic and textual environments. Many scholars have, indeed, placed Fielding squarely within the neoclassical or Augustan canon, and there are some good reasons for doing so. His extremely symmetrical and balanced chapter division in *Tom Jones*, for example, has inspired architectural metaphors that compare the overall shape of this novel with a Palladian villa. But as the complexities of his descriptive joke already intimate, Fielding's relationship to the forces of symmetry and proportion is in truth rather more complicated.

Even from within his architectural chapter division, Fielding manages to mock so-called neoclassicism by advertising different temporal lengths for each book. This running gag targets the extreme aesthetic demand articulated in texts such as John Dryden's *An Essay of Dramatic Poesy* (1668) that, in order to be natural, a play's parts "are to be equally subdivided" over twenty-four hours so that "one act take not up the supposed time of half a day, which is out of proportion to the rest, since the other four are then to be straitened within the compass of the remaining half."[57] Such disproportion is precisely what Fielding's temporal subversion of spatial structure celebrates. By having time actively bear on space in this way, and by pointing to the impossibility of maintaining the spatial and temporal purity required by neoclassicism, Fielding signals a general commitment to the embedded relationship that time and space assume in the common law and in what I take to be one of its critical instantiations, the manor.

Fielding is not the last lawyer-author in my study to bear witness to the tension between the world of common law and neoclassicism, as I will show in a discussion of William Blackstone's aesthetic in Chapter Five. But Fielding had additional aesthetic resources that have not yet been adequately accounted for, resources that better suit his vision of the possessive relation and his interest in projecting a unified human-material sphere. His description of the Allworthy estate reveals them.

IV

Just after the titular foundling of Fielding's novel has made his first appearance, Fielding offers the following description of the Allworthy estate:

The Gothick Stile of Building could produce nothing nobler than Mr. Allworthy's House. There was an Air of Grandeur in it, that struck you with Awe, and rival'd the Beauties of the best Grecian Architecture; and it was as commodious within, as venerable without.

It stood on the South-east Side of a Hill, but nearer the Bottom than the Top of it, so as to be sheltered from the North-east by a Grove of old Oaks, which rose above it in a gradual Ascent of near half a Mile, and yet high enough to enjoy a most charming Prospect of the Valley beneath.

In the midst of the Grove was a fine Lawn sloping down towards the House, near the Summit of which rose a plentiful Spring, gushing out of a Rock covered with Firs, and forming a constant Cascade of about thirty foot, not carried down a regular Flight of Steps, but tumbling in a natural Fall over the broken and mossy Stones, till it came to the bottom of the Rock; then running off in a pebly Channel, that with many lesser falls winded along, till it fell into a Lake at the Foot of the Hill, about a quarter of a Mile below the House on the South Side, and which was seen from every Room in the Front. Out of this Lake, which filled the Center of a beautiful Plain, embellished with Groupes of Beeches and Elms, and fed with Sheep, issued a River, that for several Miles was seen to meander through an amazing Variety of Meadows and Woods, till it emptied itself into the Sea, with a large Arm of which, and an Island beyond it, the Prospect closed.

On the right of this Valley opened another of less Extent, adorned with several Villages, and terminated by one of the Towers of an old ruined Abbey, grown over with Ivy, and Part of the front of which remained still entire.

The left Hand Scene presented a View of a fine Park, composed of very unequal Ground, and agreeably varied with all the Diversity that Hills, Lawns, Wood and Water, laid out with admirable Taste, but owing less to Art than to Nature, could give. Beyond this the Country gradually rose into a Ridge of wild Mountains, the Tops of which were above the Clouds. (42–43)

The act of quoting this passage immediately raises the issue of description's disembedding and objectifying potential. Removed from its textual place, the description appears to have become what Fielding had wished to avoid, a setpiece that can be appreciated on its own, stripped of its relations to its surroundings. In some ways the transportability of such a passage is built into the literary convention that Fielding follows here. This is neither a real nor a wholly imaginary scene, and Fielding pays descriptive tribute to various landed estates, including those of his patrons George Lyttelton and Ralph Allen.[58] To the extent that this description is a gift to these readers that acknowledges and repays their patronage, it is meant to be an object that can be appreciated on its own.[59] In this sense Fielding's description is linked to the conditions of production that inscribe *Tom Jones* as a whole.

Fielding's novel is the product of a precapitalist patronage system that survived into the eighteenth century and, as such, partakes of the complicated network of interest, obligation, and reputation that continues to structure social relations in mid-eighteenth-century Britain. Yet such participation qualifies the object status of Fielding's description. Because eighteenth-century social, cultural, and, to some extent, economic reproduction depended on personalized, two-way relationships, the gift Fielding offers to his patrons with this passage bears more resemblance to the gift economies observed by Bronislaw Malinowski and Marcel Mauss within "archaic" societies than the more abstract exchange systems of "mature" capitalist societies.[60] In these gift economies the gift creates and extends social bonds by traveling throughout the community without ever becoming stationary and permanently attached to any one individual or family. Within this scenario the mobility of things exists apart from a system of appropriation, finite exchange, and exclusive ownership: circulation joins inalienability.

Though Fielding's world is based on property and thus, in principle, on alienability, it is in constant denial about this. Fielding echoes the distinction between the creation of communal ties through the circulation of things and their destruction through the retention of things, for instance, when he highlights Tom's liberal habit of passing on the gifts he receives from Allworthy to sustain communal wellbeing and exposes Blifil for removing things from circulation by "hoarding" them for personal gain (144, 309). In fact, one could argue that the entire plot of *Tom Jones* is generated by the clogging up, interrupting, and diverting of the proper flow of objects and knowledge (from the abused gift of

Allworthy's initial hospitality, and representations of Tom's actions, to the letter concealed by Bridget Allworthy). The disequilibrium thus created can be redeemed only through the open circulation of the foundling Tom, whose legal construction as simultaneously belonging to everyone (*filius populi*) and no one (*nullius filius*) marks him as a communal gift, a surplus without origin and destination. It is not enough to claim, as James Thompson has stressed, that Fielding wishes to control movable property by conceiving it on the model of immovable property.[61] There is a type of movable property that Fielding embraces, and we need to distinguish between a mobility that disembeds objects from their environments by a finite exchange and a mobility that embeds objects by maintaining their circulation within a social environment – in Fielding's case, the environment of the landed estate and the system of obligation and status that sustains it. Fielding's description constitutes an object in this second sense; it stays embedded because it extends the mutual social bonds created by patronage. But what about the object described?

In one of his influential *Spectator* papers on "The Pleasures of the Imagination" (1712), Joseph Addison observed:

a spacious Horison is an Image of Liberty, where the Eye has Room to range abroad, to expatiate at large on the Immensity of its Views, and to lose it self amidst the Variety of Objects that offer themselves to its Observation. Such wide and undetermined Prospects are as pleasing to the Fancy, as the Speculations of Eternity or Infinitude are to the Understanding.[62]

The "wide and undetermined Prospects" that Addison celebrates here touch a central aesthetic nerve of Fielding's description. Addison evokes what I consider to be the dominant impression conveyed by the Allworthy estate: the sense of a lush expansiveness unrestricted by boundaries, stretching "beyond" the sea and "above" the clouds to the very limits – or so it seems – of spatial extension. This sense of "Infinitude" is communicated, more specifically, by a displacement of topographical limits. The central paragraph in Fielding's description, for instance, concludes: "for several Miles [the river] was seen to meander through an amazing Variety of Meadows and Woods, till it emptied itself into the Sea, with a large Arm of which, and an Island beyond it, the Prospect closed." After we have followed the course of the river from its spring through the lake and the entire valley, its final release into the sea seems a more than appropriate conclusion to our lengthy journey. But Fielding presses on, adding two more subordinate clauses to further expand an already wide view. When, finally, an indeterminate "beyond" is claimed to close the prospect, the idea of closure is neutralized and a sense of illimitability established. Not surprisingly, the anonymous reviewer of *Old England* in 1749 ridiculed Fielding's "great Skill in Chorography" and found it difficult "to reconcile this Description with Probability."[63]

The sense of illimitability is also evident in what I want to call the description's generic exhaustiveness, another feature that puzzled contemporary observers.[64] House, spring, fall, river, lake, sea, island, mountains, and clouds: though incomplete, this list already looks as if it derives not from an actual landscape, but from an exhaustive collection of all possible landscape elements. Connecting house, sea, and mountain in a single staggering movement, Fielding's description produces an idealized plenitude whose vital presence threatens to overflow spatial boundaries. There are, indeed, no boundaries in this landscape. Following the landscape conventions of his time, Fielding presents the Allworthy property as coextensive with the land at large. There is no perceptible beginning or end to Paradise Hall and the constant emphasis on "Variety" and "Diversity" only underscores the seemingly irreducible richness of this "Image of Liberty."

One of the crucial gardening techniques responsible for the effect of such boundlessness was the device of the sunk fence (also called "ha-ha").[65] In his *The History of the Modern Taste in Gardening* (1771), Horace Walpole considered the introduction of this device in the eighteenth century "the capital stroke, the leading step to all that has followed [in English gardening]." He describes the effect of the sunk fence as follows: "The contiguous ground of the park without the sunk fence was to be harmonized with the lawn within; and the garden in its turn was to be set free from its prim regularity, that it might assort with the wilder country without... the contiguous out-lying parts came to be included in a kind of general design."[66] The reduction of contiguity that Walpole emphasizes here as the crucial effect of the sunk fence contrasts strikingly with the landscape that Robinson Crusoe creates on his island. Despite his aim of concealment, Crusoe's drawing of boundaries and fencing in of territory were vital factors in his creation and declaration of possessive ties. Crusoe's long inventory of the island's landscape was accordingly structured by a contiguity of anxiously marked out parcels. The land had to be segmented and visible to ensure possession; cultivated and noncultivated parts were strictly differentiated. The sunk fence, by contrast, symbolizes and enables Paradise Hall's boundlessness. Without a discernible limit, Paradise Hall cannot be separated from its surroundings. The Allworthy

manor is not visible as such because it does not emerge as a piece of property, a thing that could be distinguished from its environment. Extending
Fielding's characteristic gesture, his English garden effaces the distinction
between property and land, culture and nature. When Fielding praises
the landscape for imitating nature so closely that the difference between
nature and culture vanishes, the fact of possession disappears with it.[67]
Property becomes a deeply embedded relation that structures social and
physical realities without appearing to intervene in any discernible way.
Its invisibility results from an artful naturalization that makes the manor
look like the land itself.

 Fielding's description creates a boundless space in which the eye can,
in Addison's phrase, "lose it self," yet such "Liberty" does not simply signify the absence of restraint, nor does the eye's supposed disorientation
contradict the logic of property. As Walpole's remarks underscore, the
English garden's boundlessness is the result of a deliberate construction
by the landowner. The reduction of contiguity that Walpole stresses,
however, is merely a negative description. Effacing boundaries is one
thing, producing a structured whole another. It might seem tempting to
seek such structure in the topographical directions of Fielding's description. Yet these directions slide into vagueness as Fielding moves from
"South-east," "half a Mile," "thirty foot" and "a quarter of a Mile,"
to "on the right" and "left Hand." The limited sense of structure thus
communicated is increasingly challenged by the scene's overflowing richness. In comprehending its constantly expanding variety, the reader is
ultimately thrown back to the physical boundlessness of the landscape
itself. The combination of dense variety and illimitable extent prevents
the emergence of an independent sense of space, and the most characteristic impression conveyed by this landscape is not one of precisely
articulated distances and relations, but one of what I shall call "radical
proximity," in which an extremely wide range of phenomena appears in
the closest neighborhood. This impression is caused by the dominance
of an idealized plenitude over topographic objectivity.

 To gain a clearer sense of what this means, it is helpful to consider
briefly the concept of space that continues to dominate our perception today. Recent sociological and geographical research has shown
that advanced capitalist societies tend toward conceiving of space as a
homogeneous and mathematically coherent container that can be
"filled" or "emptied." In this conception space exists as an independent, objective reality that is clearly differentiated from the objects that

occupy it.[68] That the eighteenth century was at least familiar with a different spatial logic is evident, for example, in David Hume, who argued against Locke's view that space and time are uniform, independent phenomena by asserting that "space and time are . . . no separate or distinct ideas, but merely those of the manner or order in which objects exist."[69] In this formulation our sense of space does not congeal into an objective sphere *in* which reality appears, but depends on the primacy of sensuous particulars. Offering the reverse of what may seem intuitive today, Hume's argument assumes that it is the order of things that articulates the order of space and thus insists on an embedded sense of things. Space is not abstract and general, but embodied – the result of a local configuration of things and thus directly tied to the particulars of appearance.

What Hume does here, in fact, is to offer a philosophical analogue to the common law conception of space as a fundamentally relational phenomenon – as always already possessively attached to someone or something else. The doctrine of *nulle terre sans seigneur* contradicts the notion of an empty space, and we have already seen how this sidelined the common law with regard to colonial land claims. On the other hand, Locke's position that space does exist independently would seem to agree rather well with his construction of America as a "vacant space" open to appropriation. Locke encourages this link between his political thinking on property and his philosophical thinking on space when he argues against the "Hypothesis of Plenitude" by insisting on a notion of space as a "Vacuum":

We can . . . consider the Space or Distance so imagined, either as filled with solid parts, so that another Body cannot come there, without displacing and thrusting out the Body that was there before; or else as void of Solidity, so that a Body of equal dimensions to that empty or pure Space, may be placed in it without removing or expulsion of any thing that was there.[70]

The philosophical insistence on the possibility of an empty space touches here on the legitimacy of occupation. Whereas the "Hypothesis of Plenitude" admits the notion of "displacing," Locke's belief in "empty or pure Space" recasts such forceful movement into space as a neutral and peaceful placement that has nothing to do with "expulsion." But even as space appears in this context as an "empty" thing that can be subject to simple actions such as finding, filling, losing, and keeping, it has not yet assumed the reassuring rationality of the container. The idea of an undivided and independently existing space continues to inspire Locke with considerable awe as he invokes the power of "boundless Oceans" and the "infinite Abysses of Space and Duration."[71] As Crusoe's adventures show with particular vividness, the notion of a vacant space still carries with it uncomfortable associations of the unnatural void and the *horror vacui*, of the undifferentiated hole that threatens to swallow its occupant. Hume's plenist position, on the other hand, avoids the emergence of space as an independent reality. It can be aligned with Fielding's evocation of property, which constructs a space that is overwhelmed by the variety of its sensuous elements.

In fact, the plenitude of the Allworthy landscape, its variety and extent, are pushed to a degree at which containment would pose insurmountable problems. The Allworthy estate celebrates its boundary-breaking richness. Instead of space defining and framing the location of the landscape elements, these elements themselves appear to articulate space, to expand and contract it, thus undercutting spatial homogeneity as much as our ability to distinguish between space and that which occupies it. The propertied ground of Fielding's manor aspires to a kind of fluid natural order that fuses expansiveness with proximity and generates an animated, flexible spatiality that is fundamentally at odds with Crusoe's precarious attempt to rationalize space – to cut it up into parcels and to distinguish it from the body. By contrast, Fielding's idea of space is not distinct from that of the body and thus resists the rationalizations of the natural law perspective.[72] In this way Fielding's descriptive production of space is deeply political. It mirrors his socio-political preservation of the manorial community because its refusal to disembody space, to neutralize and rationalize it, is at the same time also a refusal to distinguish between land and property. In tying us to the particulars of the place and undercutting our ability to situate them in a generalized space, Fielding privileges the landed estate over the land, the local over the national, and prepares us to view social life as embedded in, and thus characteristic of, a distinct place owned by a single individual.

The main vehicle for holding together the abundant variety and extent of Fielding's landscape is water in different and interrelated forms (spring, fountain, channel, fall, lake, river, and sea). Four basic functions of water can be distinguished. The line that connects spring to sea links the near and the remote, the copresence of spring and estuary in the same landscape associates beginning and end, and while the gradual transformation of spring into fountain, fall, lake, river, and sea enacts continuity and change, the various manifestations of water signal again the seemingly inexhaustible variety of the landscape at large. These observations indicate that the order of things at Paradise Hall rests on a logic of presence. Its generic exhaustiveness, the dominance of a varied appearance over objective parameters, and the spatial approximation of near and remote, beginning and end, continuity and change: all of these factors contribute to the impression of an idealized plenitude that precludes a sense of remoteness and absence. Nothing, indeed, seems out of reach or absent in a landscape whose overwhelming variety figures spatial extent in the concrete particular and whose topographical association of beginning, end, continuity, and change absorbs time into spatial proximity, thus eliding temporal difference and the contingencies of historical change.

This inclusive relational structure finds its most concentrated expression in the figure of the meandering stream that guides us through much of the landscape. A closer look at this figure shows the underlying principle of Fielding's idealized possessive plenum. William Hogarth's *Analysis of Beauty* (1753) offers important insights into the aesthetics of the undulating line and Fielding's descriptive construction of property.[73] Starting from the assertion that the eye has "enjoyment in winding walks, and serpentine rivers, and all sorts of objects, whose forms . . . are composed principally of what, I call, the waving and serpentine lines," Hogarth articulates the aesthetic properties of his line of beauty most completely when he states that "the serpentine line, by its waving and winding at the same time different ways, leads the eye in a pleasing manner along the continuity of its variety, if I may be allowed the expression; and which by its twisting so many different ways, may be said to inclose (tho' but a single line) varied contents."[74] The most symptomatic moment in this passage comes with Hogarth's suggestion that the serpentine line can be seen "waving and winding at the same time different ways." Capturing the tension between a generous swerving movement and the single point in time in which it unfolds, this phrase points to a crucial aspect of Hogarth's line of beauty. It conveys a relational mode whose circumstantial density defeats the order of temporal succession. This is symptomatic insofar as it stands for a more general resistance to objective parameters. The variety of appearance – of the line itself and of the "varied contents" it "may be said to inclose" – challenges not only the limits of temporal succession but also those of spatial coexistence. Hogarth's line expresses a logic of crowding that collects such a multitudinous variety into a single movement that spatial and temporal parameters cannot function as containers. Such crowding does not produce complete chaos because the serpentine line manages to unite variety and continuity. The "continuity of its variety" combines a maximum of unqualified inclusion with a minimum of directedness.

This is precisely the point at which the line of beauty discloses its most significant relational properties, which can be said to be located between two crucial associative principles, contiguity and resemblance. The line's integrative swerve produces a higher degree of connectivity than mere juxtaposition, but without creating a paradigmatic relation between the elements it pulls into its orbit. What this means can be elucidated by comparing the temporal and spatial implications of contiguity, proximity, and resemblance. Contiguity, as David Hume emphasized, describes a relational mode that directly depends on the vagaries of time and space.[75] Contiguity *is*, in fact, either temporal or spatial. As the pressures of Defoe's descriptive practice indicate, it connects elements not on account of any inherent quality they have, but solely on account of their relation *in* time or space (this is precisely what feeds Crusoe's nervous attempt to sustain a tangible physical connection to his surroundings). By contrast, resemblance establishes relations through the elements' qualities, by comparing them irrespective of their position in time or space.[76] Distinct from these two modes of association, proximity is something of a hybrid. It does not establish relations between elements on account of their qualities (by comparison), but complicates the circumstantial logic of contiguity. Promoting the dominance of appearance over quantitative or qualitative schemata, the waving line binds time and space in its exuberant connectivity. One eccentric swerve connects far and near, high and low, beginning and end. These mediatory qualities of the line keep the variety and extent of Fielding's landscape so remarkably proximate and make Hogarth's line the concentrated expression of the principle of proximity. Defying spatial or temporal abstraction as it bids the beholder to follow its circuitous spontaneity and its expansive association of sensuous features, the line figures property as a preestablished, alluringly physical relationship that eludes the differentiations and divisions between nature and culture, space and time, land and property, material and human spheres.

Fielding's use of Hogarth's line disempowers the distancing function of the eye because it demands an immediate engagement with particulars, drawing us literally into the shapes of a remarkably various landscape and denying us a defined vantage point from which we could take in the whole. We cannot be spectators while Fielding pulls us thus into the landscape. Defoe's descriptive acts in *Robinson Crusoe* labor to articulate a controlled relationship between body and environment, a relationship that is organized around distinctions between inside and outside, the visible segmentation of space and time, and the creation of a rational field for human agency. However problematic the emergence of time and space as neutral arenas for individual exertion unbounded by custom was in *Robinson Crusoe*, it tore the fabric of precedent, tenure, and usage that in common law interweaves time, space, and practice. Such interweaving is precisely the goal of Fielding's descriptive act. What we witness here is an attempt to escape distance and separation without abolishing it. As the great principle of approximation in Fielding's production of space, Hogarth's line contradicts the frame and the pictorial, it eludes time and space as objective parameters, and is able to promote the continuity of human and material spheres. If the possessive relation was subject to a hyperconscious surface manipulation in *Robinson Crusoe*, it has here become subconscious, has gone underground, is pervasive but nowhere manifest.

Such spontaneous-seeming intimacy between human and material spheres is underscored when the owner appears on the scene. His movement aligned with the rising sun (he "walked forth on the Terrace, where the Dawn opened every Minute"), his eye interlocked with the sun as for a moment both seem to "sen[d] forth Streams of Light" (43), Fielding's Allworthy reinforces the proximity already figured descriptively.[77] This is, indeed, no exceptional moment for Fielding. In his panegyric on Ralph Allen, for example, Fielding remarks that "his House, his Furniture, his Gardens, his Table, his private Hospitality, his public Benificence all denoted the Mind from which they flowed, and were all intrinsically rich and noble, without Tinsel or external Ostentation" (404). Possession is here conceived in highly personal terms, as the happy confluence of owner and owned, signifier and signified. "Denotation" is linked to a "flow," and as with the meeting "streams" of eye and sun in the Allworthy description, ownership is imagined as a spontaneous relation that blurs the boundaries between human and material spheres. Allen's things do not possess a definitive outline, a hardened surface, that would distinguish inside and outside and endow them with an interiority that could emancipate them from their context.[78] In both Allen's and Allworthy's case, possession is naturalized and the thing itself eloquently announces its participation in the person of the owner.

v

Fielding's reliance on a landscape description to embody political, aesthetic, and epistemological problems is not unusual. He was able to draw on an established tradition of political landscapes that stretched from Ben Jonson to James Thomson and could incorporate, as we have seen, the actual landscaping practices that marked the transition from the French formal gardens popular during the Restoration to the variety and extensiveness that began to characterize the English landscape garden of the first half of the eighteenth century. Still, inserting a landscape description of such length into a prose narrative struck many observers as strange, and Fielding's practice appears to have rubbed against developing genre expectations.[79] I want to argue here that in overcoming his own substantial reservations with regard to the descriptive, Fielding did not draw decisively on the traditions of topographical poetry. Important Miltonic resonances notwithstanding, his descriptive practice gained most from the writings of Lucian, the influential Greek writer of the "Second Sophistic" during the second century AD. Lucian was a central figure for Fielding, who claimed to have modeled his style on Lucian's, a style that did more than simply convey the humor for which Lucian was frequently commended.[80] Lucian was one of the great exponents of prose description during a period closely associated with the beginnings of what is usually called the Greek romance.[81] In his "Essays in Portraiture," "Essays in Portraiture Defended," and "The Hall," Lucian offers extensive and polished meditations on the art and purpose of description. These writings form part of an attempt to liberate description from a purely rhetorical exercise and to "fus[e] it with other literary possibilities."[82] Lucian's "Heracles," for example, opens with an extensive description of a painting whose scenes are marveled over by an observer who cannot make out their meaning. Eventually, a second figure joins this observer and interprets the painting for him. This interpretation turns out to foreshadow and encapsulate the argument that follows.[83]

Description is used similarly in Lucian's "On Salaried Posts in Great Houses," a topic Fielding would seem to have been in a position to appreciate. This time the description of an imaginary painting condenses and embodies a lengthy discourse preceding it. Addressing his listener, the speaker announces that he wishes "to paint you a picture of this career we have discussed, so that you may look at it and determine whether you should enter it." The picture turns out to echo Fielding's descriptive scene, for Lucian describes a "golden gateway" placed on a hill on which the allegorical figure of "Wealth" resides. In addressing the way up this hill, Lucian observes that the "slope is long and steep and slippery, so that many who hoped to be at the summit have broken their necks by a slip of the foot." The description concludes with an exhortation to the listener to "examine all details with care and make up your mind whether it suits you to enter the pictured career."[84] "Entering" the career is here equivalent to "entering" the picture, and we can now see that Fielding's remark about the broken necks his readers are risking in going up "as high a Hill as Mr. Allworthy's" contains an additional, previously invisible meaning. It is not merely an expression of Fielding's complex attitude toward descriptive acts, but a playful recommendation to the reader to be especially attentive to the scene into which he or she is led. Fielding's refusal, meanwhile, to describe the landscape around the Man of the Hill, and his framing of the episode with two withheld descriptions, also gain additional significance. These choices need to be recognized, I believe, as a validation of the initial description of the Allworthy estate (which maintains, throughout the entire novel, its status as a privileged entrance point to the narrative) and as a clear sign that the Man of the Hill cannot serve as a pattern of Fielding's communal imagination.

Fielding's allusion to Lucian in his description of Paradise Hall indicates that he considers his description as Lucian did his – namely, as an invitation to the kind of interpretational activity we have already engaged in. Through Lucian, Fielding finds a way to escape the censure of description as an extraneous embellishment, prone to disengage from its textual environment, and we will need to consider the extent to which Fielding's descriptive act can be said to constitute a kind of "proleptic simile" that condenses and embodies that which follows it.[85] What does the figure of the undulating line and the principle of proximity have to do with the rest of Fielding's text? Does their creation of a possessive ground stretch out beyond the limits of the descriptive scene?

In answering these questions, I should like to return to the point made previously concerning Tom's status as a communal gift whose open circulation redeems the limits imposed by the Blifils on the free flow of gifts. Tom's legal definition as belonging both to no one and everyone already contradicts the logic of possession, and the common law articulated this aspect of illegitimacy even further when it barred bastards from inheriting title and property, thus excluding them from a dominant mode of socio-economic reproduction. In this way the law defines the bastard as the "other" of Britain's possessive culture, a situation Richard Savage, a famous bastard whose story Fielding knew, captures in the following verses:

> Born to himself, by no possession led,
> In freedom foster'd, and by fortune fed;
> . . .
> Loos'd to the world's wide range – enjoyn'd no aim;
> Prescrib'd no duty, and assign'd no Name:
> Nature's unbounded son, he stands alone,
> His heart unbiass'd, and his mind his own.[86]

In these lines property figures as a participatory and directional force, the lack of which compels the bastard to embrace an isolation that is here sarcastically presented as liberating, but not without linking such liberty to a characteristic indirection and aimlessness. The bastard fails to be bound by the possessive paradigm, and he has literally no place within the hierarchy of ranks. As the cultural conception of bastards in eighteenth-century Britain demonstrates, bastards do not "belong" anywhere in a social structure that continues to be organized through a hierarchical sense of place, and this is what enables their wide circulatory range.[87]

As a lawyer Fielding was familiar with the laws concerning bastardy, and he draws on the legal construction of the bastard as a nonpossessive, placeless figure to make plausible Tom's extensive ramble across the uneven social spaces of eighteenth-century Britain. Because he is a bastard, Tom is uniquely qualified to lose himself in the thick entanglements of an extensive social landscape and to engage in an open-ended flotation across the established boundaries of rank and propriety. Hence his affairs with women embrace a spectrum of social and cultural possibilities, from the gamekeeper's daughter to the squire's, and from his purported mother to London's rakish Lady Bellaston. Ranging thus between country and city, lower and upper ranks, he becomes in the shortest time the dearest companion of Jacobite Squire Western, a soldier fighting the Jacobite rebellion, and a friend of a band of gypsies who comes close to being persuaded of the virtues of absolute monarchy. Fielding celebrates

Tom's essential openness to circumstance in this ironic comparison with Blifil:

Poor Jones was one of the best-natured Fellows alive, and had all that Weakness which is called Compassion, and which distinguishes this imperfect Character from that noble Firmness of Mind, which rolls a man, as it were, within himself, and like a polished Bowl, enables him to run through the World without being once stopped by the Calamities which happen to others. (760–761)

Tom's ability to be immediately absorbed by whatever situation he encounters is here contrasted with a self-enclosed mind – suggestively compared to a gleaming commodity – that is able to maintain a critical distance vis-à-vis the scenes it travels through. Blifil's self-possession is not available to the bastard Tom, whose generous openness and placelessness merge him with his environment. Though Fielding's narrator carefully keeps his readers from getting absorbed by his fiction, his protagonist is uniquely susceptible to such absorption. The effect that this has should be familiar from my discussion of description: Tom's circuitous spontaneity, his interaction with various social enclaves, ranks, and characters prevents the emergence of social space as an independent phenomenon. His lack of an observational stance propels Tom into an undulating course whose spontaneous responsiveness to circumstance privileges the concrete appearance over objective parameters. In this sense Tom operates as a figure of description that keeps the various scenes and characters he encounters embedded in the uneven social space of eighteenth-century Britain. Society does not emerge from Tom's expansive ramble as an object in its own right, as an entity that would exist separately from the self. For, paradoxically, Tom's descriptive flotation does not entail the formulation of a clear observational stance. Extending our tactile involvement in Fielding's descriptive production of physical space, Tom gives us access to social space only by participating in it. In this way the boundary between society and self is effaced. Self-consciously deployed by Fielding, description and narration turn out to be equivalent modes as Tom is utilized to extend the descriptive figure of the line into a wider social sphere. The social panorama of Fielding's novel is ultimately anchored in the world of the landed estate, and it is to this world that Tom in the end returns. Having brought together the social complexities of a modernizing society without calling on the forces of separation, Tom brings them home, into a now expanded and consolidated Paradise Hall. Named by the squire after himself, Tom turns out to be the emissary of the landed estate.

Fielding's generation of a narrative logic out of a descriptive practice allows us to recognize a systematic link between two modern observations on the eighteenth-century novel – its so-called "episodic" narrative structure and its "flat" characters. The presentist baggage of the term "episodic" becomes obvious once the kinship between description and narrative is recognized. What we have in a novel like *Tom Jones* is not an "episodic" narrative, but a narrative strategy that originates in a descriptive disposition. And what we designate, by negative comparison with the nineteenth-century novel, as a "flat" character results here from the need for an embedding social description. The "episodic" narrative and the "flat" character together respond to the demands of the descriptive in a novel that is concerned with a construction of social and political community through landed property. The extendibility of property into its surrounding environment applies both locally, within the description of Paradise Hall, and within the larger environment of the text as a whole. Fielding's preference for the "flat" and the "episodic" is far from accidental, or the sign of a technical deficiency plaguing eighteenth-century writers. It is instead a deliberate choice, and Fielding makes this clear when he associates the self-enclosed mind of Blifil with the ability to create intricate plots by "deep Scheme[s]" and "long Train[s] of wicked Artifice" (946, 657). As for Milton's devil, for Blifil the "Mind is its own place" and it is this mind and its ability to remember, withhold, and "hoard up," that creates the complex plot of *Tom Jones*. Such complexity is consistently contrasted with Tom's unassuming embedding swerve that unites the "flat" and the "episodic" to redeem the separations and depths introduced by the Blifils. If Crusoe struggled to stabilize an inner life by drawing possessive boundaries around him, Tom can efface these boundaries because he is a flat, placeless character. Untouched by the possessive individualism of Crusoe and Blifil, he is the foundling who can lose himself in the social landscape – up to a point, that is.

In using Tom as an extension of the landed estate, Fielding deftly exploits the fact that the bastard is comprehensively defined by the discourse of property. Initially astonishing, Fielding's decision to select a bastard as his protagonist turns out on closer inspection to be strategic, because he uses a figure that can never escape from the possessive culture that brands it an outsider. Tom's placelessness is the precise negative of a social structure still organized around notions of social place, and Tom's proclivity toward absorption reveals his failure to gain a critical perspective on the possessive culture to which he belongs. When in the end the illegitimate Tom returns to the manor to assume possession, we

are not witnessing a subversion of Fielding's carefully balanced traditionalist world. Instead, the bastard contributes to Fielding's conflation of the
culture of the gift that is common to all with the culture of the landed
estate, a conflation that echoes his descriptive equation of property with
the land at large as much as his anticipation of Tom's social flotation in
the possessive figure of the undulating line. And even in a more specific
political sense, Tom's bastardy fails to be subversive.

Initially, the controversial accession of a bastard to Allworthy's manor
would seem to create problems for political readings of *Tom Jones* desirous
of placing the novel in the context of the political writings I explored
earlier in this chapter. I agree with critics such as Hugh Amory, Homer
Obed Brown, and J. Paul Hunter, who have seen Fielding's concluding
deviation from the straight line of descent as validating the succession of
1689.[88] But what these critics have not addressed is the role of the bastard
in this particular context. For the bastard's position as ultimate owner of
Paradise Hall – if we follow Fielding's equation between possessive right
and royal right – would paradoxically align the legitimacy of the crown
with illegitimacy. To clarify the relationship between the Glorious Revolution and illegitimacy, it is important to recall that Fielding's novel was
not the first literary text to use the bastard in defense of the Protestant
succession. In one of the most popular poems of the first half of the eighteenth century, Daniel Defoe had already utilized the bastard figure to
defend King William, suggesting that the intermixture and unregulated
sociability of the bastard is, in fact, a highly appropriate representation of
British national identity and history. This use of the bastard dramatized
the fact that the forces of straight descent and genealogical right had
been displaced by 1688. In Defoe's *The True-Born Englishman* (1701), the
bastard comes to signify an open, nonabsolutist national history that can
no longer be measured by lines of descent, and such signification is underwritten by the same sentiment that Fielding subscribed to – the idea
that the rebellion of the royal bastard Monmouth in 1685 prefigured the
Glorious Revolution and can therefore be linked with King William's
arrival.[89] In this way Tom's bastardy calls up the revolutionary tradition that Fielding sees reemerge with Monmouth and find fulfillment in
William of Orange.[90]

Not all contemporary observers were attuned to this political dimension of Fielding's use of bastardy. Samuel Richardson for one felt
that Fielding's choice of an illegitimate hero was thoroughly misguided:
"What Reason has [Fielding] to make his Tom illegitimate, in an Age
where Keeping is become a Fashion?"[91] Richardson's exasperation over

the "spurious Brat Tom Jones" shows that he could not share the brazen comfort that Defoe found in the fact that "Spurious Generation" lay at the base of much of English life and many of its institutions, including the common law.[92] But Richardson's comment also points to a rank-specific dimension in Fielding's employment of the bastard. The "keeping" that he complains about is the keeping of mistresses, a "fashionable" practice mostly associated with the upper ranks. Such illicit relationships, as a text like Defoe's *Roxana* (1724) makes abundantly clear, produced numerous illegitimate children. His earlier political use of the bastard notwithstanding, Defoe has Roxana identify the laissez-faire production and elevation of bastards as a conspicuous aspect of aristocratic culture, and it must have appeared as such to Richardson when he heard about *Tom Jones*.[93] From the perspective of the middling ranks at least, Fielding's Tom must easily have seemed a symbol of this aristocratic practice, especially since Fielding himself still belonged to the world of wealthy patrons and noble connections.

From Fielding's perspective, however, the bastard seemed peculiarly appropriate because this figure could symbolize his understanding of 1689 more fully than one might have expected. The association of the bastard with notions of intermixture, for example, also linked up with Fielding's view of the British constitution as a "Mixture" of the "Monarchical, Aristocratical, and Democratical," a mixture stabilized, in the eyes of many political observers, only after the revolution of 1689.[94] Even more specific was the fact that *Tom Jones*'s final resolution of conflict, symbolically coincident with a diffused Jacobite threat, bypasses the better claims of the direct heir Blifil and promises to make Tom as absolute a possessor as Blifil would have been. Fielding here exploits the way in which common law bars the bastard from inheritance, but makes him perfectly capable of holding property. The only significant restriction is that, since the bastard has no relatives in law, only his own children are capable of claiming possession through the prestigious channel of inheritance. Though much lamented by some lawyers, the common law provided that landed estates and, indeed, all property, could be transferred absolutely through will or deed.[95] William Blackstone, in fact, considered the "alienation by deed" to be "the most solemn act that a man can possibly perform, with relation to the disposal of his property."[96] Thus the bar from inheritance, though socially stigmatizing, proved no legal obstacle to the possession of an estate.

The legal interventions that would have been necessary to effect Tom's accession to the property resemble what happened in 1689, and this resemblance comes into view with the basic legal distinction between "purchase" and "descent." Purchase, defined as "any means of acquiring an estate out of the common course of inheritance," played a crucial role in Blackstone's conceptualization of the revolutionary settlement.[97] Like Fielding, who completed his legal studies two years before him, Blackstone conceives of the settlement through the terms of property law and argues that "king William, queen Mary, and queen Anne did not take the crown by hereditary right or *descent*, but by way of donation or *purchase*."[98] From a lawyer's perspective, then, Tom's accession to Paradise Hall falls under the same general legal category, that of purchase, as the Protestant crown's. In both cases it is purchase and not descent that gives legitimate possession, and in both cases this solution balances the respective claims of merit and blood. For while Tom's descriptive flotation is also an extensive testing of his merit through the unmitigated forces of circumstance, the eventual revelation that he carries Allworthy blood in his veins is crucial to his integration into the sphere of the name and property. Such balancing echoes the Protestant settlement in that it, too, tried to balance merit (Protestant faith) and blood (Stuart alliance), and that echo is strengthened by the union of Jacobite and Whig estates that becomes possible at the end of *Tom Jones*. It is in this sense that Fielding's equation, developed in his political writings of the 1740s, between the right to property and the right to the crown finds expression in *Tom Jones*. Adapting the precedent of the Glorious Revolution, Fielding's constitutional vision is more expansive than the alleged oppositions of resemblance and contiguity, blood and merit, narrative and description, and it projects a less pure, more mediated social life. To that mediation the bastard's undulating course is as indispensable as its origin in the figure of the landed estate and its eventual narrative reintegration. As with so many other aspects of Fielding's text, the possessive relation draws beginning and end together and generates its own circuitous trajectory: the placeless bastard's descriptive flotation is made possible by a logic of "place," by a possessive culture that keeps the bastard's movements embedded in social space and, once his circulation is complete, activates the genealogical narrative to return him to the manor.

CHAPTER FOUR

Commodity fetishism in heterogeneous spaces

My discussion so far has, I trust, begun to indicate the extent to which novels as different as *Robinson Crusoe* and *Tom Jones* depend on an inter-mixture of persons and things in their construction of community. The violent instability of boundaries in Defoe's novel and their invisibility in Fielding's show that the communal forms these texts figure by drawing on natural and common law meet their limit in an entanglement between persons and things. True, *Robinson Crusoe* strives to create a causal rela-tionship between narrative and description (thereby placing the material under human control), and *Tom Jones* seeks a relationship of equivalence (thereby stressing the unity of human and material spheres). But these different strategies nonetheless reveal that essential – though ideolog-ically opposed – cultural resources of the first half of the eighteenth century do not lend themselves to assembling more differentiated com-munities of persons and things. Considering *Robinson Crusoe*'s difficulties in stabilizing boundaries and the depth with which Fielding imagines a possessive world of preestablished and natural-seeming continuities, one is, in fact, inclined to say that even at mid-century, British legal and political ways were still more susceptible to literary appropriations that integrated time, space, and practice than to ones that pulled apart this trinity. The *Gestalt* of the manor outlined by Edward Coke a hundred years earlier still provides the most helpful map in locating the limits of the communal in early eighteenth-century British fiction.

But while this shared trait of two such different novels presents striking evidence for the importance of landed property in eighteenth-century constructions of community, one is bound to wonder at this point how this tallies with the increasing mobility of persons and things that Fielding's *An Enquiry into the Causes of the Late Increase of Robbers* (1751) recognized as the main challenge to the manor's embedded communal forms. My reading of *Robinson Crusoe* as a text that revolves around the question of landed property may, in fact, strike some as exceptional – if not perverse.

After all, Defoe's novels in general offered an unprecedented imaginative appreciation of the new economic and psychological possibilities that arose in a society progressively founded, in J. G. A. Pocock's words, upon "the exchange of forms of mobile property and . . . modes of consciousness suited to a world of moving objects."[1] Mobility, exchange, and a widening circulation are driving forces in Defoe's fiction, and Defoe pays tribute to the "world of moving objects" in his famous comparison of land and trade as sources of wealth:

An estate's a pond, but trade's a spring: the first, if it keeps full, and the water wholesome, by the ordinary supplies and drains from the neighbouring grounds, it is well, and it is all that is expected; but the other is an inexhausted current, which not only fills the pond, and keeps it full, but is continually running over, and fills all the lower ponds and places about it.[2]

The eternally stagnant and the ceaselessly mobile form here a clear contrast, and Defoe's positive representation of trade through figures of inexhaustible currents and constant circulation has led some critics to argue that he is mainly interested in undermining or, to stay with his own image, 'overrunning', feudal modes of community.[3] But while this passage signals an antagonistic relationship between movable and immovable forms of property, it also suggests a relationship of cooperation in which the currents of trade replenish the "ponds" of the landed estate. Such doubleness is not resolved – neither here nor elsewhere in Defoe's thinking – and reminds us that the Augustan debate on land, trade, and credit "did not oppose agrarian to entrepreneurial interests, the manor to the market."[4] Even so, literary critics interested in the depiction of mobility in eighteenth-century texts frequently view circulation as an independent force that undercuts traditional, locally embedded forms of community, and projects the dehierarchized and homogenized social space characteristic of a more advanced capitalist society.[5]

The recent identification of the eighteenth century with the beginnings of a consumer society has lent this tendency additional plausibility, for it has allowed us to trace back to the eighteenth century the massive commodification and boundless circulation of things that we face under the freshly globalizing capitalism of our own present. From the perspective of our thoroughly commodified culture, Defoe's complex suggestion of a simultaneously antagonistic and cooperative relationship between movable and immovable property quickly contracts into the more conflictive scenario presented by Bram Dijkstra, who asserts that "Defoe's most persistent and emphatic economic theme consisted of an exposition of the intolerable impediments placed by the remnants of a feudalist world view upon the free and full development of a modern market economy."[6] This view does more than simplify Defoe's nuanced distinction between "pond" and "spring," land and commodities. It overlooks the extent to which Defoe's engagement with the circulation of commodities reveals fundamental similarities between immovable and movable forms of property. These similarities are symptomatic of the economic conditions of early eighteenth-century Britain and of Defoe's mercantilist assumptions. To recognize them means to recognize the distinct moment that Defoe occupies in what I see as a long and richly textured history of objectification.

This history has been abridged on a second front by critics such as Laura Brown, James Bunn, Christopher Flint, Erin Mackie, Colin Nicholson, and James Thompson, who have been drawing on Karl Marx's analysis of the nineteenth-century commodity fetish to describe the representation of things in eighteenth-century literature.[7] Yet such use of the Marxist analysis shortcircuits, it seems to me, the historical process that leads to a cultural and economic situation where Marx's argument on the modern commodity is indeed appropriate. According to Marx the modern commodity fetish is the specific result of an industrial capital whose complex appropriation of human labor generates a reified world in which commodities face us as a collection of opaque, alien objects whose origins in human needs and human labor have been erased. It is, indeed, the great project of the opening chapters of the first volume of *Capital* (1867) to unlock the hermetic surface of the commodity to recover the historical and economic processes that have led to its appearance as an objectified, independently existing "thing." Marx's key to this recovery is an historically specific analysis of the industrial labor process.

Marx is equally specific when he comments on the economic discourse of the seventeenth and early eighteenth centuries. In *A Contribution to the Critique of Political Economy* (1859), he points out that in the period we have come to refer to as "mercantilist," the "actual bourgeois economic sphere...was the sphere of the circulation of commodities. It is from the perspective of this elemental sphere that [contemporaries] judged the whole entangled process of bourgeois production."[8] The ruling paradigm of the mercantilist discourse on wealth is thus not the production but the circulation of commodities. This does not, of course, mean that human labor was not involved in the production of eighteenth-century commodities or that mercantilists did not recognize labor's importance. It does mean, however, that the most advanced analysis of economic processes in the seventeenth and early eighteenth centuries tended to locate the production of wealth not in the exploitation of human labor, but in the global circulation of goods. And this emphasis is not, as Marx is quick to make clear, the ideological cover of a ruling class that refused to recognize the actual origin of all wealth in human labor. The mercantilist preoccupation with circulation is, rather, at least in part an appropriate reflection of economic realities that differed substantially from those of the early nineteenth century.[9]

In taking the mercantilist emphasis on circulation seriously, I hope to show why it is misleading to import the industrial commodity fetish into the eighteenth century and how we might arrive at a more differentiated approach to the representation of movable things in eighteenth-century texts. I contend, in particular, that we need to supplement Marx's industrial commodity fetish with the notion of a mercantile commodity fetish that reflects the economic conditions of early eighteenth-century Britain. In temporarily returning to *Robinson Crusoe* (1719) before developing my argument further, I will show that the early modern circulation of goods and the forms of objectification it promotes are dynamically affected by a heterogeneous mercantile trading space. It is this heterogeneous space that aligns movables with certain key characteristics of immovable property.

I

The most crucial stylistic manifestation of the mobility of things in *Robinson Crusoe* is their description in lengthy and detailed lists. In this as well as other novels by Defoe, the list is most frequently used to capture the transfer of things from one location to another. In a revealing episode of *Robinson Crusoe* – the transfer of objects from the wrecked ship to the island – lists proliferate and passages such as the following are common:

I brought away several things very useful to me; as first, in the carpenter's stores I found two or three bags full nails and spikes, a great skrew-jack, a dozen or two of hatchets, and above all, that most useful thing called a grindstone; all these I secured together, with several things belonging to the gunner, particularly two or three iron crows, and two barrells of musquet bullets, seven musquets, and another fowling piece, with some small quantity of powder more; a large bag of small shot, and a great roll of sheet lead.[10]

Readers of Defoe will instantly recognize this passage. It exemplifies one of the established hallmarks of Defoe's literary practice, the detailed list of material objects featuring specific designation, quantification, and classification (here in the form of a distinction between the carpenter's and the gunner's things). The interjection of narrative moments that could bind this enumeration within the context of human activity is notably sparse, and the physicality of the objects is sharply reduced as they almost completely lack individuating characteristics. In this way Crusoe's list removes things from concrete contextualized relationships and encloses them in a zone of heightened visibility – reminding us, in fact, of the older meaning of the list as a boundary and as "'a place within which combat takes place.'" "Entering the lists" does not here mean combat, but the assembled objects are given an opportunity, now that they have been disembedded from their social ground, to enter into exclusive relationships with each other.[11] The central reason for the appearance of these objects is their accidental collection in the neutral space provided by the list. Because it creates purely contiguous relationships between material objects and elides narrative elements, the list embodies a kind of degree zero of description. It belongs to a literary mode that eighteenth-century critics such as Adam Smith and Henry Home, Lord Kames, and twentieth-century Marxist critics such as Georg Lukács and Fredric Jameson, have eyed with suspicion. What unites these writers across a considerable ideological and historical gulf is a basic resistance to the literary representation of objectified forms of social life. From their perspective the list condenses the most dreaded effects of the descriptive – a deadening emphasis on materiality that muffles human presence and a reifying cultivation of exclusive relationships among things.[12]

Lists can be seen as fundamental cultural technologies whose origins are associated with early uses of writing and reach as far back as 3,000 BC. They are easily linked to processes of modernization and objectification, but assume their specific functions within actual historical environments.[13] A number of cultural practices bear on Defoe's listing rhetoric, including the accounting habits of modern economic man, the emphasis of the "new science" on particularized observation, the linguistic demand for a return to a "primitive" syntax by which "men deliver'd so many things almost in an equal number of words," and, finally, the desire for epistemological credibility that some early modern genres articulated by concealing their inevitable selectivity through an appearance of arbitrary inclusiveness.[14] Yet the context of mercantilism promises to shed the most light on Defoe's fascination with enumerating things.[15] As the dominant form of economic discourse in seventeenth- and eighteenth-century Britain, mercantilism shaped the way in which educated figures such as Defoe conceived of the role and nature of objects within an economic and cultural formation that elevated circulation over production.[16]

The careful enumeration of goods was closely connected to the mercantilist stress on circulation and was a central element in mercantilist beliefs and policies, including those endorsed by Defoe in his economic writings. As the Act of Navigation of 1660 shows, mercantile policies specified so-called "enumerated commodities" whose export from the colonies was restricted and that had to pass through England, via English ships, before they could reach other countries.[17] One effect this had was that the 1660 act itself produced lengthy lists of things, but such enumeration was more important as an actual instrument to reinforce mercantile policies.[18] To this end a separate office was created in the late seventeenth century to keep "a distinct accompt of the importation and exportation of all commodities into and out of this kingdom; and to and from what places the same are exported or imported; in order to make a balance of trade between the kingdom and any other part of the world."[19] One of the key concepts of mercantile economics, the balance of trade, thus made enumeration an important cultural practice. Defoe recognized this not only by relying on the enumeration of goods in custom-house books in his economic writings, but also by stressing what he called the right "trading style." This phrase heads a section in Defoe's *The Compleat English Tradesman* (1725) on the style in which tradesmen should write, but it also alludes, characteristically moving between words and things, to the act of trading itself. "The nicety of writing in business," Defoe claimed here, "consists chiefly in giving every species of goods their trading names."[20] The basic act of correctly naming goods has considerable significance for Defoe, and in the passage from *Robinson Crusoe* quoted previously one can hear a distinct note of pride in the proper designation and enumeration of things. Some of the lists produced in *Robinson Crusoe* reappear, in fact, in similar form in Defoe's *A Plan of the English Commerce* (1728), and there is thus good evidence that the origins of Defoe's enumerating habits lie in the institutions of mercantile capitalism.[21] Proper designation, enumeration, and exchange go together.

Mercantile policies such as the Navigation Act and the enumerating practices it spawned were embodiments of an economic thinking that conceived of national wealth on the basis of an advantageous distribution and circulation of goods. Wealth, according to many mercantilists including Defoe, could not be "generated" domestically or internationally. Surplus could be achieved only by "attracting" a superior portion of a finite, materially existing wealth, preferably in specie. The whole notion of the balance of trade rested on a conception of wealth as naturally limited.[22] Wealth could be gained only by the proper management of the channels of circulation, a management that had to make sure that more goods were exported than imported, with the overall aim of a large amount of money entering the nation. "If it be our gain," as Defoe sums up this notion of trade as a competition for limited wealth, "it must be to their loss."[23]

Because wealth, in this conception, does not emerge from the process of production, the distribution of goods takes precedence over their manufacture. Metaphors such as "Channel," "Current," "Stream," or "Sluice" proliferate in Defoe's *Plan* and describe economic activity in terms of a circulation of goods.[24] They extend the basic image of trade as a spring, but also help Defoe to articulate a specific mercantile anxiety, described in Eli Heckscher's classic study of mercantilism as the "fear of goods."[25] In a more elaborate vision of a dangerously swollen circulation, Defoe expresses this anxiety as follows:

As the Veins may be too full of Blood, so a Nation may be too full of Trade; the fine fresh Rivers, when they run with a full and gentle Stream, are the Beauty and Glory of a Country; they water the Meadows, moisten the Earth, drive our Mills, fill our Moats and Canals, carry our Vessels, and enrich the whole Nation; but when swell'd by sudden and hasty Showers, they turn rapid in their Course, overflow their Banks, and rise to an undue Height; then they turn frightful and dangerous, drown the Country, and sometimes the People.[26]

The "glut[ting of] the Markets with Goods" that Defoe envisions with the help of his customary water metaphor shows the extent to which proper circulation is identified with the economic wellbeing of the nation.[27] National prosperity is directly linked to the process of circulation, and Defoe is ultimately not really interested in the process of production. He believes that the circulation of goods itself is productive of wealth. As Peter Earle has shown, the "chain of distribution was one of the most important elements in Defoe's economics. The more hands a commodity passed through on its way from raw material to consumer, the more employment each article gave rise to and the more wages and profits could be earned on the way."[28] Not surprisingly, Defoe's *A Tour Through the Whole Island of Great Britain* (1724–1726) consistently privileges the movement of things over their production. Defoe leaves out, as Earle notes, rapidly developing industrial areas and fails to notice new production technologies. Instead, he rhapsodizes on the immense circulation of goods from faraway places to the center of all economic activities, London, as the most important contributor to the wealth of the nation.[29] Circulation, indeed, is most productive when it is most circuitous: "The circulation of Trade is ruin'd," as Defoe writes in *The Review*, "[when] things go in straight lines that formerly took large circles."[30]

Such privileging of circulation over production is also evident in the extent to which trade (and not manufacture or labor) is for Defoe the true hero of the economy. There is, for instance, Defoe's sense that "Trade disperses the natural Wealth of the World and Trade raises new Species of Wealth which Nature knew nothing of," a statement that refers to the discovery of "the Gold of Africa and Brazil, the Silver of Mexico and Peru [which] but for Trade [had] remained undisturbed in the Mines."[31] While nature can be ignorant of its riches, trade unfailingly discovers already existing material wealth; it does not generate, but "raises" and "disperses," riches. Even labor ultimately depends on trade, as it is "Trade [that] invigorates the World, gives Employment to the People, raises Pay for their Labour, and encreases that Pay as their Labour encreases." This hierarchy of trade above manufacture is made more explicit when Defoe remarks upon how many landed estates have been acquired by "Citizens and Tradesmen." Belittling the forces of production, he notes that some have achieved this "by Merchandizing, some by Shopkeeping, and some by meer Manufacturing." Manufacturing, along with navigation, is for Defoe simply one of the "two Daughters" of trade.[32]

Defoe's habits of enumeration – the emphasis on specific designation, quantification, a plurality of things, and the absence of individuating characteristics – make his lists into versions of the "stream" he invokes to represent the productive flow of commodities. In Defoe's lists things lead a mostly collective life, and his novels, unlike the object narratives that became popular in the 1730s and 1740s, typically fail to give things individual histories. In the list the focus shifts too rapidly from one object to the next to allow concentration on any one object, and the emphasis on quantity and quick conveyance should be read as another expression of the mercantile "fear of goods." Things are not particularly valuable to Defoe as individual objects; it is their movement from one place to another that creates all the value.

In some ways, however, Defoe's taxonomic plainness and deindivid-
ualizing quantification are deceptive, and we shall later see that Defoe's
objects play an unexpectedly dominant role in certain situations. For
now, though, one cannot help but notice the marked contrast between
the mercantile and the industrial commodity suggested by these observations. As analyzed by Marx, the commodity of a more advanced
capitalism bristled with "metaphysical subtleties and theological whims"
and was, despite its innocuous appearance, a mysterious object that demanded close analysis.[33] Whereas Defoe's interest lies predominantly in
narratives of circulation, Marx's desire is to recover the origins of the
modern commodity and to devise a narrative that recaptures its lost
genesis. Because for Defoe wealth derives from the movement of things
from one place to another, attention is not focused on the object itself.
The form of the mercantile commodity draws attention rather to the
varying relationship between object and context. For Marx, on the other
hand, the modern commodity has closed itself off from contexts through
a complex process of self-mystification and has hardened to acquire an
objective appearance that invites systematic inquiry into its innermost
being.

Taking seriously mercantilist beliefs like the idea of circulation as a
productive mode has been difficult for historians of economic ideas.
The fullest and most rewarding study of mercantilist theories continues to be Heckscher's two-volume *Mercantilism*, first published in 1931.
In reading more recent histories of economic ideas, I have been struck
by how difficult it is for historians to leave behind a scenario in which,
roughly, everything preceding Adam Smith is incoherent and economically unsound but everything following Smith is a gradual advancement
to lasting economic truths.[34] But even if one is disposed to take seriously
Defoe's far from unique belief in circulation as a mode of production,
one has to wonder how this was supposed to work in practice and, in
fact, escape complete circularity. Heckscher stresses circulation, but does
not contribute much by way of explanation except to say that the issue
was highly characteristic of mercantile theories.[35] The question is under what conditions it was possible to conceive of circulation as central
to the production of wealth. An answer is available, it seems to me, in
Crusoe's simple transfer of things from the wrecked ship to the island.
This is a peculiarly charged scene in part because it enacts the defeat of
the mercantile aspiration towards open-ended circulation. Yet precisely
because it confronts the limits of circulation, this scene discloses some of
the basic forces that animate objects under mercantile capitalism.

II

The list quoted earlier is prompted by one of many visits that Crusoe pays to the wrecked ship. His exertions in this regard are remarkably energetic and they start, early in the novel, with the well-nigh miraculous movement of the stranded ship to a location where it can be reached from the shore.[36] The work of retrieval is fruitful, but after "five or six voyages" Crusoe begins to feel that he has "nothing more to expect from the ship." Yet he goes again anyway and, contrary to his expectations, finds "a great hogshead of bread and three large runlets of rum or spirits, and a box of sugar, and a barrel of fine flower" (74). This happy discovery triggers a new round of visits, but after the eleventh Crusoe finally believes that "nothing more could be found." Even so, he still goes to the ship and is astonished to find "two or three razors, and one pair of large sizzers, with some ten or a dozen of good knives and forks" as well as that "drug," money (75). This twelfth visit is lucky indeed, for a heavy storm carries the ship away during the following night. But even without the ship, additional items are disclosed as Crusoe explains that he "omitted setting down before" a number of finds, such as "pens, ink, and paper, . . . three or four compasses, some mathematical instruments, dials, perspectives, charts, and books of navigation" (82). And in case we were wondering what had happened to the ship, it suddenly returns after a six-month absence, and Crusoe's compulsive retrieval of things resumes, culminating in the following crescendo of journal entries:

May 5. Worked on the wreck, cut another beam asunder, and brought three great fir planks off from the decks . . .
May 6. Worked on the wreck, got several iron bolts out of her, and other pieces of iron work; worked very hard, and came home very much tyred, and had thoughts of giving it over.
May 7. Went to the wreck again, but with an intent not to work . . .
May 8. Went to the wreck, and carry'd an iron crow to wrench up the deck . . .
May 9. Went to the wreck, and with the crow made way into the body of the wreck . . .
May 10, 11, 12, 13, 14. Went every day to the wreck, and got a great deal of pieces of timber, and boards, or plank, and 2 or 300 weight of iron. (100)

The relentlessness of Crusoe's visits, which now aim at wresting material from the ship's body, is exposed here in the tremendous repetitiveness of the entries and the puzzling suggestion that he visited the ship "with an intent not to work" (why else go?). Crusoe manages to make an astounding forty-two visits to the wreck in all, and Defoe acknowledges the excessiveness of Crusoe's efforts when he returns to it in the sequel to *Robinson Crusoe*. There he feels compelled to rationalize Crusoe's behavior by a rather overdetermined combination of motives that include national character, providence, and prudence.[37] But such motives do not contribute much to explaining what I take to be the most basic aspect of Crusoe's activities – their fantastic inclusiveness. Marx's account of Defoe's novel stressed that exchange value does not really figure on Crusoe's island and that, because use value dominates Crusoe's solitary life, "all the relations between Robinson and things ... are ... simple and transparent."[38] I agree with Marx's diagnosis of use value as the dominant factor of Crusoe's insular existence, but I am less certain that this results in a simple and transparent relationship between persons and things.

Considered in more detail, Crusoe's transfer of goods is driven by a generalized assumption of potential, not actual, usefulness. At the moment of retrieval Crusoe has no clear sense of how useful "ten or a dozen knives," "2 or 300 weight of iron," or "two or three popish prayer books" will turn out to be, and he takes things not knowing "whether I might want them or no" (82). He is unable to evaluate and select, and what guides him is an abiding sense that they might become useful, that "every thing I could get [from the ship] would be of some use or other to me" (100). This assumption slips beyond reasonable bounds, so that in the course of forty-two visits Crusoe cannot see a single thing that does not have some potential for use – sometimes realized fortuitously, as with the empty "bag of chickens' meat" whose shreds of grain will enable him to grow barley, and sometimes unrealized, as with the money that he takes despite his assertion that he has "no manner of use" for it (95, 75).

If use value is extended to a point at which nothing can escape being useful, the criterion of utility loses its central characteristic – that of responding to a specific human need within a particular context. As Crusoe abandons evaluation and selection, he begins to see things detached from contexts. It is not clear what needs the things he collects will satisfy and in what situations they may unfold their potential for usefulness. While the list realizes a certain degree of abstraction – within its boundaries things seem to form a purely quantitative world of their own – the listed items continue to be haunted by the potential usefulness for which Crusoe appreciates them. His inflation of use value does not remove these things completely from contexts of use, but generalizes their potential role within undetermined contexts to such an extent that they acquire magical qualities. In the course of Crusoe's relentless transferring, things begin to resemble fetishes: they become protagonists in a ritual that is based on an unwavering belief in the secret and unpredictable power of things to create context and relationships once they are in the right place. It is here that Crusoe's loss of control over his actions, his inability to leave the ship alone, has its ultimate origin. Once utility becomes a universal yet un-realized aspect of all material objects on the ship, the act of transfer be-comes compulsively inclusive since, the more often such acts occur, the more transformative energy is accumulated in the form of inherently but unpredictably powerful objects. Such phantasmagoric use value forces narrative into mechanical repetitiveness, and elevates description over narration and things over persons. As selection and evaluation decline, repetition and ritual rise, making the fetish visible through generalized use value.[39]

Crusoe's transferring is not just a removal of objects from one place to another, but a ritualistic act in the far more ambitious enterprise of worldmaking in which Crusoe is engaged. In this undertaking, and de-spite frequently renewed opportunities for the isolating display of things, the list can only suggest its powers of abstraction and objectification. The preliminary nature of these powers is made clear when the list reveals its kinship to the complete disorder indicated by the "confused heap of goods" into which it literally decomposes once its contents hit the un-occupied and therefore "vacant" space of the island (84).[40] Crusoe feels oppressed by this heap: his goods "lay in no order, so they took up all my place, [and] I had no room to turn my self" (84–85). Symptomatic of the perceived absence of a ground that would position person and thing and allow for their differentiation, this brief crisis indicates that thing and self are at odds as Crusoe's radical inclusiveness clashes with the perceived vacuum of his insular space. This distressing human-material tangle is sorted out as follows:

I made large shelves of the breadth of a foot and a half one over another, all along one side of my cave, to lay all my tools, nails, and iron-work, and in a word, to separate every thing at large in their places, that I must come easily at them; I knocked pieces into the wall of the rock to hang my guns and all things that would hang up. So that had my cave been to be seen, it looked like a general magazine of all necessary things, and I had every thing so ready at my hand, that it was a great pleasure to me to see all my goods in such order, and especially to find my stocks of all necessaries so great. (86)

It is tempting to interpret Crusoe's "great pleasure to me to see all my goods in such order" as a kind of protobourgeois delight in the orderly disposal of personal belongings. But the aesthetic is not really the source of such pleasure. Something more primary is going on here, indicated by the notion of "a general magazine of all necessary things," which suddenly raises the stakes of Crusoe's homely ordering act by further exaggerating the already extensive variety of things collected on the ship. We have now reached a level at which Crusoe's heap of things comes to embody a whole world, a material reservoir so extensive and general that nothing outside it is needed and everything can be constituted from within it. "Every thing," in fact, is one of the key phrases in this passage, and it is in the oscillation between its specific (every *thing*) and general (everything) meanings that Defoe suggests something about the worldmaking ability of things. Crusoe's ordering of the heap is not simply a distribution or a placing of things, but a primary act that aligns the creation of location with the creation of order: "*Ortung*" equals "*Ordnung*," to use Carl Schmitt's terms.[41] In Crusoe's imagination, haunted as it is by visions of "savages," "wild beasts," and natural forces waiting to "devour" and "swallow" him, the island is a boundless space that threatens to absorb rather than just contain that which is placed in it. In the primary transformation of such boundlessness, the arrangement of things and the creation of place coincide. The compulsive transfer of things and the pleasure in having them "in their places" and "ready at my hand" may seem to be merely matters of practicality, convenience, or aesthetics. In fact, having things "ready at my hand" has to be understood instead as a condition of Western worldliness, and it is the assumed status of the island as *terra nullius* – as "empty" space belonging to no one – that throws these assumptions about worldliness into relief. Involving both person and thing, the crisis of the heap is the origin of Crusoe's appropriation of the island by centrifugal extension.

The contextualizing power that things have in this episode – their fetishistic ability to control human action and territorialize a "vacant" island – seems irrational, but is not therefore asymptomatic, the unique product of a particular individual facing an exceptional situation.[42] The close relation between enumeration, circulation, and mercantilism indicates that the transfer of objects from ship to island needs to be grasped as a micronarrative of the larger socio-economic conditions of *Robinson Crusoe*. As William Pietz has argued, the notion of the fetish itself emerges historically in a "mercantile cross-cultural space of transvaluation between material objects of radically different social orders."[43] It is tied to the destabilization of value created by the colonial trade of the sixteenth and seventeenth centuries between zones of starkly uneven economic development. The notion of the fetish does not emerge, as Pietz makes clear, as the identifiable institution of a discrete society, but out of the interaction between different economic and cultural zones. *Robinson Crusoe* allows us to extend and radicalize this point. Defoe's novel reveals that the destabilization of value inherent in the circulation of goods across strongly heterogeneous zones is capable of endowing any object with fetishistic qualities, no matter where the object comes from. The European attribution of an "absurd" overvaluation of European things to the "primitiveness" of indigenous cultures is a misattribution, for such overvaluation is simply a particular expression of the general destabilization of value created and exploited by mercantile capitalism.[44] Under these circumstances even the European Crusoe can become the helpless devotee of fetishistic objects, a white cargo-cultist whose feverish hopes for salvation through European things overtake every aspect of his life.

Defoe was acutely aware of the volatility of value created by the movements of mercantile trade, and his advocacy of the circulation of goods is directly linked to the assumption of a heterogeneous space. His insistence on London as the gravitational center of all movements of trade, his concern over the clogging of the "streams" and "channels" of trade, and his belief that the best trade is that "founded upon the most clear Principles of Commerce; namely, the meanest Export exchang'd for the richest Return," show that Defoe's economic space is not a rational, homogenized container that hosts a variety of economic movements.[45] The island itself is an important figure for this vision of trade, as it symbolizes a world of separate economic enclaves connected by a precarious and exclusive network of travel routes. Crusoe's location on a South American island close to the "Mouth of the great River of Oroonoque," and thus outside of the assimilated trading spaces of the British empire, is not eccentric, but a dramatic expression of the basic economic, cultural, and geographic heterogeneity underwriting the mercantile system as a whole.[46]

Fredric Jameson eloquently evokes this economy when he writes: "this is the stage Marx describes as exchange on the frontiers between two modes of production, which have not yet been subsumed under a single standard of value; so great fortunes can be made and lost overnight, ships sink or against all expectation appear in the harbor, heroic travelers reappear with cheap goods whose scarcity in the home society lends them extraordinary worth."[47] Defoe is deeply attracted to this narrative of transformation, not only in novels such as *Captain Singleton* (1720), *Moll Flanders* (1722), and *Roxana* (1724), but also in his economic writings. He identifies the origins of the English strength in trade, for instance, with those seventeenth-century seamen who "went out as Beggars and came Home Gentlemen."[48] The marvelous transformation that the seamen undergo here is closely related to the radical transformation that commodities undergo as they enter largely different economic zones. Thus in *Captain Singleton*, when his protagonist lands on the island of Madagascar and makes contact with the natives, Defoe writes:

As to our Money, it was meer Trash to them, they had no Value for it; so that we were in a fair way to be starved. Had we but some Toys and Trinckets, Brass Chains, Baubles, Glass Beads, or in a Word, the veriest trifles that a Ship Loading would not have been worth the Freight, we might have bought Cattel and Provisions enough for an Army.[49]

Such drastic instability of value makes clear that Defoe's sense of trade is still far removed from the more finely graded, uneven development of a more advanced capitalism. Although goods and funds have already entered a phase of accelerated international circulation, the institutions, modes of production, and imaginative procedures that would make us see "the earth's surface as a spatial framework in which events are contingently and temporally located" have not yet come into existence.[50] As a result, there is no generalized trust in the efficacy of modern systems of transfer or even the quantifiability of space. Such institutional trust, if one can call it that, does not really exist. In Defoe's writings the traffic of goods across national and geographical boundaries still depends on particular friendships with virtuous individuals whose services are reliable not because of professional ethos or bureaucratic rationality, but because of personal integrity – hence the proliferation in *Robinson Crusoe* of friends who manage Crusoe's international dealings in money and goods.[51] Mobility is not a generalized condition, but continues to be shaped by a heterogeneous space with small havens of personalized trust. This is why the list is the inherently unstable, momentary bridge between essentially different economic and geographic zones and fails to remove things permanently from localized contexts. It simply assists in actualizing the volatile value of things as they traverse the uneven spaces of mercantile capitalism.

It is these conditions that create the irrational expansion of use value on Crusoe's island and render it recognizable as an aspect of the more general destabilization of value cultivated by mercantile capitalism. Circulation can indeed be a mode of production in such a scenario: the movement of things across economic, cultural, and geographic boundaries can create wealth because of the marked unevenness of these spaces.[52] The transfer of goods from ship to island is a telling demonstration of this dynamic, for it reveals how the simple movement of things can transform them from basic items of daily use to fantastically powerful objects able to territorialize a perceived blank space. And even though Crusoe's things have only use value, their heightened mutability as they move from one location to another also tells us something about exchange value. For these two forms of value, strictly distinguished in Marx's analysis of industrial capitalism, are still related under an economic regime that considers circulation central to the production of wealth. What *Robinson Crusoe* suggests, and what I take to be more generally true of the traffic of things under mercantile capitalism, is that the movement of goods across different economic zones maintains a link between use value and exchange value because value emerges from the relationship between the thing and the context within which it appears.

The activation of contexts by the mercantile circulation of things can be seen, for example, in the following letter from a West Indian sugar planter living on St. Christopher's island to his cousin in Cornhill, London, written in 1676:

I promised to send you word what is most vendible in these parts. First, I shall give you as good advice as I can concerning those things you deal in, as your chairs that do not fold, your bed ticks, serges of cloth colours, your striped curtains and valances, your carpets of low prices. But too many of these things would soon cloy the country, because they are not but for the better sort. The most part here lie in hammakers, sit upon benches, clothe themselves in camies or some finer linen, and never cover the table but at meals. For your buckrams, printed stuffs, white serges, hangings, or cushions, I would counsel you never to send any more, till you hear I have sold these.[53]

This letter shows how the business of trading across substantially different economic zones connects exchange value and use value. Even comparatively simple items such as chairs, valances, and curtains do not seem to fit the needs and practices of the islanders, and the sugar planter assumes that "bed ticks," "chairs," and "buckram" will not find a place in a culture that relies on "hammakers," "benches" and "linen" for sleeping, sitting, and clothing. He thus compares in considerable detail two social and cultural contexts of use and shows how the mercantile search for exchange value necessitates a specific consideration of the different ways in which material objects mediate the social and cultural practices of England and St. Christopher's island. Because mercantile trading spaces are uneven, the relationship of things to their social and cultural contexts is brought to the fore while the cultivation of relationships among things, independent of any distinct contexts of use, recedes. Although the sugar planter expresses a clear interest, in some of his other letters, in the kind of advantageous trade Defoe envisions when he speaks of the "meanest Export exchang'd for the richest Return," it is equally clear that such a trade thrives on evading (even as it dialectically promotes) the general equivalency between things diagnosed by Marx for more advanced commodity cultures.[54] However critically one may view the facile glorification of the merchant that David Hume offers when he describes his role as that of a benevolent knowledge broker between geographic zones "that are wholly unacquainted, and are ignorant of each other's necessities," one also has to concede that such a statement touches on a genuine feature of a mercantile economy.[55] Mercantile exchange value engages significantly with the specifically context-bound value of use.

Robinson Crusoe's transfer of goods taunts us with yet another insight when it indicates, as I noted earlier, a kinship between use value and fetish value. In his account of industrial capitalism, Marx states categorically that the fetish value of the modern commodity arises out of exchange value, out of the exclusive relationships things cultivate among themselves. While all commodities combine use and exchange values, the industrial commodity is dominated by the latter. It becomes a fetish precisely because it has managed to remove itself from the concrete contexts of human need and human labor and has thus contributed to a "separation of man from things," which now confront each other as objectified realms of social experience.[56] Increasingly complex patterns of production and labor division, a massive expansion of the variety and number of objects produced, and constantly growing spheres of exchange have caused such separation. Things now define each other quantitatively, as equivalencies, and appear as abstract objects that disguise their origin in human need, labor, and use.

Marx recognized, of course, that the modern commodity fetish had historical precedents. But while he studied the available ethnographic literature on "ancient fetishism," to use W. J. T. Mitchell's phrase, he does not appear to have appreciated the link between use value and fetish value.[57] This is, no doubt, in part connected with his critique of religion and the prominent role the fetish began to play in eighteenth-century accounts of "primitive" religions.[58] But the realization that the fetish, insofar as it embodies a mixture of human and material spheres, is an important aspect of the materialist vision of human life is already implied in Marx's sense of society as a complex "*Stoffwechsel*" or "metabolism" between human and material spheres.[59] As Pietz's materialist reading of Marx's use of the fetish suggests, the scandal of the modern commodity for Marx is not that it signals an interdependence of persons and things.[60] Marx's materialism recognizes such interdependence as a condition of human existence. What is upsetting about the industrial commodity is that it has removed itself from the context of human use and labor and established for itself an independently existing world of self-defining objects that measure and determine us – who have, after all, produced this material world.

While Crusoe's objects also exert power over him and to that extent resemble the industrial commodity fetish, they derive their power from a different source. It is not the exclusive relationship among themselves that gives things their power in *Robinson Crusoe*, but their dependence on the cultural, economic, and geographic contexts within which they exist. The workings of the mercantile fetish are emphatically context-bound, and the mutability of the mercantile commodity indicates that it has not hardened into an independent material reality. The uneven spaces of mercantile capitalism do not only "volatilize" value, they also produce a porous commodity whose identity is shaped by the markedly different zones it inhabits. This allows for a complete or partial transformation of previous contextual identities – an aspect Nicholas Thomas has emphasized in his study of colonial exchange in the Pacific – or a forceful resurgence of the original context within the new one.[61]

Robinson Crusoe reveals, then, that the difference between an object defined by use value and one defined by mercantile fetishism lies not in their participation in the world of human needs and production. This they share. The difference lies rather in the mode of their interaction with that world. The power of the fetish, as Pietz points out, lies in its "gathering" ability, its capacity to transform a perceived "negative" space into a "positive" spatio-temporal structure.[62] Charged by the encounter with an essentially different economic and geographic space, Crusoe's objects assume intentionality and take on an originary function within the contextualizing narrative of utility. Of course, these temporarily intentional objects eventually return to the status of objects that respond in more specific ways to Crusoe's needs. As long as they have fetish value, they have an actively contextualizing function, but as soon as they assume specific use value, they are contextualized through human practice and become passively useful in Crusoe's concrete attempt to survive. Use value and fetish value under mercantile capitalism thus

represent versions of contextualized modes of being whose main difference lies in the distribution of agency between persons and things. Unlike
the modern commodity fetish, Crusoe's fetishes remain recognizable as
human extensions, as being directly involved in the process of human
reproduction.

Defoe's place in the long history of commodification can thus be clearly
differentiated from the early nineteenth century and the forms of objectification that Marx analyzed for this later period. *Robinson Crusoe* forces
us to expand the conceptual repertoire with which we approach the
commodity, and this not merely because it presents us with a capitalist
commodity type that cannot be accounted for in the terms of Marx's
well-known analysis of the industrial commodity. What is at least equally
important is that, by linking use value and fetish value, *Robinson Crusoe*
makes visible the idealization of use value that plagues many Marxist
accounts. The transparency that Marx himself thought characterized
the relationship between persons and things under use value is shown
to possess an opaque element in its kinship to more ancient forces of
fetishism. Such kinship exposes the notion of an economy governed by
use value as an anthropocentric vision that remains blind to the primacy of the communal and the full spectrum of possible person-thing
relationships.

But Defoe's place in the history of commodification also resists being
captured by the conceptual distinction between movable and immovable property. What is perhaps most striking about Defoe's engagement
with things is that it undermines our almost instinctive assumption that
global circulation defeats local associations and uproots the objects it
"displaces." Because he views circulation as a productive force, however,
Defoe has to recognize that the commodity bears a primary relationship
to ground, a relationship that ineluctably shapes its identity. And because mercantilism keeps the object-ground relationship alive – in fact,
depends on it – it also modifies the traditional distinction between movable and immovable forms of property. If landed property is traditionally
defined by an essential embeddedness that binds value in the ground,
the mercantile commodity partakes of this quality to the extent that it,
too, depends on a similarly primary relationship to ground. As *Robinson
Crusoe* shows, the mercantile fetish is even able to recreate this primary
relationship in distant places. In this sense the mercantile commodity
is less than fully alienable; it retains the imprint of its earlier existence.
It is precisely the encounter between this original cultural, economic,
and social imprint and the fundamentally different environment of the

island that generates the fetishistic energy necessary for these objects to territorialize a "vacant" space and to recreate a culturally specific type of groundedness. Any fundamental distinction between movable and immovable forms of property, then, cannot hinge on the criterion of transportability. The circulation of an object does not necessarily mean that its original associations are lost – and it does not mean that we are automatically dealing with an object whose exchange value becomes its dominant characteristic.

Defoe's novel thus complicates the distinction between movable and immovable property in two ways. As immovables resist becoming fully mobile and movables reveal immobile characteristics, *Robinson Crusoe* discloses a dependence on a primary ground whose preestablished grav-itational force cannot be escaped – not by the island, not by commodities, and not by Defoe's characters. The rambling habits of Crusoe and many of Defoe's protagonists, their impossibly various and interminable lives, along with the constant need to identify such habits and lives as excessive and even perverse, have to be recognized as the constrained expression of a desire to break free of embedded modes of being. Yet this desire to push open a neutral space and time of unlimited social and economic possi-bilities cannot be normalized at this historical juncture.[63] In this sense Crusoe's forced confinement on the island constitutes not only a religious chastening of the "original sin" of mobility, but a drastic demonstration of spatial dominance, of the continued socio-economic and existential presence of a primary relationship to ground that binds both persons and things. Exchange value has not yet established dominion over a wide and general enough sphere to uproot persons and things comprehensively, and the assertion of use value over exchange value on the island also mirrors the triumph of an uneven space over the mobile individual.[64] In such a scenario the list merely adumbrates, in miniaturistic form, the general equivalence things will acquire under the more advanced capitalism analyzed by Marx.

III

Robinson Crusoe's disclosure that the groundedness of things is stronger than the suspending powers of the list is not an isolated moment in the history of the representation of things in eighteenth-century Britain. I want to argue, in fact, that the prevalence of embedding over dis-embedding modes is symptomatic of the novelistic depiction of things in the first half of the eighteenth century – and that it is so beyond

the immediate economic context of mercantilism. Samuel Richardson's
Pamela, for instance, reveals such prevalence on the level of social space.
As with *Robinson Crusoe, Pamela*'s main drama is initiated by a crucial
transfer of things. Shortly after the death of Pamela's mistress, her son,
Squire B., calls Pamela into her "Lady's Closet." Writing to her father,
Pamela describes this scene as follows:

> Pulling out her Drawers, he gave me Two Suits of fine Flanders lac'd Headcloths,
> Three Pair of fine Silk Shoes, two hardly the worse, and just fit for me; for my old
> Lady had a very little Foot; and several Ribbands and Topknots of all Colours,
> and Four Pair of fine white Cotton Stockens, and Three Pair of fine Silk ones;
> and Two Pair of rich Stays, and a Pair of rich Silver Buckles in one Pair of the
> Shoes. I was quite astonish'd, and unable to speak for a while; but yet I was
> inwardly asham'd to take the Stockens; for Mrs. Jervis was not there: if she had,
> it would have been nothing. I believe I received them very awkwardly; for he
> smil'd at my Awkwardness; and said, Don't blush, Pamela: Dost think I don't
> know pretty Maids wear Shoes and Stockens?[65]

The transfer of goods in the insulated space of a lady's closet gives rise
here to a listing rhetoric that resembles Crusoe's. Pamela's consistent
emphasis on numbers and specific designations, the breathless recur-
rence of the copula "and," and her dogged determination to present a
complete account closely echo Crusoe's predilections. As Defoe's listing
rhetoric is translated into a domestic setting, it no longer organizes the
flow of goods between the uneven economic, cultural, and geographic
spaces of mercantile capitalism, but between the uneven social spaces of
a patriarchal society.[66]

On the surface the gifts Pamela receives here are meant to consolidate the vertical dependence of servant on master. They require no
return because they are simply meant to reinforce already existing "ties
of honour and gratitude" (146), as B. phrases it at one point. But B.'s
conventional gesture strays beyond its proper bounds in the quantity
and lavishness of the things it offers and in the inclusion of a sexually
more suggestive article, the stockens. As Pamela later realizes, B.'s gesture does not so much consolidate an existing relationship, as initiate
a new one of private exchange in which beautiful objects are meant to
elicit a return in sexual favors. Pamela hesitates before this engrafting of
a private exchange on to a social custom and responds to the "dangers
of Plenty," as her parents will describe B.'s "astonishing" lavishness, by
attempting to capture its objects in a meticulous list. This list reproduces the characteristic dynamic already observed in Defoe, whereby

the traveling of objects across uneven spaces, because it is bound up with moments of abstraction and quantification, activates an increased awareness of social, cultural, and economic contexts. In *Pamela* this happens even within the list. Repeatedly noting how "fine" and "rich" the things are and reminding us of their owner, Pamela draws our attention to the social sphere to which these things belong, but that awareness is tied to a neutralizing scrutiny. Quantity and quality, measurability and social meaning, isolation and context begin to rub against each other as Pamela patiently displays the rank-specific grammar of things in the colorless medium of middle-class accounting.

Yet despite the rising tension between the potentially limitless extendibility of Pamela's quantitative method and the overwhelming plenitude and intrinsic richness of upper-class objects, Pamela's list ultimately fails to resist the charm of B.'s objects. As she eagerly points out that her foot is just like her lady's was and that the shoes are therefore "just fit for me" – an ambiguous formulation that oscillates between the physical fit of things and the propriety of wearing them – Pamela reveals how irresistible these dazzling objects are and how quickly they are associated with potential social transformation. And it is not just the suggestion that upper-class wealth may actually be appropriate to her that bears this out. Contained in the concern with the fit of her lady's shoes is also an allusion to Cinderella, one of the most potent and popular folk myths of social transformation, which was popularized in England through Robert Samber's translation of 1727.[67] Cinderella's magical unrecognizability as she is moving between high and low ranks – eventually resolved by the fit of a shoe – is developed in *Pamela* with a specific emphasis on the powers clothes derive from the exclusiveness with which they belong to qualitatively different social spaces. When Mrs. Jervis fails to recognize Pamela in her plain dress and Pamela's father fails to recognize her in her rich dress (60, 257), the novel adopts a fairytale motif to make a point about the mutual exclusiveness of hierarchical social spheres. It does so by emphasizing how the alignment of social and private selves in such a society allows rank-specific clothes to shape a person's identity. What may seem like a residue of romance in a text canonized for its "realism" thus turns out to be a "realistic" portrayal of a social structure that relies on qualitatively different and hierarchically ordered social spaces. Within this context Pamela's comparison of feet and her sense of the "fitness" of the shoe constitute an audacious play with social distinction veiled by a seemingly modest quantifying impulse.

Pamela's compromising entanglement with things becomes evident when she fails to act decisively in the early stages of the novel. Here she contemplates escape:

Sometimes I thought I would leave the House, and go to the next Town, and wait an Opportunity to get to you; but then I was at a Loss to resolve whether to take away the Things he had given me or no, and how to take them away: Sometime I thought to leave them behind me, and only go with the Cloaths on my Back; but then I had two Miles and a half, and a By-way, to go to the Town . . . (36)

In the end she fails to form a clear resolve, and her confusion has a great deal to do with the power B.'s things have gained over her. Charged by the traffic across ranks, these things have cast a spell over Pamela. They function here as fetishes, but once again as fetishes of a kind with which we are not very familiar. Their power does not derive from the human labor they entrap and conceal to confront us with an alien materiality, but from their deep embeddedness in distinct social spheres. Because they are removed from their original sphere, these objects can demonstrate their power of social belonging: they confuse and immobilize Pamela. Eluding the disenchanting grasp of the list, B.'s gifts transfix Pamela, and it is they as much as everything else B. undertakes that collapse the "Distance between a Master and a Servant" (44), as Pamela terms it, and that make her "forget . . . what belongs to me" (35), a phrase that captures the unity of property and propriety. Given Pamela's enchantment by things, it makes sense that, when she finally thinks she is leaving B., her preparations take the form of a sorting and rationalizing of things, a literalized attempt to "recollect" what "belongs to her."

She creates three "bundles," each of which contains a distinct group of objects: things she received from her lady, things given by her master, and those things she can "properly call my own" (78). In creating these three collections, Pamela distinguishes past, present, and future. The first "bundle" contains things she received along the established path by which social hierarchies reproduce themselves. They are gifts from her lady and were meant to be worn "in her Service, and to do Credit to her bountiful Heart" (80). But since this life is now inescapably lost and the things can no longer function as gifts that reinscribe social obligation, Pamela wishes to leave them behind. The bundle of her master's things (some of which we encountered in her list) is now clearly identified with a corrupting exchange relationship: "if I would not do the good Gentleman's Work," Pamela reasons, "why should I take his

Wages?" (80). The third bundle, finally, contains the things she is going to take with her and they are almost exclusively determined by immediate use value.

Pamela's ordering act thus rationalizes her past, present, and future lives by identifying three distinctly different and clearly regulated communities of persons and things. But despite this attempt at disentangling herself from things and taming the forces of fetishism, Pamela's concerted act of "recollection" is self-defeating. For while she gives these three collections of objects distinct identities, she also undermines these distinctions by turning them all into "bundles." To the extent that they are now ready for travel – as Pamela herself is – the differentiation between her "dear third bundle" (81) and the "second wicked bundle" (80) becomes questionable. We are thus not surprised when we learn that these bundles quickly follow her to her new location (111). Pamela's history of things, indeed, cannot rest until finally, briefly before her wedding, she again adorns her body with the objects contained in her bundles. She is transformed and thinks "herself a Gentlewoman once more," but this time with gratefulness "for being able to put on this Dress with so much Comfort" (256). The contents of the "bad" and the "good" bundles now figure together as "good things" (256), and Pamela finally abandons all attempts to rationalize her relationship to the gifts she received. In this way the passage of things across an uneven social space paves the way for the social transformation of persons.

Pamela's emphasis on the power of things invites reconsideration of so-called object narratives, in which commodities take on narratorial functions. A subgenre with growing popularity in eighteenth-century Britain, these narratives have been seen by a number of critics as conspicuous expressions of a modern consumer culture and modern forms of objectification. From the perspective of the readings I have offered in this chapter, this is no longer the immediately striking argument it once seemed. For objects that have the distinctly human capacity of narration simply testify to the continued fluidity between human and material spheres. Such fluidity is perhaps most dramatically expressed by Tobias Smollett's contribution to the genre, *The History and Adventures of an Atom* (1769), in which the object narrator incorporates itself variously with persons as well as things. But even beyond this perhaps most extreme example of a "fully miscible world," the assumption of narratorial functions by objects should be seen as an indication of the peculiar power the circulation of commodities gains in a society structured by an uneven, hierarchical social space.[68]

This view is confirmed by an anonymous narrative such as *The History and Adventures of a Lady's Slippers and Shoes* (1754), whose title might be alluding to a famous issue of *The Tatler*, in which its "censor" was scandalized to find "fine wrought Ladies Shoes and Slippers put out to View at a great Shoemaker's Shop" (intriguingly, Richardson himself could not find much scandal in such exhibition and associated it with his own descriptive practice).[69] Featuring objects not only as narrators, but also as protagonists, *Lady's Slippers* belongs to a group of works that became increasingly popular in the 1740s and 1750s. They began to displace earlier object narratives whose affiliation with the genre of the "secret" or "scandalous" history made objects the convenient and entirely passive witnesses to political and court intrigues.[70] *Lady's Slippers* supplements and extends the role the shoe plays in *Pamela*, and its references to *Rape of the Lock* and, more obliquely, *Pamela* itself, suggest that we need to read these object narratives alongside more canonical works.[71] The narrative of the slippers and the narrative of the shoes both start with a stylized story of production that celebrates, with some anxiety regarding even a basic division of labor, the marvelous qualities achievable by uniquely gifted master craftsmen.[72] The scene of production is thus far removed from industrialized forms of labor and it is clear from the outset that such rarefied objects belong to the upper ranks. It is here, in the upper ranks, that the main narrative begins to depict a rapid and seemingly interminable circulation across different social spheres.

The irresistible and radiant attractiveness of the shoes as they cross rank divides is strongly emphasized.[73] We see, for example, a "housekeeper" eagerly take the newly acquired shoes into "her chamber":

[She] surveyed us a long time with flushed cheeks and sparkling eyes, till at length excess of joy loosened her tongue; Well, these will suit my pink sack charmingly . . . Ye dear pretty things, you'll see me dress'd as well as any mistress ye ever had; my turn is now coming to be lady. There's a foot! let any princess of the empire match them . . . Next Sunday, my pretty rogues, ye shall go on, till when I'll wrap you up very carefully.[74]

These kinds of encounters occur frequently and I see them as striking representations of a premodern commodity culture. Passages such as the above were, of course, written with a view to warn against an excessive attachment to luxury, ornament, and mere appearance. But it would be shortsighted not to see how the articulation of such moral themes is shaped by the distinct characteristics of a commodity culture that thrives on heterogeneous spaces and transformation. The fairytale allusions recur in this passage, and they arise out of the peculiar dynamic that objects acquire in uneven social space. As long as objects are thus distinctly and exclusively associated with social rank, their mere circulation will be an absorbing narrative spectacle – as absorbing, indeed, as the objects themselves become in scenes like these. There is a remarkable closeness between persons and things on display here as the new owner tenderly addresses her "dear pretty things" and her "pretty rogues," a closeness that is fueled by the fantasy of social transformation the shoes make realizable. Such closeness is merely the reverse, it seems to me, of the reader's close contact with the object narrator – a circumstance that would seem to reinforce rather than undercut the morally questionable attachment to things that the narrative as a whole wishes to expose. Contradictions such as these underscore the fluidity of the boundary between human and material spheres and expose the difficulty of moral exhortation against luxury in a culture where an uneven social space endows commodities with absorbing charms.

These considerations should also generate a rereading of some of the more canonical verse representations of commodities. John Gay's or Alexander Pope's efforts in this area, for instance, need to be recognized as specific engagements with the properties of the mercantile commodity. The epic conventions that frame Pope's famous scene of Belinda's toilet, for example, accentuate the magical powers of the "glitt'ring spoil" that "breathes" and "glows" with its colonial origins and quite literally transforms Belinda, raising "her Charms," awakening "Grace," and calling "forth all the Wonders of her Face."[75] This association of commodities and transformation is repeated later in the poem, in a scene of objects that has found far fewer commentators. Here the genesis of Belinda's bodkin is traced back to paternal seal-rings that, in a process of cultural deterioration, were gradually transformed into maternal adornment (the "vast buckle" of the "Widow's Gown"), an educational tool (the "infant Granddame's Whistle"), and then into Belinda's mother's bodkin, which in the poem assumes the function of a knife.[76] Again Pope uses an epic convention, and again it is to foreground the mutability that characterizes the mercantile commodity. What Pope emphasizes in both these scenes is that the power of things is context-bound: their transfer from "India" and "Arabia" to Belinda's dressing table and their mutability as they become attached to different owners points to a conception of objects that sees them as unstable and destabilizing. Itself prone to constant shape-shifting, Pope's commodity can also shift a person's shape. On the one hand, this view of the commodity certainly confirms the gendered associations that small objects attract: a glance at *Epistle to a Lady* confirms that Pope associates mutability and instability with women. But on the other hand, it also shows that Pope is alluding specifically to the mercantile commodity, whose powers of transformation endow Pope's poem about small things with genuine cultural authority. As the mercantile fetish is able to reanimate epic conventions – in Pope, but also, for example, in Gay's *The Fan* – these conventions help to reveal that the culture of objectification in early eighteenth-century Britain is bound up with notions of transfer and transformation.

In *Pamela, Robinson Crusoe,* and narratives such as *Lady's Slippers,* the attempt to create a neutral space between persons and things is hampered because the circulation across qualitatively uneven social, geographic, cultural, and economic zones promotes, precisely by mobilizing things, their ability to entangle, immobilize, and transform. Such abilities echo the entrapment Pamela and Crusoe experience with regard to the immovable properties (island and estate) on which they are confined. Despite all efforts to strengthen them, the distinctions between persons and things and body and space turn out to be weak in these texts. In the end Pamela's and Crusoe's circulation follows the pattern traced out by the objects. Though Richardson's novel is in many ways more conservative, it shares with Defoe's work and *Lady's Slippers* a basic spatial logic that shapes the movement of persons and things alike. All three narratives derive their energies from the movement of persons and things across an uneven, qualitative, and embodied space, and from the strains experienced in the attempt to reshape a communal form that tends to integrate material and human zones. Even though Pamela and Crusoe try to carve out uninvadable private enclosures that resist the defining powers of the heterogeneous spaces around them, they both have to submit to their gravitational pull.

That Henry Fielding agreed with this spatial logic in principle is already indicated by his strategic choice of a protagonist who can circulate freely precisely because he occupies no social ground, no social position. Fielding's reading of *Pamela,* which recognizes that the mobility of things in the novel is closely linked to Pamela's mobility, makes this point explicit. In *Shamela* (1741), his great parody of Richardson's runaway success, Fielding singled out "the using of all manners of means to come at ornaments of their persons" as one of the fatal "instructions" *Pamela* offered to "servant-maids."[77] The impropriety of Shamela wearing her "mistress's gowns" is pointed to repeatedly, and Fielding directly parodies Richardson's penchant for lists.[78] Not surprisingly, Fielding's pronounced endorsement of the virtues of the "flat" character who cannot achieve differentiation from the social environment is matched by a portrayal of movable property that is deeply invested in controlling the transformative powers unleashed by circulation in an uneven social space. In *Tom Jones* women who wear their betters' clothes invariably cause public scandal and uproar, and from banknotes and bibles to muffs, pocketbooks, and even intellectual property, Fielding takes extreme care to mark all movables with clearly recognizable and even ostentatious signs of individual ownership.[79] To ensure that things are, as Fielding puts it, "at all Times ready to be restored to the right Owner" is a driving concern in *Tom Jones*.[80] Nothing is lost in Fielding's novel that is not returned, a pattern that James Thompson has judiciously characterized as *Tom Jones*'s "comic rule of conservation under which it is finally impossible to lose anything."[81]

Fielding's desire to curb the circulation of things leads him to withdraw them from the largely collective life they lead in Defoe and Richardson and invest them with individualized histories that enact the inevitable-return pattern I have mentioned. That individual things in Defoe and Richardson usually do not stay around long enough to acquire sustained symbolic, sexual, or sentimental values provides, indeed, additional evidence that these novels perform their textual work on things under conditions of a material culture that remains wedded to social structures. Even the often sentimental *Pamela* fails to extend its emotional charge to individual objects. One of its most prominent sentimental scenes – Pamela's creation of the bundles – derives its emotional energy not from the fond consideration of individual objects, but from the propriety that Pamela displays in arranging these objects according to their social provenance, their groundedness in distinct sets of social relationships. She literally embraces the "dear bundle," and in doing so does not show affection to individual or collected objects, but to the social relationship they constitute.[82] Things remain in the bag, as it were, and fail to emerge as foci of emotional projection.

Fielding, of course, was not prepared to stress these conservative aspects of Richardson's text, and his decision to tie movables to their origin by imprinting them with a return narrative reveals considerable anxiety and care. In his most extensive object narrative in *Tom Jones* – the "Adventure of the Muff," as Tom eventually calls it – Fielding shows that his narrative resistance to transformative circulation also protects against more modern forms of objectification. Early in his novel this muff becomes an important object in the love relationship between Sophia and Tom. Having learnt that Tom has bestowed some of his growing tenderness on her muff, Sophia suddenly becomes warmly attached to an object she had originally intended to give away. This muff reappears throughout the novel, but its most important appearance occurs during the scene at Upton Inn. Tom and Sophia are both staying at the inn, but they are not aware of each other's presence. When Sophia at last finds out that Tom is there, she also hears that he is in bed with another woman. Determined to resume her journey at once, she decides to leave Tom a memento of her presence:

The Reader will be pleased to remember a little Muff, which hath had the Honour of being more than once remembered already in this History. This Muff, ever since the Departure of Mr. Jones, had been the constant Companion of Sophia by Day, and her Bedfellow by Night, and this Muff she had at this very Instant upon her Arm; whence she took it off with great Indignation, and having writ her Name with her Pencil upon a Piece of Paper which she pinned to it, she bribed the Maid to convey it into the empty Bed of Mr. Jones.[83]

The most conspicuous aspect of this passage is undoubtedly its bawdy sexual play with the two meanings of the term "muff." Few eighteenth-century readers would have been able to ignore this dimension, as the term appears to have been widely known to signify female genitals, an association facilitated even further by the details of Fielding's scene. What Sophia is doing here on this level is, quite simply, placing her sexual organs in Tom's empty bed, reminding him not only of her presence, but, more specifically, of Tom's unfaithfulness. The message is blunt: Tom should attend to Sophia's body rather than anyone else's.

Yet apparently the punning abilities of the muff cannot be trusted to do their work alone, and Sophia feels compelled to append a name tag to this suggestive object. I would venture to say that this is rather bizarre. If Tom is as attached to the muff as the fervent kisses he earlier bestowed on it indicate, why does he need to be reminded of the muff's owner? Given the affective value of the object and the fact that we are not in an age of industrial mass production, should not Tom be able to pick out Sophia's muff among a hundred others? Sophia seems not to trust Tom's memory, and her doubt is shown to be justified when it turns out that Tom would indeed have had trouble recognizing the muff without her tag. By contrast, Parson Supple, who later also appears at the inn, does not need the assistance of a written notice. Even though his relation to Sophia is remote, he immediately recognizes the muff when

Tom parades it in the inn's parlor.[84] What are we to make of the trouble Tom has in recognizing Sophia's muff?

The most obvious explanation is that the muff simply does not work for Tom as a representation of Sophia. It is not an evocative object whose associations with another, absent object are so strong that it automatically calls up the latter. If one revisits Squire Western's house, where the muff is initially treated with affection, one quickly realizes that there the muff had an eminently practical function. It served literally as a means of bringing Tom and Sophia into contact, and it organized an illicit, physical traffic of secret kisses and embraces. In this context the muff is simply a means to an end, a transportational device without an identity of its own. Consequently, as Tom notes, the muff recedes into invisibility in Sophia's presence.[85] Even at its first appearance in the novel, the muff is thus not an object that acquires recognizability, and Tom's later failure to identify it as Sophia's is simply a result of the muff's original pragmatic status.

Tom's seemingly curious response when the muff turns up at Upton, then, has little to do with forgetfulness and everything to do with a virtuous inability to mediate absence symbolically. For Tom the muff does not *represent* Sophia or her genitals, and it cannot divert Tom's sexual energy from its original object – in Tom's world, such diversion is reserved to other women. And while the muff is sexually suggestive, it is not a sexual object in its own right, a differentiation that is preserved in Fielding's reliance on the pun to generate his sexual meaning. The pun depends on the copresence of at least two meanings and fails to elevate the one over the other. It is the constant oscillation between the two meanings that generates the pun's specific power. Such reliance on punning keeps the object attached to its original meaning even as sexual connotations are activated. Fielding's unwillingness to let the muff acquire an independent meaning is also signaled by the name tag. The name tag extends Fielding's consistent habit of inscribing the owner's name on all forms of mobile property in the novel and thus prevents the object from assuming a meaning that would be grounded in itself, without distinct reference to the person to whom it belongs. Because the circulation of the muff does not awaken unpredictable forces or endow the object with an independent identity, Fielding escapes both older and newer forms of objectification. He reveals the muff's pragmatic essence in a comic scene of nonrecognition that presents the muff without an independent identity and therefore without the ability to stand between persons, in whatever capacity.

But while the muff does not face us as a separate material object, Fielding does hint that Tom learns a lesson about objects from Sophia. At Upton the muff has for her already become a "constant Companion by Day, and her Bedfellow by Night." After his comic nonrecognition, Tom follows suit and we see him, further on in the novel, retiring "with his two Bed-fellows [Sophia's] Pocket-Book, and the Muff."[86] There is a suggestion here that Tom is beginning to adopt what was considered to be a typically female attachment to small objects, yet Fielding again refuses to give the muff a clear identity, as he now pairs it with another object belonging to Sophia. Together these suggestive "bedfellows" resist the individuating pressure that could have been exerted on a single thing; their joint representation of Sophia defuses a specific symbolization.

These readings of various histories of things should have made it clear just how consistently things in these texts fail to match modern notions of objectification. In all of these instances, the notion of the Marxist commodity fetish with its characteristic emphasis on generalized exchangeability and self-enclosed materiality fails to provide much insight. The communal forms we are dealing with here embed persons and things in concrete social, economic, and cultural contexts, preventing their emergence as separate objects that could begin to cultivate exclusive relationships and bounded identities and thus escape the condition of groundedness. The commodity culture evident in all of these texts still bears the imprint of a mercantile economy in which heterogeneous spaces, circulation, and transformation sustain the context-bound life of persons and things.

IV

In *An Inquiry into the Nature and Causes of the Wealth of Nations* (1776), Adam Smith attempts to place the mercantile commodity in a remote historical past. In an account of the changing relationship between movable and immovable property that sketches, with the broad strokes of conjectural history, the encounter between manorial modes of community and the growing forces of international trade, Smith explains:

The silent and insensible operations of foreign commerce and manufacturers . . . gradually furnished the great proprietors with something for which they could exchange the whole surplus produce of their lands, and which they could consume themselves without sharing it either with tenants or retainers . . . For a pair of diamond buckles perhaps, or for something as frivolous and useless, they exchanged the maintenance, or what is the same thing, the price of the maintenance of a thousand men for a year, and with it the whole authority and weight which it could give them. The buckles, however, were to be all their own, and no other human creature was to have any share in them; whereas in the more ancient method of expence they must have shared with at least a thousand people. With the judges that were to determine the preference, this difference was perfectly decisive; and thus, for the meanest and most sordid of all vanities, they gradually bartered their whole power and authority.[87]

In this dramatic replacement of patriarchal social bonds that encompass "a thousand men" by an individualistic fixation on "a pair of diamond buckles," Smith puts the feudal lord in the position of the savage chief whose ignorance prompts him to "barter" entire kingdoms for the dazzling objects of the colonizer. The mercantile commodity appears in all its irrational splendor and Smith gleefully insists that the great landowners sold "their birthright in the wantonness of plenty, for trinkets and baubles, fitter to be the playthings of children than the serious pursuits of men" (I:439).[88] Smith's conjectural sketch outlines the social, economic, and psychological transformations caused by the increasing circulation of rarefied objects under an expanding commerce. It emphasizes the violence of the initial encounter between two fundamentally different forms of property. The localized social cohesion of a political economy based on feudal ties of personal dependence and obligation centered in the owner of expansive lands and radiating outwards in generous hospitality is suddenly undermined by what Smith calls "the greatest of all superfluities" (I:229), the diamond. The inherent splendor of the mercantile object, when retrieved from the "diamond mines of Golconda and Visiapour" (I:193) and brought into an environment that depends on embedded modes of social and economic being, causes a concentration and narrowing of attention whose intensity rechannels the excessive outward communal orientation of the "more ancient method of expence" (according to which possession is shared and social) into the exclusive and the personal. In this way the movable goods of mercantile traffic break the socio-economic network of the expansive landed estate.

Smith appreciates the consequences of this early encounter between movable and immovable property and celebrates, under the rubric of unintended consequences, how the landlord's modern form of expense on luxury items provided by merchants and artificers promotes the breakdown of an unwieldy manorial estate into smaller units. Forced to raise rents to satisfy his increasing appetite for luxury goods, the feudal lord initiates the gradual establishment of more independent forms of ownership. Because he has to pay more, Smith argues, the tenant begins to demand greater control over his property, which he is then more motivated to improve. But while the mercantile commodity causes a first approximation of movable and immovable property by promoting smaller, independently held parcels of land, this historical development, positive as it is on one level, is for Smith nonetheless an aberration that violates "the natural course of things" (I:441). As his pejorative representation of the diamond buckle indicates, this is no straightforward celebration of the rise of movable property. While Smith elsewhere concedes that our pursuit of frivolous trinkets is beneficial even as it is deceptive, his account of mercantilism makes clear that the circulatory logic of the mercantile commodity is precisely what he wishes to expose as an outmoded and, indeed, misleading conception of the creation of wealth.[89]

Smith's lengthy, scathing attack on mercantilism indicates just how widespread its assumptions still were in mid-eighteenth-century Britain, and he argues that there are important reasons why such beliefs should be especially tenacious in Britain. Of all the countries of Europe, he suggests, Britain was particularly vulnerable to what he calls the "mean and malignant expediences of the mercantile system" (II:126) because of its extensive seacoast and navigable rivers, which predisposed it to be "the seat of foreign commerce" (I:442).[90] For Smith the ascendance of mercantilist beliefs and practices in the seventeenth and eighteenth centuries inverted the natural scheme of national development according to which "the greater part of the capital of every growing society is, first, directed to agriculture, afterwards to manufacture, and last of all to foreign commerce" (I:405). "The trade of exportation" – absolutely central to the mercantilist model of wealth – has for Smith "the least effect" on national prosperity (I:387).

While he grants historical validity to Defoe's claim that trade is the mother of manufacture, Smith sharply attacks "the violent operation ... of the stocks of particular merchants and undertakers" through which manufactures unnaturally became "the offspring of foreign commerce" (I:429). He acknowledges the remarkable capital that mercantilism has been able to collect, but quickly points out what a "precarious and uncertain possession" is wealth derived from international trade. Merchant capital, in Smith's eyes, does not "belong to any particular country" and the merchant himself "is not necessarily the citizen of any particular country" (I:444–445). Mercantile stock is always "out of sight" and so violates what Smith sees as the "natural" inclination of every individual to have his capital – to quote a constantly repeated formula – "under his own immediate view and command" (I:475–476).[91]

"Distant sale" (I:429) and slow, indirect returns (I:390–391; II:144) are the risky conditions of a mercantile exchange that suspends capital and keeps it from being "secured and realized in the cultivation and improvement of . . . land," in the form of either agriculture or its proper "offspring," manufacture (I:444, 431). The volatility of value created by the precarious trade across uneven economic zones renders the merchant equally fickle and unreliable – prone to "remove his capital" because of "a very trifling disgust" (I:444–445) and likely to abandon "sober virtue" to revel in "expensive luxury" at the expense of "productive labour" (II:127–128). "All the different regulations of the mercantile system," Smith claims, "necessarily derange" natural patterns of distribution (II:146). The unceasing mobility that drives mercantilism, its nervous pursuit of advantageous circulation, and its cultivation of heterogeneous spaces amount for Smith to a dangerous rootlessness that leaves wealth disembodied, invisible, volatile, alien, and produces commodity forms capable of inducing an irrational, blinding absorption to which even the merchant himself easily falls prey (II:127–128).

It is no surprise, then, when Smith at one point begins to associate a central part of the mercantile economy with the properties of the mercantile commodity: "To the undiscerning eye of giddy ambition, [the great commerce of America] naturally presents itself amidst the confused scramble of politics and war, as a very dazzling object to fight for. The dazzling splendor of the object, however, the immense greatness of the commerce, is the very quality which renders the monopoly of it hurtful" (II:143–144). Smith's history of the mercantile commodity thus exposes it as a disembodied, shifty, and dangerously dazzling object – the forceful opponent of stable, nationally rooted forms of wealth. But if he thus dramatizes the conflict between movable and immovable forms of property, Smith's ultimate intention is to reestablish, on a different level, the similarity between these forms. In his account the destructive encounter between mercantile commodity and manorial community yields modern property forms that bind movable and immovable wealth in the productive native soil and the bounded outline of a homogenized national space.

I have spent some time on Smith's attack on mercantilism because I believe that its intensity, far from constituting an uncharacteristic outbreak that one can pass over fairly swiftly, is actually integral to understanding those of Smith's economic assumptions that have been recognized as essentially modern. The normative, measured tone of Smith's exposition in the first three books is deceptive and needs to be brought into contact with the more vitriolic aspects of his attack on mercantilism in the fourth. Even the opening passage of the *Wealth of Nations* on the division of labor, while also a critique of the physiocratic notion that manufacturing is "unproductive," is equally a polemic against the continuing influence of mercantile ideas. Smith's striking example for the division of labor – the pin factory – is calculated to shock the reader into realizing that a new way of conceptualizing wealth has arrived that is centered on production, not circulation. This shift is addressed explicitly only later on when Smith notes that "the prejudices established by the commercial system [i.e., mercantilism] have taught us to believe, that national wealth arises more immediately from exportation than from production" (II:22). Yet to alter the reader's understanding of commodities and even his or her perception of things is already the object of the opening description of Smith's most famous commodity, the pin. Its display is carefully designed to achieve maximum contrast with the lure of the mercantile fetish.

Smith's use of the pin should be seen as a catachresis, a violent yoking together of radically different meanings by which one of the smallest, simplest, and most utilitarian objects – mostly used and produced, as Kathryn Sutherland reminds us, by women – reveals the inner workings of that commanding totality, the wealth of nations.[92] Smith is careful to stress this dynamic and points repeatedly to the "trifling" nature of his representative commodity, its remarkable smallness, designed to "supply the small wants of but a small number of people" (I:7). It is not hard to see how stark a contrast this establishes with the "frivolous ornaments of dress" (I:193) Smith criticized in the figure of the diamond buckle.[93] His representation of the pin replaces the emphasis on circulation and blinding absorption in his account of a cultural revolution induced by "trinkets and baubles" with an emphasis on arrest and visibility. For Smith, as his comments on description in *Lectures on Rhetoric and Belles Lettres* underline, such an emphasis implies divisibility.[94] Among the many advantages of the pin Smith importantly includes that "those employed in every branch of the work can often be collected into the same workhouse, and placed at once under the view of the spectator" (I:78). His interest in visibility and comprehensibility may have been influenced by François Quesnay's success in focusing and grounding the circulation of the national economy in a single image in his *Tableau Economique* (1758).[95] In a letter to Mirabeau, Quesnay (whom Smith met in 1766 and to whom he wished to dedicate the *Wealth*) stresses the visibility produced by the tableau: otherwise "elusive ideas" are "fixed securely in the imagination by the tableau," allowing viewers "to picture [these ideas] as a whole in their order and interconnection at a single survey, so that we can contemplate them at ease without losing anything from sight."[96] Smith draws us into a similar spectatorship when he describes, in concentrated phrases that quickly succeed each other, the operations of the pin factory:

One man draws out the wire, another straights it, a third cuts it, a fourth points it, a fifth grinds it at the top for receiving the head; to make the head requires two or three distinct operations; to put it on, is a peculiar business, to whiten the pin is another; it is even a trade by itself to put them into the paper; and the important business of making a pin is, in this manner, divided into about eighteen distinct operations (I:8).

Here we have the manufacture of the pin "placed at once under the view of the spectator." Smith manages to "collect" into one sentence the activities that take place in a single workhouse. The pin proves a fortunate example, as its divisibility has clear limits. While Smith foregrounds the several parts that constitute the pin, he can present them quickly, within one sentence, and thus balance the divisibility of the object with syntactic wholeness. The problem with other commodities, as he explicitly concedes, is that their divisibility is too extensive and would thus frustrate the "conciseness" and "vivacity" that he considers essential to "lively" description.[97] Even under conditions of modern manufacture, the pin is a simple enough object to keep divisibility and comprehensibility in close contact: the spectator does not become lost in the contemplation of all the different parts that come together in the production, and Smith can maintain the transparency he needs to differentiate the manufactured commodity from the irrational, absorptive splendor of the mercantile commodity.

But while he wants to break the infantilizing grip of the mercantile commodity, Smith's descriptive creation of immediacy, visibility, and comprehensibility is equally careful to avoid an objectifying distance between persons and things. His requirements for a successful description evolve around a basic connectedness between human and material spheres. His preference for an individualized perspective on things (what he calls "indirect description"), the insistence on a human presence within the descriptive scene, or even the use of such terms as "liveliness" and "animatedness" as criteria for a successful evocation of inanimate objects all confirm his desire to link human and material spheres. He associates the criterion of "liveliness," in fact, with the challenge of descriptively combining concision and circumstantiality. To meet this challenge he recommends that "every member of a sentence represent at least one and if possible two or three different circumstances," a recommendation clearly illustrated by his strongly circumstantial description of pin production, which shows the "wire," for example, within the context of five distinct operations.[98]

Such circumstantiality, indeed, is for Smith closely allied to spectatorship. In *The Theory of Moral Sentiments* (1759), the notion of the spectator plays a crucial role in Smith's articulation of sympathetic relationality. "Sympathy," he states, "does not arise so much from the view of the passion as from that of the situation which excites it."[99] In order to feel sympathetic, we cannot rely on a spontaneous, immediate response, but "have to take time to picture out in our imagination the different circumstances of distress" and "its minutest incidents," the deliberate contemplation of which defines the attitude of the "spectator."[100] Sympathy for Smith is thus associated with "moderation" and even "mediocrity," a middle ground between the extremes of immediate, passionate identification and detached observation.[101]

In the description of the pin factory, Smith creates distance between observer and scene, but strives to preserve an involvement that now no longer derives from an unreflective, absorptive link with the object, but from a deliberate consideration of the circumstances from which the object emerges. By thus drawing attention away from the immediate physicality of the object and on to the set of circumstances that produce that physicality, Smith balances distance and involvement, avoiding the absorptive qualities of the mercantile commodity without yielding to an objectifying differentiation between persons and things. His view of the manufactured commodity is designed to break through the circulatory paradigm of mercantilism by tying the forces of transformation and the creation of value to a clearly localized, visible, and rational process of production. Rearranged along chronological lines, Smith's account of the rationalization of property begins by depicting the mercantile commodity as a radically disembedded, capricious object that undermines manorial forms of embedded community and then proceeds by associating the small landed estates that emerge from the decline of the "great proprietors" with the security and reliability of the manufactured commodity. In the manufacture, as on the small landed estate, capital is "under [the owner's] own immediate view and command," and in both cases such visual-tactile closeness establishes a sympathetic relationship that is based on the detailed knowledge of circumstance. "A small proprietor," as Smith explains in a passage that could equally well apply to the manufacturer, "knows every part of his little territory [and] views it all with the affection which property, especially small property, naturally inspires" (I:441). The overall direction of commercial development that Smith articulates moves from the vast, diffusive, obscure, and open-ended to the small, concentrated, visible, and closed: from the inclusive social patterns of ancient expense to the exclusive personal patterns of modern expense; from the unwieldy, inefficient manor to the manageable parcel of land susceptible to proper improvement; from the heterogeneous spaces of international trade to a homogenized home market (I:151, 456); from the circulation of numerous goods to the production of a single commodity; from the workman of undivided labor whose attention "is dissipated among a great variety of things" to the workman of divided labor, whose "whole ... attention comes naturally to be directed towards some one very simple object" (I:13). In this sense the opening description of the pin already expresses the economic, psychological, and epistemological reorientation of communal form that Smith wishes to effect.

v

The space between person and thing opened up by Smith's view of commercial society – a space that, I have been arguing, remains unmapped in a mercantile economy – depends on an act of concentration that evolves around smallness, simplicity, and divisibility. In this sense *The Wealth of Nations* constitutes a significant attempt to rationalize attention to small objects in a culture that continued to view commodities within the mercantile context of unpredictable transformation, volatile value, and irrational absorption. For Smith the locus of transformation and value is not the collective circulation, but the circumstantial constitution of small objects, and such constitution is localized and thus comprehensible through the moderate attitude of sympathetic observation.

Smith was not alone in refiguring the mercantile community of persons and things in this way. While his book had a long gestation, its publication in the 1770s, during one of the highpoints of the cult of sensibility, has more general cultural significance. Seminal texts in the sensibility tradition such as *A Sentimental Journey* (1768) and *The Man of Feeling* (1771) articulate a move from circulation to sympathetic relationality that is closely connected to Smith's project. Together these texts begin to rupture a communal imagination that relies on notions of an embodied, uneven space and on a tangible continuity between human and material spheres. They show that, ultimately, circulation itself is not able to effect the transition to more modern communal forms. To reshape the relationship between persons and things in eighteenth-century Britain requires the interruption of a circulatory logic that makes movement across space central to transformation.

Laurence Sterne's *A Sentimental Journey* undermines the forces of circulation by unsettling the relation between traveler and environment. As Yorick's extensive catalogue of different types of traveling makes clear, the act of traveling itself comes under some scrutiny and Yorick's sentimental traveling is a separate and newly established mode of conveyance. "Sentimental commerce," as Yorick also calls it, is a mode of traveling guided by the need to find objects that "call forth my affection" and to overcome the "many impediments in communicating our sensations out of our own sphere." The desire to find things "to connect myself to" determines Yorick's scattered and spontaneous movements and renders the travel itinerary secondary to the narrator's need for connection.[102] This search for moments of sympathetic relationality breaks down conventions of beginning, end, arrival, and departure. More importantly, it defies elements of travel as basic as movement and destination. *A Sentimental Journey* refuses to circulate, and, rather like the "see-saw" of Yorick's one-seated chaise, the "Desobligeant," is not animated by travel, but by the erratic and self-indulgent acts of the sympathetic imagination. The "Novelty of my Vehicle," as Yorick refers to the mode of sympathetic transport exemplified by the Desobligeant, does not consist in its ability to provide movement through physical space.[103] Yorick's encounter with the Desobligeant suggests rather that such novelty springs from the way in which sensibility appropriates the trappings of travel for its own separate ends, ends that have little to do with the description of different countries, constitutions, and manners, and everything to do with the opportunistic cultivation of moments of sympathetic connection. To be "moved" – to be transformed – is here no longer the effect of a circulation across heterogeneous spaces, but of capture by sympathetic contact. The standstill that Yorick comes to when he feels the pulse of the "grisset," holds the hand of the unknown lady, or imagines the situation of a prisoner is always elevated over the movements of travel.[104]

Closely related issues are raised in *The Man of Feeling* when the narrator suggests that "in the velocity of the modern tour, and amidst the materials through which it is commonly made, the friction is so violent, that not only the rust, but the metal too is lost in the progress." Instead of gaining polish through "frequent collision," the modern traveler is here envisioned as losing substance by circulation in a wider sphere. Henry Mackenzie's protagonist Harley is unlikely to gain at all from traveling, for he has a "consciousness, which the most delicate feelings produce."[105] The opening of Mackenzie's novel thus points to the same tension between sensibility and circulation that Sterne identified, and this tension is articulated further in the pages that follow. For while the man of feeling is sent on a journey to London and is there exposed to various characters and situations, scenes of sympathetic relationality puncture the episodic narrative to such an extent that Mackenzie's text, like Sterne's, begins to resemble a series of tableaux. Both authors depart in this way from a narrative and economic mode that presents circulation across uneven spaces as central to the creation of value.

"Sentimental commerce" is unfamiliar with the mercantile fear of goods and clogged circulation; it is devoted to finding and sustaining moments of intensified contact that enclose the singular object and arrest movement. Mackenzie gestures towards this distinction when he states that he wants to avoid the "entanglement" and "intricacies" of a novel, wishing instead to present "recitals of little adventures, in which the dispositions of a man, sensible to judge, and still more warm to feel, had room to unfold themselves."[106] Achieving this shift from dispersal to concentration, from the wide landscape in which it is possible to lose oneself to the small room in which a sensible and feeling disposition can burgeon, frequently means arresting circulatory movement. All outward motion is suspended in Mackenzie's carefully circumstantial scenes, whose pathetic force derives from a visual concentration that makes verbal engagement difficult and often reduces the observer to tears. The man of feeling is, significantly, a man of seeing – a man of concentrated viewing:

In some of these paroxisms of fancy, Miss Walton did not fail to be introduced; and the picture which had been drawn amidst the surrounding objects of unnoticed levity, was now singled out to be viewed through the medium of romantic imagination: it was improved, of course, and esteem was a word inexpressive of the feelings which it excited.[107]

What is happening here in miniature is precisely the process of affective concentration that Mackenzie wishes to achieve in his text as a whole. The mental image of Miss Walton, focused and isolated through a particular medium, gains ascendancy here over a distracting environment in the same way in which the sentimental tableaux displace and arrest the "intricacies" of Harley's episodic adventures. Created by Harley's imagination, the idealized "picture" acquires an agency of its own and excites feelings that defy verbal representation.

This movement toward pictorial isolation becomes even more explicit in Chapter Forty, "The Pupil. A Fragment." In this brief episode the European travels of a noble youth are brought to a halt by the realization that one of his fashionable companions has been involved in ruining a family. The young traveler sees this family for the first time when a little boy implores him and his benevolent tutor to visit some poor people in a nearby prison. He is led "through a dark passage" and a "little door" and is then presented with the following scene:

On something like a bed lay a man, with a face seemingly emaciated with sickness, and a look of patient dejection; a bundle of dirty shreds served him for a pillow; but he had a better support – the arm of a female who kneeled beside him, beautiful as an angel, but with a fading languor in her countenance, the still life of melancholy, that seemed to borrow its shade from the object on which she gazed. There was a tear in her eye! the sick man kissed it off in its bud, smiling through the dimness of his own![108]

We are here almost literally given a room for unfolding our feeling disposition. The description is carefully separated from the preceding textual material by the "dark passage" and the "little door" that frames the image, just as when, in the closely related scene in *A Sentimental Journey*, Yorick imagines the situation of a prisoner by "look[ing] through the twilight of his grated door to take his picture."[109] We are forced to stand still and contemplate a framed scene whose self-conscious pictorialism, circumstantial detail, and undisturbed intimacy provoke an emotional response that is predicated on our distance from it. We are not allowed into this tableau – it presents itself as an object, a "still life" whose seclusion and visual arrest render us passive. It "fixes" our eyes in the same way in which Harley's eyes are so frequently "fixed" by the scenes that silence him and draw out tears.[110] Gazing and crying, indeed, are not coincidentally central motifs of this silent image. Their presence indicates how this passage wants to be read: we have room to unfold our emotions, but we are meant to sit still, without the ability to participate in the scene in more tangible ways.

In Mackenzie's text our arrest in the room of feeling – our sentimental commerce – is achieved by a considerable amplification of pictorial elements. Even while a simple narrative dimension persists in this moving picture, its careful framing and separation from its textual environment suggest a growing willingness to differentiate between description and narrative. Such differentiation, in fact, is heightened to such an extent that *The Man of Feeling* inverts what has traditionally been seen as the dominance of narrative over description. Its multiplication of pictorial scenes places narrative at the "service" of description, merely providing opportunities for the display of the tableaux, which are at the heart of the text. Their vitality hinges on their status as separable objects. Just as the scene itself is carefully framed and thus objectified, the episode as a whole is a "fragment" whose obvious incompleteness draws attention to its objectlike separability and transportability – as does, indeed, the entire book. A found manuscript, it is described as "torn," a "bundle of little episodes, put together without art," a "medley" containing some "very trifling passages" of curious emotional power. Such self-consciousness about the text's status as a brittle and divisible object transforms the act of reading into an act of concentrating on the "trifling" and the "little."[111] It is not "odd," as the fictitious editor of the Harley manuscript notes, that he "should have wept" over such trifling things, for such an emotional response is precisely an effect of the concentration on the small visual objects that make up Mackenzie's and (as Barbara Benedict has shown) numerous other sentimental texts.[112]

A few words need to be said at this point about Michael Fried's *Absorption and Theatricality* (1980), which has dealt so influentially with some of the issues that have concerned me in this chapter. Readers familiar with Fried's work will have noticed that I use the term "absorption" in distinction from "visual arrest." Fried's reading of Denis Diderot strives to align these terms, and Fried would undoubtedly argue that Mackenzie's tableau – which so closely fits Diderot's criteria of silence, simplicity, visuality, emotionality, and absence of the beholder – induces a state of absorption.[113] But as my argument in this chapter should have made clear, I see absorption as a participatory mode that breaks down the boundary between observer and object – a process that is prevented by a scene as carefully framed as Mackenzie's. Here the fluid comprehensiveness of absorption is reduced and refined to a clearly focused relationship of distance. Organized around a single sense, sight, the scene produces an emotional response, but at the price of exclusion from broader participation, from actual involvement. While my disagreement with Fried may stem in part from the difference between eighteenth-century Britain and France, it seems to me that the conceptual problems are compounded even within his own text when Fried tries to link his notion of absorption with a painterly tradition that invites the observer to enter the picture, to become part of its scenes.[114] In the descriptive tradition that I have traced here, this convention belongs to what Mackenzie might call the "entanglement and intricacy school" (embodied, for example, in Fielding's description of Paradise Hall), and needs in my view to be clearly distinguished from the increased enclosure and distance developed by the school of sentimental concentration.

Sentimental commerce, to return to my argument, is centrally about increasing the intensity of sympathetic connection by creating pictorial effects of enclosure, distance, and absence. Despite its efforts in this regard, *The Man of Feeling* is in the end ambivalent about its sentimental effects. It draws attention, in fact, to the difficulties of balancing detachment and absorption along the lines suggested by Smith's account of sympathetic relationality. Mackenzie foregrounds simplicity, divisibility, and circumstantiality, but his protagonist reveals the potentially deleterious consequences that sympathetic relationality can produce – even as such relationality is celebrated. I have already touched on the "fixed" gaze that so frequently accompanies Harley's acts of sympathetic viewing. Such emphasis on fixation is literalized at the end of the novel with Harley's death. As Harley's final glance on Miss Walton first "fixes" her and then "closes" into death, the gaze of sympathetic relationality is associated with a deathlike fixation. Harley's dead body, as the final scenes of the novel make clear, becomes itself a sentimental spectacle, a visual object that cannot be approached and that induces speechlessness and tears in the spectators, who are themselves reduced to mute objects.[115] In this way the novel reveals the interdependence of lively feeling and deathlike fixation, communion and absence, intimacy and distance, a paradox that is painfully inscribed into every scene of sympathetic relationality.

A Sentimental Journey seems eager to evade such fixation by cultivating, as Jonathan Lamb has pointed out, a "mobile reciprocation between things, ideas, and words where the importance of an event is measured in terms of the layered ideas it creates and is created by."[116] But Sterne's interest in "the affection that inanimate things will create in us" (to use Mackenzie's words) yields a configuration of persons and things that is ultimately compatible with Mackenzie's.[117] The use Yorick makes of the snuffbox he received from the deceased monk is representative: "I guard this box, as I would the instrumental parts of my religion, to help my mind on to something better: in truth, I seldom go abroad without it; and oft and many a time have I called up by it the courteous spirit of its owner to regulate my own, in the justlings of the world."[118] Sterne's allusions to relics and conjurations satirize Yorick's sentimental attachment to the box, but that attachment is nonetheless celebrated and escapes the contexts of religion and magic that Sterne mobilizes. What matters here is the way in which concentrating on the box provides mental definition when the "justlings of the world" become overwhelming. Such definition is brought about by the box's ability to "call up" that which is absent and dead. The object is thus allowed to do what Fielding had so carefully denied the muff. It has insinuated itself between persons and has acquired an identity that is independent of its pragmatic function within the contexts of normal use. As Yorick's mind gains definition by gazing on the inanimate object, the object begins to call up and reanimate a figure that has died. The sympathetic connection thus interlocks person and thing in a mutually defining communication that releases them both, through the power of sympathetic relationality, from their immediate contexts. Yet the various collisions generated by this encounter – between presence and absence, life and death, human and material – become eventually overwhelming, prompting Yorick to "burst into a flood of tears."[119]

The urgency with which such moments of connectivity are sought out, the elaborateness with which they are staged (sometimes ironically, sometimes not), and the curious unsustainability that characterizes them (typically concluding with a tearful breakdown) signal considerable cultural anxiety. Unlike Benedict, who associates such anxiety with efforts to control and restrain excess of feeling, I view the complicated enactments of sympathetic relationality in texts like *The Man of Feeling* and *A Sentimental Journey* as constructive: these enactments begin to produce a world that exists at a distance, a world that can be reached only through the special exertions of the sympathetic imagination.[120] While cutting through the complexity of a social life that is no longer felt to be within the grasp of circulation, the series of intense and fleeting contacts these texts exhibit cannot be stabilized and take on narrative flesh. It is, paradoxically, precisely their emotional excess that links moments of sympathetic relationality to the rise of modern forms of objectification. For it is such excess and the emotional concentration that goes with it that begins to introduce a crucial tension between ground and figure, between the world as a neutralized backdrop and an individual finding definition in the cultivation of isolated moments of intensified contact. As persons and things give each other definition, visibility, and emotional depth, they remove themselves, at least temporarily, from the established divisions of social space and in their disembedding encounter experience simultaneously heightened intimacy and increased distance.

In the light of the cultural work done by sentimental texts, John Mullan's complaint that "it is difficult . . . to explain how the lament for 'particular attachment' can be an even, refined, or sublimated response to specific social or economic changes" must seem premature.[121] For it is precisely the search for and cultivation of such "particular attachment," of sentimental contact, that not only enacts an opening and widening of the sphere of sociality that strains beyond the personalized hierarchical strictures of the old society, but in fact produces a sense of "general detachment." This dialectic is crucial, for it initiates a fundamentally modern play between absence and presence that breaks up the grounded modes of being referred to earlier. It dissolves the social immediacy that characterizes a text like *Tom Jones*, whose reliance on manorial modes of community translates into a rejection of mediation as a means to construct social and psychological cohesion, and thus keeps persons and things embedded in the established divisions of social space. As long as space is constructed in this way as qualitative and uneven, narrative and description maintain a fundamental alliance, whether that alliance is exploited and manipulated, as in Defoe's and Richardson's transformative circulation, or whether it is protected and fostered, as in Fielding's disembodied circulation. Even in Richardson's texts, whose reliance on the epistolary activates this aspect to some extent, the play between absence and presence is critically reduced because the localized context dominates. The longing for an original or lost state has little force in narratives that acknowledge the transformative powers of a heterogeneous spatiality: that state is either abandoned or reinstated, but not dwelled on as an unreachable aspect of a present situation. Clarissa's brutally irreversible loss of home, station, and family provides perhaps the most poignant commentary on the remarkable power of eighteenth-century social spaces to achieve fundamental transformations.

In Smith, Mackenzie, and Sterne, however, we start to see a move away from the entanglement of persons and things that underwrites the economic and narrative worlds of Defoe, Richardson, and Fielding. The continuity between human and material spheres is here interrupted. Circulation ceases to be a paradigm of production, just as narrative ceases to incorporate a descriptive dimension. Instead, these texts do their cultural work by constructing self-enclosed rooms, separate spatial units whose frame, simplicity, and circumstantiality enable a silent visual concentration. Such concentration sets in motion a disembedding play between absence and presence whose forceful emotional effect is predicated on the "unreachability" of the evoked scenes. That these moments of sentimental contact are frequently unsustainable and that such unsustainability is nervously associated, in both Sterne and Mackenzie, with a concern over emasculation, points, among other things, to the strains that accompany such a basic refiguration of communal patterns. Yorick's and Harley's breakdowns indicate that the escape from circulation is precarious and that the play between absence and presence is not easily sustained against the pressures of social groundedness and its masculinist pedigree.

When I turn next to Ann Radcliffe and the Gothic novel, it is with the conviction that we can find in these texts a further elaboration of the problems of political economy that have been raised here. In fact, Ann Radcliffe's texts are crucial because they engage far more directly than Sterne's or Mackenzie's with the issue of the relationship between sensibility and landed property. While they reveal the tremendous staying power of the manor as a communal form, they also make the manor visible with revolutionary clarity.

CHAPTER FIVE

Ann Radcliffe and the political economy of Gothic space

Students of the eighteenth-century novel have been strongly impressed with the architectural qualities of *Tom Jones*. Ever since, in 1953, Dorothy van Ghent compared the structure of Henry Fielding's novel to a Palladian mansion, many have been intrigued by a metaphor that seems so appropriate to the self-conscious constructedness of Fielding's fictional world. But critics such as van Ghent, Frederick Hilles, Martin Battestin, and J. Paul Hunter may have been too eager to include *Tom Jones* in an Augustan canon.[1] Their Palladian analogy has at least obscured the fact that Fielding's archetypal English manor is not crowned by a neoroman villa, but by a Gothic mansion, an architectural style extremely compatible, as Fielding's friend Hogarth suggested, with the aesthetic of the undulating line that shapes so much of what Fielding does in *Tom Jones*.[2] If one wants to venture any architectural comparison, the irregular extensions of the Gothic seem much more congenial to Fielding's swerving figurative mode and his mocking of neoclassic regularity in literary structures. Fielding's preference for the Gothic, in fact, is symptomatic in a wider literary-historical sense if such a preference is recognized as a subtext to Ann Radcliffe's Gothic romance and its refiguration of Britain's possessive culture.

Fielding's Paradise Hall stands at the beginning of a period of intensified ideological uses of Gothic architecture. I wish to explore such uses in legal and political discourse in order to shed some light on what interpretations of Radcliffe's novels have left by and large in the dark: the historical significance of the Gothic castle. In Gothic novels, as Norman Holland observes, the castle has an "immense structure of possibility." Its figurative potential has generated a variety of psychological readings whose range Holland indicates when he states that the castle can represent "unchanging hardness, undifferentiated parents, parents differentiated into hard father and yielding mother, or sexual father and idealized mother."[3] Depending on one's critical outlook, this list may seem amusing or not, but whatever our response, we should not dismiss psychological readings of Gothic space too quickly. "Much of the best criticism of Radcliffian Gothic," as Claudia L. Johnson has recently reminded us, "has been psychoanalytic at least in part because it has been so easy to believe that decaying castles could not possibly represent actual, material features of the European countryside inscribing the still surviving feudal past."[4]

It is only during the past fifteen years or so that historicist approaches have been able to assert themselves against the dominance of psychoanalytic readings, but Radcliffe's texts have not always benefited from such approaches. Critics such as Barbara Benedict, David Durant, and Ronald Paulson, for example, have seen the castle as a negative representation of revolutionary turmoil and Radcliffe as a conservative critic of the unrestrained emotional excesses allegedly licensed by the French Revolution.[5] More recent work by Johnson and Robert Miles has begun to correct this conservative view of Radcliffe, but the readings of the novels remain hesitant, prepared only to recognize "a vaguely progressive political critique."[6] The most that historically-minded critics have been willing to grant Radcliffe is a finally indecisive fluctuation between poles of neoclassic and romantic aesthetics, aristocratic and bourgeois values, sublime and picturesque views – a fluctuation that raises progressive and even radical possibilities, but is not willing to pronounce them in a more straightforward way.[7] I believe a stronger case can be made for Radcliffe's critical intervention into the culture of the 1790s; it is a case built on a clearer sense of the extent to which Radcliffe's novels recognize the continuing social, political, and imaginative centrality of landed property in late eighteenth-century Britain, and on a more detailed positioning of her work vis-à-vis the French Revolution and its British reception.

Critics who associate Radcliffe's Gothic with a conservative response to revolutionary turmoil neglect an important chronological factor. During the time when Radcliffe was writing her first three novels (1789–1791), public debate over the French Revolution was far from endorsing Edmund Burke's passionate critique of the new French government. On the contrary, newspapers of the day seriously wondered whether the *Reflections on the Revolution in France* (1790) were not the product of a distempered brain. The progressive *Gazetteer and New Daily Advertiser*, for instance, suggested in January 1791 – three weeks before Radcliffe's husband William became its editor – that Burke's "manifest state of irritation" would quickly deteriorate into "downright madness" if one contradicted his arguments.[8] Burke needed treatment, not engagement. A confident rejection of his arguments remained the dominant response for some time. As late as May 1792, Charles James Fox could denounce the *Reflections* in a parliamentary speech as a "libel on every free constitution of the world."[9] Even when, in February 1793, Britain declared war against France, "fairly moderate members of the opposition, in and out of Parliament, believed [the war] to be the ploy of an aggressive, aristocratic English government against the peace-loving, humane, and united people of France."[10] While Burke's conservative reaction seemed on the fringes of reasonable argument, a positive response to the Revolution was still within the mainstream of English political opinion when Radcliffe was writing her first three novels. Given this chronology, it is debatable whether Radcliffe's readers perceived the Gothic castle as symbolizing the subversive turmoil of revolutionary France.[11]

Radcliffe's response to the events in France, elusive as it may seem initially, becomes more discernible when one links several dispersed clues, the first of which is found in her third novel, *The Romance of the Forest* (1791). At a point in the novel when Radcliffe presents her version of an ideal social order, the national characters of the French and English are compared. When a ringing denouncement of the French people's "wretched policy, their sparkling, but sophistical discourse, [and] frivolous occupations" is offered, Radcliffe goes out of her way to assure the reader that the *ancien régime*, and not contemporary France, is meant. Employing the unusual device of a footnote urgently introduced in the middle of a sentence, Radcliffe intervenes: "It must be remembered that this was said in the seventeenth century."[12] While this carefully qualified critique of France falls short of expressing actual sympathy for the Revolution, the urgency of the intervention suggests a desire to shield contemporary France from undeserved criticism.[13]

More substantive clues emerge from Radcliffe's *A Journey Made in the Summer of 1794 through Holland and the Western Frontier of Germany* (1795). While in Germany, Radcliffe witnessed France's military conflicts with its neighbors and received first-hand accounts of the French terror. Personal contacts with French noble emigrés inform her of the "private malice of Robespierre's agent," and she includes in her published travel account a description of the discriminations endured by the French nobility. One of the reports she hears on the progress of revolutionary sentiment in France suggests that "such a change of manners and the course of education had taken place, that the rising generation were all *enragées* in favour of the Revolution."[14] Under the influence of these impressions, Radcliffe appears to begin to concede that the "wretched policy" of the *ancien régime* did have some merits. Referring to the French emigré officers she has met, she notes: "Had the old system in France, oppressive as it was, and injurious as Englishmen were once justly taught to believe it, been universally administered by men of their mildness, integrity and benevolence, it could not have been entirely overthrown by all the theories, or all the eloquence in the world."[15] There is a hint of defensiveness in this remark as it registers the English transition from longstanding rejection of the *ancien régime* to the recent discovery of its comparative virtues.

Radcliffe's animated justification of the English condemnation of France's "old system," her insistence on the latter's "oppressive" and "injurious" character, reveal discomfort with the recent change of English opinion, even as Radcliffe tries to adopt a more tempered outlook. That such an outlook does not come naturally is made clear when, elsewhere in her travel account, she alludes to the events in France and charges, now with an eye to England, that "the praises of liberty [are currently] endeavoured to be suppressed by the artifice of imputing to it the crimes of anarchy" – a brave statement to make, as Miles notes, in the increasingly oppressive atmosphere of the mid-1790s.[16] Despite the fact that, by the time Radcliffe undertakes her journey, Burke's dire prediction of revolutionary terror had largely come true, she resists vindicating the *ancien régime*. Seen in the context of her persistent unease over prerevolutionary France and her embrace of "liberty," the urgent footnote of 1791 testifies not to a sudden concern for historical accuracy or political circumspection, but rather to a strongly developed belief in the injustices of France's old political system. Behind it, one may surmise, lay a desire to protect from abuse a political revolution that in Radcliffe's eyes promised a change for the better. Even in 1794 she looked back longingly, on her return to England, to "the now distant shore of France, with Calais glimmering faintly, and hinting of different modes of life and a new world."[17]

These observations should put to rest the claim that "Radcliffe's gothic underworld speaks for her pessimistic estimation of the modern world."[18] In fact, Radcliffe had considerable hopes concerning the "modern world," and her Gothic castles, their location in Europe notwithstanding, are not monitory figures of a debased revolutionary modernity – quite the contrary. The rich semantic environment inhabited by the Gothic castle in eighteenth-century England indicates that it had more profound associations with the domestic scene than with revolutionary France, and more with the past's grip on the present, than the attack of the present on the past.[19] The *Monthly Review* may have commented, in reviewing *The Romance of the Forest* in 1792, that "the days of chivalry and romance [are] (ALAS! as Mr. Burke says,) for ever past," but it also has to concede that "castles and forests remain," and that literature may legitimately use such settings to create "surprise."[20] For Radcliffe, of course, more was ultimately at stake than creating surprise, and the political responsiveness of her novels is evident in the use she makes of strategically displaced castles and forests. As Jane Austen's early parody of the Gothic novel indicates, Radcliffe's settings were European, but her readers saw English landscapes.

Austen's *Northanger Abbey* (1818) rests on a simple premise: the assumption that some readers of Gothic novels set in Europe applied what they read all too literally to eighteenth-century England. As far as Austen is concerned, the main problem with Catherine Morland's voracious appetite for Gothic novels is that she fails to see that they do not portray indigenous manners. Catherine's mistake, however, is understandable. The foreign settings of Radcliffe's novels were not entirely persuasive, and some readers complained of anachronisms and an inaccurate portrayal of foreign manners.[21] It is in this respect that *Northanger Abbey*'s patient insistence that one should read Radcliffe's novels without thinking of eighteenth-century England becomes significant. For such insistence acknowledges the genuine power that Radcliffe's temporally and spatially imprecise settings had in conjuring blurry imaginative scenes that appeared eminently translatable into other contexts. Catherine's obstinate identification of Northanger Abbey as a Radcliffian setting is not idiosyncratic or simply ridiculous; it is a legitimate response to Radcliffe's technique. Austen's parody presents this response as representative of wider cultural habits, which, thanks to Radcliffe's "hazy" settings, applied to contemporary England what appeared in the guise of a European past.

Such cultural habits, I want to suggest, were facilitated by a marked awareness of the Gothic as a distinct figure of British political economy, an awareness that peaks, after its emergence in the first half of the eighteenth century, during the Revolution Controversy of the 1790s. In the following pages I argue that conservative uses of the Gothic castle opened up the possibility of picturing the epistemological, sociological, and political contradictions of Britain's possessive culture, and that this possibility was realized in Radcliffe's spectacular descriptions, whose cultural impact is evident in the force with which they imprinted themselves on the minds of contemporary readers.[22] The spatial politics of Radcliffe's descriptive acts have not been adequately analyzed. This is a significant problem not only because Radcliffe's importance in the history of the novel, as Walter Scott realized, is tied to her descriptive practice, but because this practice acknowledges the cultural need for a clearer visualization of Britain's continued reliance on landed property as its most privileged figure of political and social community.[23] Description is so crucial in Radcliffe's texts because it is a central arena for her engagement with political economy, flowing from her profound awareness that the spatial dominates Britain's possessive culture. For a politically oriented criticism, her highly deliberate descriptive acts are nothing less than attempts to exorcise what Mary Wollstonecraft called the "demon of property" in 1790, and we shall see that this is true in a far more specific sense than one might expect.[24]

I

Set in sixteenth-century Sicily, the narrative of *A Sicilian Romance* (1790), Radcliffe's second novel, evolves around a secret contained in an old and neglected part of the "large and irregular fabrick" of Mazzini castle.[25] The mysterious sounds and lights that issue from this part of the Marquis Mazzini's property pique our curiosity from the very outset, yet we do not learn the cause of these disturbances until the end of the text, when the young Julia Mazzini, having escaped the castle in Chapter Four, returns to it in Chapter Fourteen. Julia is forced to flee because her tyrannical father insists on marrying her to an undesirable suitor. She finds refuge first in an ancient abbey, but as the Marquis soon catches up with her, she has to continue her flight. Having temporarily fallen into the hands of robbers (who confine her in another decayed abbey), Julia extracts herself – only to be again pursued. At this point of her lengthy and torturous escape from Mazzini Castle – in one of the last chapters of the novel – she decides to hide in a cavern. Her decision brings us to a narrative turning point that repays close analysis.

Julia follows the cavern to "its inmost recesses." Apprehending further pursuit, she discerns "a low and deep recess in the rock," which she enters "on her knees, for the overhanging craggs would not suffer her to pass otherwise." This recess is "terminated by a door. The door yielded to her touch, and she suddenly found herself in a highly vaulted cavern, which received a feeble light from the moon-beams that streamed through an opening in the rock above." Hearing again the voices of her pursuers,

Julia "fled from the door across the cavern before her, and having ran a considerable way, without coming to a termination, stopped to breathe. She imperfectly surveyed the vastness of the cavern in wild amazement." At this point Julia realizes that she is lost in the windings of the cavern; she cannot trace her way back and decides to wait for morning. The spare light that soon enters through an opening in the rocks enables her to find another door, which opens upon "a dark passage." Groping along its "winding walls," she finds yet another door which admits her into "a small room, which received its feeble light from a window above." To her "inexpressible surprise" Julia realizes that "she was now in a subterranean abode belonging to the southern buildings of the castle of Mazzini" and finds, to her utter consternation, her mother, believed dead for fifteen years (172–175).

Julia's remarkable discovery may seem like a tediously prepared and highly improbable resolution of the mystery that haunts Mazzini Castle from the very first pages of the novel. The puzzling lights and sounds and the dilapidated state of the castle's southern wing are now attributed to the Marchioness's fifteen-year confinement, perpetrated by a husband who wished to marry another woman. Yet, fantastic as this denouement may seem, it is also curiously appropriate and contains a number of revealing ironies. There is, first of all, the fact that Julia fails to find her mother during the fifteen years that she shared the same residence, but eventually stumbles accidentally upon her room, having approached from an entrance that seemed far removed from the castle. Secondly, she can only "find" her mother after she is literally "lost" in the windings of the cavern. Finally, her "return" to the castle is the outcome of an attempt to "escape" (before she enters the cavern, Julia is on her way to a harbor to leave Sicily for good). These ironies, of course, can be readily accounted for by invoking providential design, and this is in fact what Julia does when she exclaims to her mother that "providence . . . has conducted me through a labyrinth of misfortunes to this spot for the purpose of delivering you!" (181). Yet Radcliffe simultaneously works on a less allegorical and more materialist level. On this level the curious interdependence of losing/finding and escaping/returning points to the political economy of Radcliffe's Gothic space.

Let us recall that Julia's entrance into the cavern is a double removal. She first follows the cavern "to its inmost recesses" and then enters, on her knees, through a small opening, into another "deep recess in the rock." It would seem that this ordeal has lodged Julia in a deeply secluded natural space. Yet the double removal into nature so patiently described results in the stunning discovery of a door in the middle of the rock. Enfolded in nature's interior, Julia finds a sign of property, and what had seemed a removal into a deep natural space now becomes a penetration of an even deeper natural-cultural space. This uncanny mixture of the natural and the cultural recurs in the next stage of Julia's journey, when she finds herself in that hybrid space, the "vaulted cavern." And while the cavern assumes architectural traits, the castle is characterized by natural ones. It is described, early in the novel, as containing a "wild hall" and exhibiting an "air of wild desolation," a "proud sublimity, united with singular wildness" (40, 45, 46). Not incidentally, when Julia's brother Ferdinand explores the interior of the castle, he is, like his sister in the cavern, "quickly lost in the windings of the place" (40). It seems but a small step, indeed, from the "vaulted cavern" to the "cavernous hall," and in this way Radcliffe deliberately blurs distinctions between nature and culture, inside and outside, beginning and end.

Such blurring establishes Mazzini Castle as a space of uncontrollable, complex extension, and the interdependence of escape/return and losing/finding is the result of a space whose expansiveness disables penetration by deliberate action. Indirection is the key to the secret of Mazzini Castle and the reason why only the accidental transition from "removal" to "penetration" can uncover what lay concealed for fifteen years. This means, however, that the course of action is dictated by the setting, that the resolution of the plot depends on the penetration of this Gothic space. Julia's progress, the progress of the plot, and the progress of reading depend on submitting to the unpredictable turnings and twistings of Mazzini's Gothic space. In order to find resolution, a directionless narrative has to find its unconscious way through a dense, obscure descriptive scene. Such submission of action to setting, narrative to description, time to space, characterizes a ritual of passage that reveals the crimes of the Marquis Mazzini and ultimately, after the Marquis's death ends his cruel reign, liberates us from spatial domination. No longer under the spell of the interdependence of escape and return, Julia and her family can leave Mazzini Castle and Sicily at the end of the novel.

The blurring of contrasting categories seen by many critics as a sign of Radcliffian wavering is in this case the specific manifestation of a political economy based on landed property.[26] For what Radcliffe's novel suggests is that the dominance of Gothic space and its confusing – in fact, terrifying – blurring of nature and culture, beginning and end, inside and outside, is a concrete manifestation of the Marquis Mazzini's land-based powers. In fact, Radcliffe is careful to highlight that these powers derive directly from a particular relationship to the land when she has Julia's mother explain that "the marquis . . . has not only power to imprison, but also the right of life and death in his own domains" (180).[27] This means that the marquis's jurisdictional rights are strictly related to his landed possessions and that he is able to determine justice by right of property. His rule exemplifies the local integration of land and law that finds its most prominent English expression in the indispensable link between manor and court baron.[28] The marquis's formidable manorial rights are given concrete form in the overpowering complexity and subterranean connectivity of Radcliffe's Gothic space. Sicily's landscape is literally permeated by feudal power, the land drawing you in and back even as you want to escape, the grasp of landed rule foreshortening the distance between center and periphery. In this manner Radcliffe endows landed property with an intentionality all its own. Matter is animated in the Gothic spaces of Radcliffe's novels, and this continuity between human and material spheres figures a patriarchy whose powers to rule derive directly from the land. When Julia discovers her mother at the center of a labyrinthine landed order, she not only finds the marginalized other of a male property regime, but recognizes that the exclusive association of possessive rights and judicial authority is a particularly oppressive social and cultural paradigm – the ultimate source of her and her mother's ordeal. The interrelation of nature and culture, property and land, judicial and territorial authority that *Tom Jones* was still able to present as the cheerful epitome of English liberty is here transformed into a source of near endless confusion and terror.

It may still seem that the marquis's territorial powers exemplify a historically remote European feudalism, but Radcliffe's text actually invites us to connect the political economy of Gothic space to the concerns of the late eighteenth century. At one point of her interminable flight, Julia seeks refuge in "the obscure recesses" of an ancient abbey. Radcliffe focuses initially on Julia, but she quickly adopts a more general tone and gives us a view of the abbey that does not rely on Julia's perception:

The view of this [large magnificent mass of Gothic architecture] revived in the mind of the beholder the memory of past ages. The manners and characters which distinguished them arose to his fancy, and through the long lapse of years he discriminated those customs and manners which formed so striking a contrast to the modes of his own times. The rude manners, the boisterous passions, the daring ambition, and the gross indulgences which formerly characterized the priest, the nobleman, and the sovereign, had now begun to yield to learning – the charms of refined conversation – political intrigue and private artifices. Thus do the scenes of life vary with the predominant passions of mankind, and with the progress of civilization. The dark clouds of prejudice break away before the sun of science, and gradually dissolving, leave the brightening hemisphere to the influence of his beams. But through the present scene appeared only a few scattered rays, which served to shew more forcibly the vast and heavy masses that concealed the form of truth. Here prejudice, not reason, suspended the influence of the passions; and scholastic learning, mysterious philosophy, and crafty sanctity supplied the place of wisdom, simplicity, and pure devotion. (116–117)

The impersonal "beholder" who is here imagined distances this passage from the immediate concerns of the narrative and makes room for more general reflections. For a while we seem to be drifting away from the sixteenth century as Radcliffe's remarks on how such buildings call up strange manners reflect a common cultural habit of eighteenth-century England. We seem to be moving back into greater historical specificity when "rude manners and boisterous passions" enter the picture, and Radcliffe describes the "progress of civilization" in terms that call up Scottish Enlightenment accounts. The gradual refinement she sketches tracks a movement from the unrestrained, public satisfaction of the most immediate, basic desires to a world in which far more subtle, less visible, private, and interiorized means lead to refined ends. General as it is, this account seems applicable to sixteenth-century Europe without provoking much contradiction, but a glance at William Radcliffe's writings shows that the progress of civilization outlined here could also apply to more modern times. William's study of law probably fueled his interest in questions of political economy, but his wife was an equally interested inquirer into such issues, as her preface to the *Journey* indicates.[29] In one of his editorial interventions into Baron Holberg's *An Introduction to Universal History* (1787), William appears to anticipate Ann's sentiments about the progress of civilization. "As force is less," he states on the same process of refinement, "strategem is greater; there is now, in the common business of life, more circumvention and subtility of contrivance, and the same end is now obtained with greater certainty by the invisible machinations of artifice."[30] The same transition from visible and public force to invisible private artifice is here shown to be true of modern societies, and Ann's account no longer appears as historically specific as it first seemed. In fact, I believe Ann is not that interested here in addressing the sixteenth century. Instead, she uses a vague historicist veil (lifted again at the end of my quotation when she refers to "scholastic learning") to articulate sentiments that have to do with her own historical moment.

This is probably most strikingly the case with the passage that describes the "sun of science" breaking through the "dark clouds of prejudice." Prejudice was a politically charged term at this time and it would gain even greater political explosiveness with the publication, two months after *A Sicilian Romance*, of Burke's *Reflections*.[31] The progressive newspaper that William began to edit and write for in January 1791, for instance, drew repeated attention to the political connotations of the term "prejudice" within the context of the French Revolution, both before and after the publication of Burke's famous attack.[32] Perhaps even more significant is that at this point in her text Radcliffe returns to the contemplation of the Gothic structure that generated her initial observations on the course of civilization. In a crucial sentence she notes, closing in on the recent revolutionary events in France, that "through the present scene appeared only a few scattered rays, which served to show more forcibly the vast and heavy masses that concealed the form of truth." Radcliffe is developing a trope here that would become well-known in the political debates of the 1790s. She is close, for example, to James Mackintosh, who would describe the situation in 1791 by stating that "the political light which is to break in on England should be 'through well-contrived and well-disposed windows, not through flaws and breaches, through the yawning chasms of our ruin'."[33] The same trope appears in a poem composed in the same year, Helen Maria Williams's "To Dr Moore," which dramatically contrasted the obscurity of the Gothic castle with the "scanning" movements of enlightened reason. Radcliffe is identifying, then, the process of visualization that long-established, traditionalist institutions were seen to undergo in the confrontation with a Revolution that was frequently associated with the forces of light and science. I would even go so far as to say that Radcliffe is here telling us something about her own text, which itself dramatizes, as we have seen, the discovery of truth underneath "vast and heavy masses," and whose extensive descriptive rendering of Gothic space could be seen to "scan" the interior of an overpowering ideological structure.

I will say more later about this aspect of Radcliffe's novels and about Mackintosh and Williams, but at this point I wish to extend my argument that *A Sicilian Romance* employs the Sicilian backdrop to rediscover in a superficially alien setting issues and concerns very much connected with eighteenth-century England. For this is also true of the marquis's territorial jurisdictions, a theme that seems removed from contemporary indigenous problems. I have already pointed out that territorial jurisdictions were a subject of heated parliamentary debate in 1747 and that such

manorial rights were far from anachronistic.[34] Even though their practical communal relevance declines significantly, by the early 1790s their
ideological importance rises sharply. Radcliffe recognizes their continued political relevance when she uses the term "territorial jurisdictions"
to describe the constitutional arrangements of Cologne in 1794.[35] The
question of "manorial rights," moreover, figures in the political debate
of the 1790s over the Revolution. The *Critical Review*, for example, in dis-
cussing an early history of the French Revolution in 1792, agrees with its
author when he questions "whether it would be just or even popular in
England to abolish all prerogatives of lords of the manor, the remains of
a Gothic legislation." "We have little doubt in saying," the reviewer adds,
that such remains constitute "a greater grievance than any which have
been so ostentatiously produced."[36] Similarly, Mackintosh's extremely
popular reply to Burke's *Reflections*, his *Vindiciae Gallicae* (1791), not only
observed that "tithes, feudal and seignorial rights" were defended "as
the most inviolable property" in 1790s France, but pointed up more generally the persistence, from the Middle Ages, of "Gothic manners" that,
while they have lost "direct influence," exert their "indirect influence"
with "increasing vigor."[37] These are more than isolated examples. They
illustrate the larger case I am making about the remarkable staying
power of the manor as a paradigm of social and political community in
eighteenth-century England. In my view, it is precisely the perceived persistence of "manorial rights" and "Gothic manners" that gives Radcliffe's
novels their cultural and political vitality and that motivates what, from
our perspective, can seem an incongruous historicism.

Mackintosh's progress of civilization – conceived, like the Radcliffes',
as a movement "from ferocity and turbulence" to "tranquillity and refinement" – acknowledges the peculiarly transitional nature of English
political history when it argues, against Burke, that "the age of chivalry
is not past."[38] Ann Radcliffe's seemingly unspecific progress testifies, I
suggest, to a similar recognition. She, too, realizes the historical persistence of ancient ways, and that is why her account of historical change
can modulate across the sixteenth and eighteenth centuries. The suggestion of such fluidity between past and present, in other words, does
not in fact indicate lack of a "proper" historicism, but expresses rather a
distinct historical vision in which a process of transformation cannot be
assigned to a distinct period because it is still incomplete and ongoing.

A related point might be made on the level of geography. Just as
Radcliffe brackets, at least at this point of her career, problems of
anachronism, she also does not worry about anatopism. She is as willing

to see "Swiss scenery" in the English countryside as she is to show us an "English pleasure ground" modeled on eighteenth-century tastes in seventeenth-century France. Her outlook in the 1790s resists the concern with the "mutual fit between anachronism and anatopism" that would become, as James Chandler has argued, a "major preoccupation for a wide range of writing in British Romanticism."[39] This would eventually change, as her growing antiquarian interests and her posthumous historical romance *Gaston de Blondeville* (1826) indicate, but for now Radcliffe's work is marked by a deliberate fluidity that defies both the subtle differentiations of region and period and the sweeping homogenizations of "empty" time and space that accompany the increased concern generally with anachronism and anatopism. Radcliffe's times and spaces still resist being defined as discrete points against neutralized backgrounds. This resistance, it seems to me, is motivated by a critical engagement with property and its ability, within the British context, to safeguard a transitional culture by limiting the differentiating play between absence and presence, past and present.

True, Radcliffe conjures a "striking contrast" between Gothic manners and "the modes of [the beholder's] own times," but she also suggests an equally striking familiarity with those manners when she asserts that the "memory of past ages" is "revived in the mind of the beholder." The contemplation of the Gothic structure, in other words, does not activate an imaginative reconstruction of something that has been lost, but rather causes something to become apparent that is already lodged in the mind: this is why Radcliffe talks about a *revival* of the "memory of past ages." The bond between the present and the past is not broken, and when such a break is suggested – in the contrast between "prejudice" and "science," "dark cloud" and "sun" – Radcliffe is quick to emphasize a gradual process that has just begun to send "a few scattered rays" through a vast Gothic structure whose extensions are only now becoming visible. In this way Radcliffe, Mackintosh, and the *Critical Review* acknowledge that one is dealing with "remains" and "relics" of Gothic institutions in 1790s England, but that these remnants continue to exert their influence – a recognition that is facilitated by the "light" that emanates from France and throws English institutions into relief.

Radcliffe's attribution of territorial jurisdiction to the marquis, then, is politically astute. It identifies the integrated communal form of the manor as a distinct historical liability. Legal historians, in fact, have long recognized the profound effect that "the feudal identification of government and property" has had on British legal and political institutions.[40] What

I take to be the crucial aspect of Mazzini's landed power – its merging of jurisdiction and domain, government and property – exerted significant influence long before and throughout the eighteenth century, and I have already noted that even Daniel Defoe treated it as the self-evident basis of governmental authority. Against the legal equation Fielding used to address this issue, Radcliffe offers a robust reminder that the argument for the relation of government and property has its roots in specifically gendered, oppressive manorial power structures. Her Italian romance is no escapist fantasy. In an age that saw itself increasingly in terms of politeness, commerce, and movable forms of property, Radcliffe's novel recalls that landed property and feudal traditions continue to inform political institutions and ideological structures.[41] The question of territorial jurisdictions touches a central chord of a whole way of thinking about the relationship of law, land, and property, and Radcliffe's depiction of Mazzini's territorial powers is a significant indicator for the position her novel occupies in eighteenth-century political culture. That position can be clarified further by turning to the eighteenth-century debate over the English constitution, which was itself informed by the tie between property and government. The relevance of this debate for a discussion of Radcliffe's Gothic novel is borne out not only by Radcliffe's stress on the link between government and property, but also by one of the debate's important ideological figures: the Gothic castle.

II

The early Gothic revival of the 1740s and 1750s loosened the association of Gothic architecture with Catholicism and contributed to the rise of Gothic architecture as a national style in a Protestant country – a style that combined political and religious meanings by suggesting "an analogy between the breakup of the Roman empire by the Goths and the demands of the humanist reformers of northern Europe for religious freedom."[42] The primitive parliamentarianism introduced by the German Goths into England and the Protestant tradition became jointly synonymous with English liberty in such early examples of the Gothic revival as Lord Cobham's Temple of Liberty.[43] Contrasted with the rising respectability of the Gothic style, neoclassicism and its Palladian branch in architecture were increasingly perceived as unrepresentative of a vernacular nationalism. This trend emerged as early as 1739, when the *Gentleman's Magazine* printed an essay in which an anonymous author described the "constitutional Reverence" he felt whenever he entered one of those "old hospitable Gothick Halls," a political feeling disabled by the "imperfect Imitation of an Italian Villa," which, in an age of refined taste, so often replaces the "venerable Paternal Castle."[44] As a subsequent reference to Magna Carta underscores, this essay indicates that for those who wished to eulogize native English liberty, the Gothic's political associations presented a far more attractive paradigm than Palladio's Roman pedigree.

One who eventually also felt this attraction was William Blackstone, the first lawyer to bring English law from the Inns of Court into the university. Blackstone has been appreciated by critics of the Gothic novel for his famous use of the Gothic castle as a figure of the law and the constitution, but even so I believe his significance has been underestimated.[45] Blackstone's imagination is deeply infused with a sense of the spatial, and his ability to see the common law and the English constitution spatially subsequently defines a cultural pattern that animates texts by Burke, Radcliffe, Williams, and others. The earliest evidence we have of Blackstone's interest in the spatial is his unpublished manuscript "Elements of Architecture," which he wrote between 1743 and 1747.[46] At this early point of his life, he embraces a neoclassical paradigm and extols the virtues of proportion, usefulness, harmony, and symmetry. His exposition is frequently interrupted by criticisms of the Gothic, which sometimes come, by his own admission, with considerable "Indignation." "The Gothic Order" to Blackstone is simply "that wch in any manner whatsoever differs from ye regular antique Architecture: so that when a Building can be reduced to no other Order, it is then perfectly Gothic; wherefore we can expect no settled Rules of Proportion, since that would destroy the very Essence of that Order." For him "Confusion & Gothicism" go together, and he warns that "any Tincture of Gothicism [should be] watchfully kept under."[47]

Blackstone wrote his architectural treatise while studying law at Middle Temple (where William Radcliffe began his legal studies in 1783), but his early experience with the common law prompted a painful realization. A letter to his uncle from 1745 documents the initial encounter between the most exalted branch of English legal learning and Blackstone's architectural preferences:

I have sometimes thought that ye Common Law, as it stood in Littleton's Days, resembled a regular Edifice: where ye Apartments were properly disposed, leading one into another without Confusion; where every part was subservient to ye whole, all uniting in one Symmetry: & every Room had its distinct Office allotted to it. But as it is now, swoln, shrunk, curtailed, enlarged, altered & mangled by various & contradictory Statutes &c; it resembles ye same Edifice, with many of its most useful parts pulled down, with preposterous Additions in other Places, of different Materials & coarse Workmanship: according to ye Whim, or Prejudice, or private Convenience of ye Builders. By wch means the Communication of ye Parts is destroyed, & their Harmony quite annihilated; & now it remains a huge irregular Pile, with many noble apartments, tho' awkwardly put together, & some of them of no visible Use at present.[48]

Gone seem to be the fond hopes Blackstone had before he entered Middle Temple of illuminating the common law's "mystic, dark, discordant lore" through classical learning.[49] The confusing extensions of the common law Gothic contradict all the standards Blackstone was simultaneously eulogizing in his "Elements." What he finds instead is a space with which readers of Radcliffe's novels would later be familiar: the confusing connections between apartments, their occasional uselessness, the irregular shape, and the sense of unmanageable spatial extension are also prominent aspects of Radcliffe's depiction of Gothic space. However much his letter may still hold out the hope of restoring the common law to its original symmetry and proportion, Blackstone's desire to use Enlightenment language to describe a body of learning rooted in medieval traditions ultimately had to be adjusted. The time for this adjustment came when his lectures on the common law, begun at Oxford in 1753, reached what would eventually become volume three of the *Commentaries on the Laws of England* (1765–1769). In the following famous passage, Blackstone accepts the law's asymmetries and inconsistencies and justifies them by a metaphor whose cultural valence had gained considerably through the Gothic revival of the 1740s and 1750s. Speaking of the law, Blackstone states:

We inherit an old Gothic castle, erected in the days of chivalry, but fitted up for a modern inhabitant. The moated ramparts, the embattled towers, and the trophied halls, are magnificent and venerable, but useless. The inferior apartments, now converted into rooms of convenience, are chearful and commodious, though their approaches are winding and difficult.[50]

Blackstone here relinquishes his vision of the common law as a "regular Edifice" and presents instead a slightly modernized Gothic castle that retains all its ancient appurtenances. Although the taste for the Gothic among the gentry had become notorious by the early 1750s, Blackstone's embrace of the Gothic metaphor is more than an appeal to a crucial segment of his intended audience, "our gentlemen of independent estates and fortune."[51] Because it unites a certain aesthetic with the national

myth of the English constitution and its liberties, and because it represents landed property – the central concern of the *Commentaries* – the
metaphor of the Gothic castle can be complexly intertwined with the
common law. That complexity is only increased by Blackstone's allusion
to the popular notion of English constitutional rights as an inheritance.
"We inherit an old Gothic castle" – with this phrase Blackstone ties
together the themes of property, common law, and the English constitution in a single image. Such conjunction is particularly prominent after
1689, and we have already observed it in Fielding's use of the real estate term "entailment" to legitimize the Protestant succession, and will
encounter it again in the Revolution Controversy of the 1790s, when
Burke refers to the notion of British liberty as an "entailed inheritance."
F. W. Maitland has best summed up this pattern by remarking that "our
whole constitutional law seems at times to be but an appendix to the law
of real property."[52] Blackstone's decision to endorse the Gothic castle
made it the image of this pattern. Through his detailed sense of the spatial, Blackstone endows the Gothic with a remarkable epistemological
eloquence.

Blackstone's immediate reason for introducing the castle metaphor
is the "intricacy of our legal process," as he phrases it. The "fictions
and circuities" that cause such intricacy result from the common law's
gradual development.[53] Here, indeed, lies the basic appeal of the Gothic
metaphor: the common law, just like the ancient castle, grows by accretion. It is a structure that cannot be reduced to a simple plan because
it evolves out of centuries of legal practice. As the *Commentaries* amply
demonstrates, England's national law is not a finite body of written rules,
but an extensive, uncodified mass of legal learning whose only reliable
record is the history of actual judicial decisions. Since the law embodies
the accumulated legal wisdom of ages, it acquires an independent intentionality, a fetishistic sanctity that makes legal innovation a difficult
enterprise. For instance, even though many of the old feudal actions, as
Blackstone emphasizes, "were ill suited to that more simple and commercial mode of property" that developed after the Middle Ages, the
common law judges could not simply abolish these actions:

[They] wisely avoided soliciting any great legislative revolution in the old established forms, which might have been productive of consequences more numerous and extensive than the most penetrating genius could foresee; but left them
as they were, to languish in obscurity and oblivion, and endeavoured by a series
of minute contrivances to accommodate such personal actions as were then in
use, to all the most useful purposes of remedial justice.[54]

This passage precedes almost immediately Blackstone's introduction of the castle metaphor and pinpoints some of its epistemological implications. Because the fabric of the law results from a complex and lengthy process of growth, cognitive penetration – however much desired – can never be complete. There will always be those seemingly abandoned rooms with no "visible purpose." Since it embodies the accumulated legal wisdom of English society, the law resists complete comprehension by the contemporary observer, and this holds true not only for the past, but also for the future. Even "the most penetrating genius" could not predict what would result from substantive tampering with the "old established forms" of feudalism. Thus, although the "moated ramparts, the embattled towers, and the trophied halls" have lost the function they had in an age of feudal regionalism, the fact that they have no visible use is no reason for pulling them down. Blackstone suggests that it is only our necessarily limited historical comprehension that makes these structures *seem* useless. They are, however, integral to the entire building and must not be violated. The best one can do is to let them "languish in obscurity and oblivion."

In Blackstone's view this logic prompted the judges to employ those "minute contrivances" that allowed them to retain the feudal actions while circumventing some of their consequences. As the "old Gothic castle" is "fitted up for a modern inhabitant," the approach to the modernized part remains "winding and difficult" because it has been constructed around the old part. Nonetheless, the apparently "useless" is secured from the harsh theoretical criticism it had drawn in Blackstone's letter of 1745. The "swoln, shrunk, curtailed, enlarged, altered & mangled" structure of the common law that caused so much displeasure then evinces now the wisdom of the English legislative process and of the English constitution as a whole. While Blackstone emphasizes historical process through the Gothic metaphor and thus leaves behind the normative aesthetic still operative in the letter to his uncle, the same metaphor also indicates the strictures he placed on change. Blackstone's castle is remarkable in this respect because it accomplishes the concrete coalescence of past and present. Through the castle the past tangibly intrudes on the present and structures the latter's practices. For a legal system that locates the law not in a permanent body of written rules, but in the precedent of judicial decisions, the appropriateness of such a traditionalist notion of history should be evident. Gothic architecture illustrates this notion perfectly as it embodies strikingly the past's participation in the present. The sprawling accretions of the Gothic condense the historical process into stone – they bind time in space – and thus enable the temporally remote to become the spatially near. Spatial and temporal extensions align, space constituting the tangible limit of duration. The continuing presence of the past hinges on this articulation of time through space.

The remarkable range of Blackstone's metaphor, however, does not stop here. The extensions of the ancient castle also bring nature and culture together. In his letter to his uncle, Blackstone had blamed the deformed state of the common law on the "Whim, or Prejudice, or private Convenience of ye Builders." Once a lecturer on the common law, Blackstone believed that such seemingly chaotic agency is no longer a flaw. He now points out – still working in the immediate context of his Gothic metaphor – that only "absolute governments" are able to reshape their law in a single, coherent effort. For England's mixed government the process of legal change cannot be instantaneous; it unfolds over long stretches of time, is in principle never complete, and relies on the more or less uncoordinated contributions of numerous judges.[55] If this process causes the "great variety" of English laws as well as a "very immethodical arrangement," that is certainly lamentable – yet such complexity is also evidence of the "excellency of our English laws." Even if they can "breed a confusion of ideas, and a kind of distraction in the memory," English laws compensate for such inconvenience by adapting their "redress exactly to the circumstance of the injury, and do not furnish one and the same action for different wrongs, which are impossible to be brought under one and the same description."[56] Looked at closely, then, "Whim, Prejudice, and private Convenience" do not necessarily produce an arbitrary body of law. Even if certain parts of that body may be confusing, its gradual amendment by multiple agents prevents the injustices that come with legal abstraction and guarantees long-term cohesion.

The explanation for this surprising transition from "Whim" to "excellency" lies in a diffusion of agency that makes it impossible, in the final analysis, to assign a closely defined cause for legal change. Without a clear beginning or end, legal change can never be reduced to a "moment" of change – one might even say that the very concept of a "moment of change" is contradicted by the strictly accretive nature of the common law. The crucial consequence of such diffused agency is that the law takes on a life of its own. Its institution is naturalized; it becomes a self-sufficient reality that can be added to – in a slow, incremental manner – but that cannot be subtracted from on account of its organic connection to the past and the unpredictability of future effects.

Blackstone manages to intertwine his constitutional vision with his architectural metaphor to such an extent that the work of figuration seems like no work at all: his metaphor becomes as much a natural expression of his legal philosophy as his legal philosophy naturally calls up the metaphor. Unsurprisingly, therefore, the figure of the Gothic is also adept in capturing the accretive order of English law. Nature and culture cannot be kept separate in a structure whose growth has no clear beginning and end, follows no recognizable overall design, is subject to extreme gradualism, and seems, finally, strangely authorless, an irreducible assortment of numerous occasional improvements. The castle's status as an inheritance reinforces this idea of accretion because it evokes the crossgenerational transmission of a single, inviolate estate. Under conditions such as these, the English constitution ceases to be a clearly identifiable institution. It represents the sedimentation of a national life whose cultural identity is preserved in the manner of nature. The Gothic castle, indeed, is an image of "second nature," of a cultural pattern that has been continued for so long that it seems like nature.

It is presumably this circumstance that made the castle metaphor interesting for Burke, the "champion of property," as Wollstonecraft called him, and the most prominent defender of the English constitution in the 1790s.[57] An early admirer of the *Commentaries* and an almost daily presence in the *Gazetteer* under William Radcliffe, Burke uses the castle metaphor a number of times in his *Reflections*.[58] He compares the *ancien régime*'s constitution with "a noble and venerable castle," and the same image recurs when Burke makes his case for the Glorious Revolution as an event that conformed to constitutional precedent:[59]

The two principles of conservation and correction operated strongly at the two critical periods of the Restoration and Revolution . . . At both these periods the nation had lost the bond of union in their ancient edifice; they did not however, dissolve the whole fabric. On the contrary, in both cases they regenerated the deficient part of the old constitution through the parts which were not impaired. They kept these old parts exactly as they were, that the part recovered might be suited to them.[60]

Like Blackstone's, Burke's castle metaphor pictures the continuous influence of past over present, conveys an image of time bound in space, and invests the constitution with a self-sufficient groundedness, the pattern of which can be imitated, but never remade. This is an order equipped with an independent intentionality that fetishistically commands its own preservation – the "regeneration" of deficient parts has to be modeled on the intact remains to ensure the integrity of the fabric, regardless of use-fulness, convenience, or clarity. Burke's emphasis on the primacy of an established pattern in the ground (a term used extensively in the *Reflections* in stark opposition to "circulation"[61]) makes this passage a concentrated expression of a "nomos" in Carl Schmitt's definition: "the immediate figure within which the political and social order of a people becomes spatially visible."[62] What Burke's subtle blending of spatial and communal metaphors achieves is a joining of "*Ortung*" (location) and "*Ordnung*" (order) that is formally similar to Crusoe's primary ordering act on his island, but establishes a configuration of community that, unlike Crusoe's, aspires to the integration of time, space, and practice characteristic of common law.[63]

The importance of Burke's castle figure was not lost on his con-temporaries, who quickly recognized its ideological force. In her response – published a mere twenty-eight days later – to Burke's *Reflec-tions*, Wollstonecraft emphasizes the "great deference" Burke pays to Blackstone in presenting English liberty as an inheritance, and she directly refers to Burke's use of the castle metaphor to explain 1689.[64] Echoing an earlier passage in which she described the English constitu-tion as a "heterogeneous mass," she challenges Burke's figure: "Why was it a duty to repair an ancient castle, built in barbarous ages of Gothic materials? Why were the legislators obliged to rake amongst heteroge-neous ruins; to rebuild old walls, whose foundations could scarcely be explored?"[65] Wollstonecraft here forcefully exposes Burke's irrational devotion to the foundational qualities of an established national ground which, in her view, defies the attempt by legislators to preserve the nomos of the English nation. Nothing can be deciphered on the ground and its divisions fail to indicate the pattern of the English constitution.

Wollstonecraft's powerful recognition of the primacy with which law, ground, and community come together in the traditionalist vision is echoed in James Mackintosh's *Vindiciae Gallicae*, which carefully differ-entiates constitutional approaches by contrasting recurrent images of Gothic architecture with images of the "machine" and the "mecha-nism of society."[66] In describing the progress of the French Revolution, Mackintosh observes how the National Assembly had to decide "whether, from [the monarchy's] ruins, fragments were to be collected for the re-construction of the political edifice."[67] The French, of course, decided against such an approach and sent a clear signal that "*the Gothic Govern-ments of Europe have lived their time*" (Mackintosh's italics). This also holds true for England, and Mackintosh stigmatizes "the mysterious nonsense" propagated by the "Cokes, the Blackstones and Burkes" as a "Gothic transfer of genealogy to truth and justice."[68] To Hannah More, on the other hand, the French developments seemed decidedly dangerous. In her *Village Politics* (1793) she defends the sanctity of established usage by protecting a "fine old castle," which "only underwent a little needful repair at the Revolution," but whose current "decays," "dark closet," and "inconvenient room[s]" do not justify any "pull-me-down works."[69] For Helen Maria Williams, though, such protection of the works of the past for their own sake was irrational and amounted to attributing a "chemic power" to time.[70] In Williams's description of England's constitutional Gothic space, time is insufficiently differentiated from practice, and this makes it a qualitative force with mysterious powers of repression. These powers become tangible in the figure of the Gothic castle.

These examples give some idea, I believe, of the pressure that the French Revolution placed on the structure of the English constitution and what had become, thanks to the exertions of Blackstone, Burke, More, and others, its darling figure: the Gothic castle. The "freedom of dispute" in matters of government bemoaned by Bishop Samuel Horsley in 1793 promoted a wide circulation of the basic assumptions underlying the traditionalist argument for the English constitution, and that circulation was crucially facilitated – reaching even the less educated classes for which pamphlets like More's were written – by the castle metaphor.[71] Blackstone is central to these developments not only because his ultimate endorsement of the Gothic exemplifies the movement away from the neoclassical vocabulary that was later to be adopted by the French Revolutionaries and their sympathizers, but also because his articulation of the conservative vision drew so deeply on the figurative potential of the castle. This was clear even to young Jeremy Bentham, one of Blackstone's students, who recognized the importance of the castle metaphor when he organized his early attack on the *Commentaries* around Blackstone's use of figurative language. But despite his gibe that Blackstone "turn[ed] the Law into a Castle" and should have "kept clear of allegories," his teacher established a powerful pattern that radical critics such as Mackintosh linked to a distinct Gothic tradition stretching from Coke to Burke.[72] The irony here is that the depth of Blackstone's articulation of the castle metaphor only exposed the English constitution to wider visibility and thus to the kind of trenchant critique Bentham had already produced by 1776. In the end, Blackstone's attempt to illuminate the Gothic structures of English law through the conventions of Enlightenment discourse prepared the ground for the concerted radical critique of the 1790s. Blackstone and Burke are in this sense central contributors to the increased ideological visibility of English constitution and common law in the 1790s.

When William Godwin turned to the Gothic novel in 1794 to portray the inescapable, repressive extensions of landed power, he acknowledged the same need Radcliffe had acknowledged four years earlier when she finished *A Sicilian Romance*: in order to expose the conservative reliance on landed property as a model of political and social community, this model had to be made available experientially, in the medium of fiction, by capitalizing on the ideological visibility the English constitution acquired in the final quarter of the eighteenth century. Radcliffe's novels have to be placed in the wider context I have sketched here because, by translating landed property into Gothic claustrophobia, they participate in lifting the veil from basic assumptions of the traditionalist argument for the English polity. One of the central mechanisms for Radcliffe's cathartic disenchantment of her strategically displaced Gothic spaces is the device of the "explained supernatural." Unlike the real terror of novels such as Horace Walpole's *The Castle of Otranto* (1764) or Clara Reeve's *The Old English Baron* (1778), the explained supernatural of Radcliffe's text serves a critical function. In Walpole and Reeve the traditional property regime is restored by supernatural intervention, and the arousal of fear is intended to instill respect for the proper succession of property. The abandoned and sealed rooms in the castle of *The Old English Baron* — a conceit this novel made popular — record the crimes of the past in ghostly appearances, but only to reinstate the proper heir, purify the reign of landed power, and assert the sanctity of an established division and distribution of property. Reeve's novel thus narratively confirms Blackstone's point about such rooms as the indispensable depositories of the past whose apparent uselessness merely veils a deeper necessity that may suddenly and unexpectedly surface. In Radcliffe the supernatural is not the manifestation of a transcendent force that restores the order of inheritance, but typically the temporarily misinterpreted symptom of a repressive system of landed rule. In novels such as *A Sicilian Romance* or *The Romance of the Forest*, fear vanishes only with the dissolution of such rule, and the final disenchantment of the Gothic castle signals the defeat of manorial rule by suggesting the breakdown of the oppressive union of government and property, law and ground.

My claim that not only landed property in general, but the English property regime in particular, is exposed in Radcliffe's Italian romance finds its strongest support in the specific sources of the supernatural.

One of these is the entrapment of narrative in space. The complexity of the Gothic castle, its "swoln, shrunk, curtailed, enlarged, altered & mangled" form, to echo Blackstone, is the ineluctable conduit of narrative sequence. Through such capturing of temporal sequence in landed property, Radcliffe narrativizes the spatial articulation of time in the traditionalist castle metaphor. The narrative resolution of *A Sicilian Romance* is directed against such capture, and the cathartic effects of eventual release are heightened by the novel's extensive lingering in the zone of confinement. To reach resolution Radcliffe's plot has to thread through a labyrinthine Gothic space, and the supernatural spell of landed power – its binding of time and practice in space – is broken only by Julia's ritualistic passage through the dark extensions of the Gothic castle.

These extensions and the dominance of space over time that they embody are also responsible for the unsettling merging of past and present at Mazzini Castle. The perplexing layout of Mazzini Castle is the main reason why the Marchioness's fifteen-year confinement remains undiscovered. Had it not been for the castle's contorted interior, Julia's brother would have found his mother during his first search, early in the novel. But the past's secret is not easily retrieved from such a complex structure. Paradoxically, the castle prevents the present from discovering the crimes of the past while it promotes the constant intrusion of the past on the present. The mysterious lights and sounds emanating from the castle's southern wing keep the past alive in the present while the castle's complex arrangement impedes the past's emergence from obscurity. In a curiously literal sense, the marchioness's long imprisonment reveals that the castle's accretions house time, transforming temporal distance into an impenetrable spatial vicinity. Exposing the fetishistic grip of the past on the present that Blackstone and Burke enforced, Radcliffe depicts the superior ability of Gothic space to let things "languish in oblivion" as integral to a repressive property regime.

Just as integral is the mixture of culture and nature. At Mazzini Castle the oscillation between nature and culture that Burke's argument on the English constitution tried to fix (by calling it second nature) is reanimated and becomes itself a source of the supernatural, the uneasy manifestation of boundless landed power. The denouement of *A Sicilian Romance*, then, not only concludes a ritualistic passage that breaks the spell of spatial dominance, it also reveals that the blurring of human and material spheres, of culture and nature, and the coalescence of past and present are central aspects of such dominance and need to be overcome as well. As Radcliffe makes the traditionalist epistemology available experientially, she reveals second nature itself to be the source of a false supernatural. If Blackstone and Burke invest the English constitution with a structural complexity whose reproduction is beyond the ability of any contemporary observer, Radcliffe appropriates their architectural metaphor and presents its epistemological implications as the ultimate source of an overwhelming terror. In the castle's seemingly supernatural activities, second nature's blending of human and material spheres becomes scary. Radcliffe's fiction manages to turn the epistemological matrix of late eighteenth-century traditionalist thought inside out and presents it as a source of delusional fear.

III

In her early novels Radcliffe does not formulate an alternative to her Gothic spaces and the dependence of narrative on description. The castles of Athlin and Dunbayne in her first novel, for instance, are both Gothic structures, even though the latter represents an avatar of feudalism while the former is inhabited by a more enlightened clan. An alternative space to feudalism is also missing in *A Sicilian Romance*. Although the remainder of the Mazzini family finally abandon Mazzini Castle and move to the Italian mainland, we lack a description of their new surroundings. The relief from confinement and pursuit offered in this novel's landscape descriptions remains occasional, for these descriptions do not coalesce around a distinct site and only temporarily suspend an otherwise evenly oppressive Sicilian scene.[73] Natural landscape, as Julia's passage through the cavern demonstrates, is never quite dissociated from the realm of landed power. All of this would change, however, in 1791 with *The Romance of the Forest*, Radcliffe's third novel and the first she published under her name. Landscape description in this text is no longer an occasional practice: it becomes central to the formulation of a political and aesthetic alternative to Gothic space.

The idealized landscape scenes surrounding Leloncourt, a small village in the Savoyan Alps, serve as a critical refuge for Adeline, the heroine of *The Romance of the Forest*. Radcliffe's figuration of this alternative space renders it impervious to the extensions of feudal power. The representative of such power is the Marquis de Montalt, in whose ancient Gothic abbey Adeline languishes for most of the novel. The narrative function and structural form of this Gothic space resemble Castle Mazzini's in *A Sicilian Romance*. Indeed, Radcliffe's third novel executes an even more deliberate deployment of the Gothic castle, its initial description in

Chapter Two serving as a "proleptic simile" in the same way that Fielding's description of Paradise Hall did. In both cases the reader enters the novel through a descriptive scene whose features articulate fundamental textual patterns. As in Radcliffe's previous novel, the confusing and seemingly inexhaustible Gothic space contains a secret that Adeline has to retrieve in order to redeem the "forlornness of her circumstances."[74] Hidden apartments close to "the ancient foundation" of the abbey contain evidence of the murder of Adeline's father, and it is this evidence that will lead Adeline to recover family ties she thought she had never had (114). Although narrative progression is again closely aligned with the penetration of Gothic space, Radcliffe's third novel delays Adeline's full comprehension of the evidence she finds; her discovery of a bloody dagger and an old manuscript does not coincide with narrative resolution. The most substantial intervention in the process of resolution occurs in the concluding third volume of the novel, when Adeline finally escapes from the abbey to join the family of La Luc, clergyman of Leloncourt.

The first description of Leloncourt, given on Adeline's arrival, already exhibits the characteristic vocabulary of Radcliffe's alternative political and aesthetic space:

[The village] stood at the foot of several stupendous mountains, which formed a chain round a lake at some little distance, and the woods that swept from their summits almost embosomed the village. The lake, unruffled by the lightest air, reflected the vermil tints of the horizon with the sublime scenery on its borders, darkening every instant with the falling twilight. (241)

In contrast to Radcliffe's boundless Gothic space, the potentially threatening aspects of this landscape are checked by the insertion of carefully maintained distances. The "stupendous mountains" form a chain around the lake "at some little distance" and the "sweeping woods" embosom the village only "almost." Rendered less imposing by this circumspect articulation of distance, mountains and woods are restrained even further discursively by being subsumed under the category "sublime scenery." And while this "scenery" is then enlarged by the introduction of the horizon, such expansion is again captured within the borders of the lake, whose serene surface mirrors the landscape as a whole. The concluding emphasis on change adds the final touch to this picture of a restrained sublime: even though it describes a darkening, the conclusion dispels the scene's potential for perceptual arrest by subjecting it to gradual temporal progression. The overarching tendency of this landscape is to make the vast "safe" by breaking it down through the insertion of numerous frames. Framing describes not only the lake's pictorial function, but also the final temporal bracketing and the categorical subsuming of woods and mountains. In all these instances the immediate impact of a possibly overwhelming materiality is softened by the interposition of borders, reflections, and gradual change. The sublime's potential for dynamic and dimensional shock is assiduously restrained.

Temporal and spatial framing is especially crucial for Radcliffe's anti-Gothic space. This is demonstrated in the initial description of La Luc's house, which echoes the structure of the previous passage:

His chateau stood on the borders of a small lake that was almost environed by mountains of stupendous height, which, shooting into a variety of grotesque forms, composed a scenery singularly solemn and sublime. Dark woods, intermingled with bold projections of rock, sometimes barren, and sometimes covered with the purple bloom of wild flowers, impended over the lake, and were seen in the clear mirror of its waters. The wild and alpine heights which rose above were either crowned with perpetual snows, or exhibited tremendous crags and masses of solid rock, whose appearance was continually changing as the rays of light were variously reflected on their surface. (247)

Although the sublime and uncontrollable forces of nature are here amplified, the same interaction between borders, reflection, and gradual change tames the potential threat. As previously with the village, the lake is only "almost environed," this time by the mountains; it reduces their size and smoothes their grotesque forms by reflecting them on its placid surface. Similarly, the "continual change" noted in the concluding sentence – again foregrounding the secondary activity of surface reflection – melts the imposing materiality of the scene into uncomposed variety and thus reenacts temporally what the spatial intermingling achieves a few lines earlier.

Such cultivation of an intricate variety seen through different frames signals a picturesque approach to landscape. In the 1790s this approach underwent a fresh theorization. As Uvedale Price's *An Essay on the Picturesque* (1794) shows, the picturesque of the 1790s deliberately departed from the English landscape garden's reliance on "mere extent" and serpentine lines by complicating the eye's "merry chace." Price commended Hogarth's emphasis on intricacy, but rejected "smoothness, undulation, and serpentine lines" as the attributes of Lancelot Brown's merely beautiful and hence inferior landscapes. Dissociating Hogarth's "wanton chace of the eye" from "soft winding shapes," Price disavowed the close relation Hogarth had stipulated between intricacy and the line of beauty.[75] He was pleased to point out, in fact, that "Hogarth had a most enthusiastic admiration of what he called the line of beauty, and enthusiasm always leads to the verge of ridicule, and seldom keeps totally within it."[76] For Price the eye's chase is no longer associated with the undulating line, but with the "deceitful maze through which it wanders without knowing where to fix itself," a phrase lifted straight from Burke's *A Philosophical Inquiry into the Origin of Our Ideas of the Sublime and Beautiful* (1757).[77] Although the passage in Burke is concerned with beauty in the Hogarthian sense (ironic, given Price's desire to differentiate himself from Hogarth), it actually depicts a loss of control as the observer tries to contemplate the "neck and breasts" of a beautiful woman. Burke's more extensive formulation, which details how "the unsteady eye slides giddily, without knowing where to fix or whither it is carried," indicates that Price's interest in the passage has to do with its resistance to a predictable, gradually unfolding alignment between object and observer.[78]

One could say a number of things at this point about the emergence of picturesque theory out of a moment of self-defeating male gazing, but my main point here is that Price's transfer of Burke's "deceitful maze" into landscape cuts against the integrative emphases of Fielding's and Hogarth's undulating line. While theirs was a participatory vision that brought human and material spheres into tangible contact, Price's distances and even estranges the human from the material.[79] Intricacy, partial concealment, and impenetrability were the attributes of a landscape whose irregularity could no longer be held together by an "eternal undulating sweep," as Richard Paine Knight ridiculed Brown's landscapes.[80] To avoid the perplexities of the sublime, however, these qualities had to be articulated through the limiting of extent and the framing of the landscape's material. According to Price, painting was a useful school for gardeners because it showed how "many of those objects, that are scarcely marked as they lie scattered over the face of nature, when brought together in the compass of a small space of canvas, are forcibly impressed upon the eye."[81] By emphasizing borders and the collection of various elements into a "small space," the picturesque ensured affective concentration even as it increased the intricacy of its variety.

Although Radcliffe's novel precedes Price's essay by a few years, the texts share basic assumptions about landscape aesthetic and promote closely related ways of seeing. Unlike not only Fielding's landscape, whose illimitable extent had equated property and land and anchored scenery in the house and its owner, but also Radcliffe's own presentation of

Montalt's Gothic abbey and Mazzini Castle, La Luc's chateau is completely incidental to the landscape at large. Even when subsequent paragraphs return to the chateau, it never anchors the landscape, nor are its borders with natural scenery unclear: "The chateau was not large, but it was convenient, and was characterized by an air of elegant simplicity and good order. The entrance was a small hall, which opening by a glass door into the garden, afforded a view of the lake, with the magnificient scenery exhibited on its borders" (248). The desire for framing is most palpable here in the suggested scale. The extreme suggestion of this passage is that the tremendous scenery that dwarfed La Luc's home in the initial description can now be viewed from the inside of his small house through a door frame. While it may seem that the surrounding scene enters the house, what really happens is the establishment of a controlled and distanced relation to the outside. The unusual device of a glass door is highly suggestive in this regard. It alludes, on the one hand, to the pictorial function of the "clear mirror" of the lake and creates, on the other, an impression of transparency and openness that strongly contrasts with the profusion of secret (and frequently locked) doors in the seemingly interminable interior of de Montalt's Gothic abbey. The sublime's capacity for shock and absorption is, quite literally, domesticated, and the magnificent scenery is "exhibited" – offered up for the detached contemplation of the viewer in his home. In these opening sentences of its description, the house functions as a *camera obscura*, a circumstance that already signals the altered valence of property in Radcliffe's text. In Radcliffe's description inside and outside, house and landscape, property and land are clearly distinguished, and as the house is transformed into a viewing device, human and material spheres are distanced from each other.

Even the Gothic – symbol of male landed power and source of terror earlier in the novel – is transformed into an aesthetic spectacle when it appears within Radcliffe's alternative space. When La Luc, his daughter, and Adeline, on one of their frequent excursions into the mountains, come upon a ruined Gothic castle, they rest to enjoy the prospect. The "deep meditation" that the group soon falls into is commented on by Adeline: "The stillness and total seclusion of this scene, . . . together with that monument of faded glory on which the hand of time is so emphatically impressed, diffuse a sacred enthusiasm over the mind, and awaken sensations truly sublime" (264). Adeline's formulaic account identifies the castle as a symbol of transience, its "faded glory" signaling that the feudal powers that still animate de Montalt's crumbling abbey are here a thing of the distant past. The binding of time in space that I identified earlier as an important aspect of traditionalist notions of community is dissociated from property and landed power and becomes a source of unmitigated aesthetic pleasure. Time is still embodied in stone, but it is no longer a figure for the actual participation of the past in the present. Instead, the "hand of time" becomes a symbol for the ephemerality of all things human. And even though, in a poem inserted earlier into her narrative, Radcliffe had shown the Gothic castle "sleep[ing] on the smooth wave in trembling beauty" (262) (suggesting that the aesthetic may only be feudal power's unsteady sleep), her political and aesthetic paradise remains undisturbed by landed rule.

Radcliffe's alternative space thus establishes a clear contrast with the Gothic spaces of Mazzini Castle and de Montalt's abbey. It invites comparison to *Tom Jones* not only because of Fielding's Gothic preferences, or because Leloncourt is referred to more than once as a "paradise," but also because Radcliffe, in keeping with her picturesque approach, presents the illimitable extent of the English landscape garden as an extension of the Gothic abbey, a disorienting "boundless" space that symbolizes the feudal powers of the Marquis de Montalt.[82] It makes sense, then, that Leloncourt's descriptive order of things, unlike the Allworthy manor's, is not structured by a spatial extension and generic exhaustiveness held together by the integrative qualities of the serpentine line. Instead of resisting the pictorial by employing an embedding figurative mode, Radcliffe relies on simple images with few basic elements. These elements, however, vary greatly in themselves. In the descriptions I quoted, for example, the woods are "sometimes barren, and sometimes covered with the purple bloom of wild flowers," the mountains extend into "a variety of grotesque forms," "crowned with perpetual snows" or exhibiting "masses of solid rock," and continually change under the impact of different light effects. The attention with which Radcliffe's description treats detail and change creates variety independent of the generic exhaustiveness and boundary-breaking illimitability that characterized Fielding's spatial logic. To stabilize such concentrated variety, Radcliffe makes extensive use of the frame, which replaces the serpentine line as the principle of cohesion. This replacement provides a basic measure of the difference between *Tom Jones*'s and *The Romance of the Forest*'s figuration of persons and things, a difference that is also evident, as we have seen, in Price's critique of the passion for "mere extent" and the serpentine line.[83]

While Fielding's landscape, through the serpentine line, drew readerly attention into the physical features of the landscape – thus mimicking

Squire Allworthy's tactile relation to his possessions – Radcliffe's landscape is predicated on the creation of distance between viewer and scene.
The emergence of temporal and spatial frames as media *through* which
landscape is perceived bars the reader of *The Romance* from the possessive incorporation that Fielding's description invited, and it redefines the
locus of variety along with the status of detail. The undulating line articulates variety through extent and inhibits a sustained focus on detail. Its
mode of operation is cumulative, and it inspires an inclusive, participatory relation whose confident sweep signifies the stability of a possession
that is conceived in terms of a continuity between human and material
spheres. By contrast, Radcliffe's frame limits extent, replaces tactile involvement with pictorial detachment, and invests the individual landscape element itself with variety. It is no longer a lengthy chain of diverse
elements that creates variety but the diverse appearance of a few select
landscape elements. Not the objects themselves, but "the tints, and the
lights and shadows of objects, are the great characteristics of picturesque
scenery," as Price pointed out.[84] One of the crucial results of this transition from the undulating line to the frame is a beginning dissociation
of spatial and temporal planes from sensuous particulars, and their consequent emergence as dimensions mediating appearance. In Fielding a
virtually boundless appearance resisted spatial and temporal limits, its
exuberant extent itself offering the only indication of measure. A different emphasis develops in Radcliffe's landscape, where appearance is
mediated by temporal and spatial parameters.

   Radcliffe's description of landscape self-consciously departs from the
embedding figuration of time, space, and practice in the Gothic castle.
Disentangled from narrative persecution and the feudal grasp of the
marquis, Leloncourt's descriptive spaces represent aesthetic and political freedom by creating distance between observer and scene and by
mediating appearance through spatial and temporal frames. Such framing is precisely the activity that the Gothic setting refuses by binding
time in space and by interrelating nature and culture, past and present.
The setting of Leloncourt lacks the embedding relationality of manorial rule, and Radcliffe's framed landscape reasserts the distinctions
that are buried in Gothic space. We are presented not only with a vision
of nature that is meant to be uncontaminated by the intrusions of culture
and the dominant powers, but also with an inversion of the traditionalist
relation of time and space. As time emerges as the measure of space in
Radcliffe's ideal landscapes, its sedimented existence in the Gothic castle
comes to an end.[85] By confronting the viewer with a framed scene of

incessant change and partial visibility, Radcliffe's landscapes destabilize a confident possessive grasp as the viewer has to adjust to a ceaseless, simultaneous play of "innumerable tints and shades" (247). Such destabilization is only enforced by the theme of mutability and loss routinely invoked by Radcliffe's landscapes. Scenes that are "darkening every instant with the falling twilight" and "continually changing" testify to a volatility of appearance that confronts the viewer with a fundamental transience that evades the possessive imagination. The constant possibility of withdrawal and permutation would be too disorienting, however, without the interposition of frames that, by imposing limits and distance, render the radicalized variety of the picturesque manageable.

While Radcliffe cultivates this picturesque way of seeing to resist the propertied perspective developed in a novel such as *Tom Jones*, how specific her descriptions are in figuring an alternative social and political community is less clear. If Radcliffe's descriptive practice can be seen to escape a political economy based on the incorporating tendencies of landed property, does her account of Leloncourt also offer a more positive formulation of social and political community? Radcliffe emphasizes that, as part of Savoy, Leloncourt is subject to feudal rule, and she honestly describes an impoverished countryside. She is quick to point out, however, that La Luc's village is different. As Adeline approaches her new home, the impoverished peasant children we have seen earlier disappear and we are informed that Leloncourt "was an exception to the general character of the country, and to the usual effects of an arbitrary government; it was flourishing, healthy, and happy; and these advantages it chiefly owed to the activity and attention of the benevolent clergyman whose cure it was" (240). But while the narrator makes La Luc's village the exception to Savoy's feudal economy, she evades a specific statement on how La Luc's "activity and attention" contribute in practice, as she claims they do, to Leloncourt's "flourishing" condition. All we learn is that "the philanthropy which, flowing from the heart of the pastor, was diffused through the whole village, and united the inhabitants in the sweet and firm bonds of social compact, was divine" (277). Unlike Fielding's Squire Allworthy, who is identified as a property owner and whose benevolence frequently takes the form of financial relief, La Luc's benevolence is abstract, a sentiment that is not grounded in the possessive division of soil but "flows" from the heart. Despite her initial reference to feudalism, Radcliffe consistently evades considerations of property in her subsequent depiction of La Luc's ideal society. What we get instead, as these passages suggest, is a political economy of sympathy apparently powerful enough to displace the detrimental effects of a feudal regime.

The temptation to dismiss this as a hopeless idealization may seem strong, but it should be resisted. The idea of sympathy itself has economic implications, as my discussion of the mercantile commodity in Chapter Four showed, and they need to be unfolded for Radcliffe's idealized village. When looked at closely, La Luc's sympathy is not simply the groundless effusion of an overflowing heart. Claudia L. Johnson has gestured toward the material base of La Luc's benevolence by suggesting that it is fueled by the sentimental relationship to his dead wife, but this relationship warrants further scrutiny. In addition to the heterosexual bias that Johnson uncovers, La Luc's relationship to his dead wife also provides insight into the history of objectification that concerns me.[86]

While La Luc has no possessive relationship to the land, he develops a remarkably intense sentimental relationship to a certain "spot" around which a small object gathers his energies. This small object is the "rustic urn" (273) that La Luc erects after his wife dies, a memorial that is doubly informed by topophilia because it is erected on the "spot" that La Luc's wife loved most and thus on the "spot" that, after her death, becomes his favorite place. So closely attached is La Luc to this place that because of it he is reluctant to leave Leloncourt. One day an emergency makes departure inevitable and La Luc drives away:

Every scene of the adjacent country called up, as he passed, some tender remembrance. He looked towards the spot consecrated to the memory of his deceased wife; the dewy vapours of the morning veiled it. La Luc felt the disappointment more deeply, perhaps, than reason could justify; but those who know from experience how much the imagination loves to dwell on any object, however remotely connected with that of our tenderness, will feel with him. This was an object around which the affections of La Luc had settled themselves; it was a memorial to the eye, and the view of it awakened more forcibly in the memory every tender idea that could associate with the primary subject of his regard. In such cases fancy gives to the illusions of strong affection, the stamp of reality, and they are cherished by the heart with romantic fondness. (279)

I find this passage extraordinary. It addresses the central problem of the attempt to refigure the community of persons and things through sympathetic relationality. *A Sentimental Journey* and *The Man of Feeling*, as we saw, both disclose with considerable force that the sentimental connection produces a world that exists at a distance. Yorick, Harley, and Radcliffe's "forlorn" protagonist Adeline experience a radical homelessness that is dialectically linked to the affective concentration and intensification characteristic of sympathetic relationality. What Radcliffe attempts here is to move from the precarious, fleeting, and selective contacts of "sentimental commerce" to a sense of "sentimental dwelling" that establishes a durable groundedness through sympathy, independent of possession. By emphasizing how the "affections" of La Luc – who is himself a displaced emigrant – have "settled" around the urn, and by pointing out that the imagination loves to "dwell" on objects related to loved ones, Radcliffe aims to stabilize the volatile play of absence and presence that otherwise besets the sympathetic imagination. In using the language of settlement and dwelling, however, she also invests the sentimental object with considerably more cohesion and force than a writer such as Sterne. La Luc's repeated visits to this memorial, the energy he derives from it and redistributes as benevolence through his community, make this spot the center around which Leloncourt coheres. La Luc's urn has, indeed, acquired powers of its own. When he is unable to see his memorial on departing, La Luc is affected "more deeply . . . than reason could justify." It is not sufficient to *think* of his wife or the memorial; La Luc needs the actual physical and visual presence of the urn to activate his feelings. The urn does not contain his wife's ashes, but it is nonetheless more than just a representation of his absent wife that could be replaced by another representation. It is the thing itself that acts on La Luc, and even though Radcliffe suggests that the absent wife is "the primary subject" of La Luc's "regard," it is the urn that "awakened more forcibly in the memory *every* tender idea" associated with her. And what the object begins is completed by the "fancy" that gives the feelings triggered by the urn "the stamp of reality." So successful is the urn in acting on La Luc that "the illusions of strong affection" seem real and La Luc is thus transported back to an emotional state he experienced while his wife was alive. What is irredeemably absent becomes fully present again. Without the urn this transformation cannot take place and this is the source of La Luc's unreasonable disappointment. Such sentimental dwelling is here a life-giving force that sustains the frail La Luc as much as the surrounding village, and one should note that Radcliffe goes out of her way to stress that La Luc's dependence on this spot is not the folly of an aging or effeminate man. *Any* imagination, as she stresses, "loves to dwell" on objects that are in any way related to something or someone we value. No tearful breakdown interrupts the presence of the absent, and Radcliffe appears to have stabilized the constitutive tension of sensibility. Yet there is a price to be paid.

Radcliffe's economy of sympathy suggests that the only way to overcome the painful distancing inevitably produced by sensibility's affective concentration is a further deepening of the relationship between person and thing – to a point, in fact, where material reality reaches out to you as a familiar part of your self. Such deliberate fetishization attempts to regain a sense of belonging within a structure of feeling – sensibility – that promotes the differentiation between ground and figure. While it admits absence into the center of the communal structure, Radcliffe's sentimental dwelling ultimately strives to leave behind the divisions that sensibility had thrown up. Making the urn a material, not a symbolic, force, Radcliffe reverts to a premodern fetishism whose powers render presence and absence, life and death, past and present interchangeable. No finally compelling border keeps these spheres apart, and in this way Radcliffe remains indebted to the communal form of the manor. She here reveals a yearning to erase the divisions that characterize modern communal forms and return to the logic of integration that had marked Fielding's Paradise Hall and, less serenely, the Gothic spaces of her own devising. In this way Radcliffe's works consciously register the considerable losses incurred by the demise of landed property as a communal paradigm. What the psychoanalytic tradition would come to describe as the inability to mourn successfully by replacing the lost object with a new one is here not a failure, but the enabling condition of La Luc's communal character. Radcliffe's sensibility thus fully acknowledges the force of death and absence, but cuts short the painful play of absence and presence I analyzed for Sterne and Mackenzie by making the fetish a figure of unrestricted, direct communion.

Despite her forceful critique, Radcliffe does not leave behind the communal model of property, and this is made clear not only by Leloncourt's actual grounding in feudalism, but also by Adeline's inheritance of landed property that makes possible her final removal to Leloncourt. In keeping with her belief in the continued influence of feudal institutions, Radcliffe only displaces, and does not ultimately replace, the order of property. The Gothic castle can be disenchanted, but its actual transformation in history does not find an imaginative outlet in novels predominantly concerned with the figuration and refiguration of space. No developmental link connects the Gothic and picturesque spaces of Radcliffe's novels, and as change is consistently imagined in terms of spatial removal, these zones remain juxtaposed islands whose structures may be shown, but never transformed. Place remains fundamental to

Radcliffe's imagination and she consistently presents certain "spots" – Naples, Leloncourt, La Vallee – as indispensable to personal and social bliss.

This approach would change only with writers such as Maria Edgeworth or Sir Walter Scott, who made the decline of landed property's communal function the subject of entire novels, and who were able to do so because they began to project time and space as contentless dimensions within which change can be located. Radcliffe does not take this step, and retrospectively even her picturesque scenes do not seem fully committed to stabilizing the distance between observer and scene. Although time and space emerge as mediators, they are still tied to appearance in descriptions that use the landscape itself – its lakes, mountains, and constantly changing lights – as spatial and temporal frames. While these frames establish some distance between material and human spheres, some of the continuity that connected these spheres in the realm of property remains, and we can glimpse this not only in the frame's participation in the landscape, but also in the animation and intricacy's of the landscape, which, even as it departs from Gothic space, also recall its confusing blend of the human and the material. In this way Radcliffe resists the forces of modern objectification even as she recognizes that they liberate us from the manor's communal form. Of all the novels that I analyze in this book, hers confront most directly the dialectic tension that characterizes the history of objectification. In Radcliffe the promise of disembedded modes of being – of a final differentiation between ground and figure – is never pure. It is always tinged with an explicit sense of lost communion with the world and an attempt to reestablish the plenitude and interconnectedness that had once characterized human existence. In Edgeworth's and Scott's texts, by contrast, the picturesque and Gothic spaces that coexist vaguely in Radcliffe are temporally and spatially located, and the following chapter will take a close look at how *Waverley* (1814) charts the losses and the gains that come with such location.

CHAPTER SIX

Scottish law and Waverley's museum of property

Sir Walter Scott once likened the experience of reading *Tom Jones* – the "first English novel" in his estimation – to a boat ride. The reader, he reflected, "glides down the narrative like a boat on the surface of some broad navigable stream, which only winds enough to gratify the voyager with the varied beauty of its banks."[1] Scott's first novel, *Waverley; or, 'Tis Sixty Years Since* (1814), pursues a similarly winding course through historical territory already important in *Tom Jones*. Its eponymous hero wanders through the confusing political landscape of the 1745 Jacobite rebellion, wavering between England and Scotland, Hanoverians and Jacobites, Lowlands and Highlands, duty and inclination, history and romance. Only at the end of the novel, with a somewhat abrupt shift of political and personal allegiances, does Edward Waverley arrest his ambulatory course. He distances himself from the rebellion and the Highlands and marries Rose Bradwardine, daughter of the Lowland Jacobite Baron Bradwardine. Echoing Fielding's ending, Scott's denouement restores all the property that was lost in the scuffle of the rebellion and unites Jacobite and Whig estates.

But while Scott's ending celebrates the return of lost property to its original owners, *Waverley* is not a comedy of things, and this is – at least in part – because it is not an English but a Scottish novel. The comic overtones of *Waverley*'s final scene, when Baron Bradwardine reclaims his temporarily forfeited estate, mask a serious engagement with the irremediable changes wrought by the last Jacobite rebellion. For Scott these changes signal the beginning of a fundamental transformation of Scotland as a whole. To capture this transformation he invokes the figure of the boat ride again in *Waverley*'s famous last chapter, but he now uses it differently:

There is no European nation which, within the course of half a century, or little more, has undergone so complete a change as this kingdom of Scotland. The effects of the insurrection of 1745, – the destruction of the patriarchal power of the Highland chiefs, – the abolition of the heritable jurisdictions of the Lowland nobility and barons, – the total eradication of the Jacobite party, which, averse to intermingle with the English, or adopt their customs, long continued to pride themselves upon maintaining ancient Scottish manners and customs – commenced this innovation. The gradual influx of wealth, and extension of commerce, have since united to render the present people of Scotland a class of beings as different from their grandfathers, as the existing English are from those of Queen Elizabeth's time . . . But the change, though steadily and rapidly progressive, has, nevertheless, been gradual; and, like those who drift down the stream of a deep and smooth river, we are not aware of the progress we have made until we fix our eye on the now distant point from which we have been drifted.[2]

Waverley enacts this surprised and incredulous look back, measuring the change between 1745 and 1814, and not quite believing it. Two complementary factors – the sudden vision of the distance between past and present and the subtle drift that has created it – mark the unique historical and aesthetic constellation out of which *Waverley* grows. The winding stream is here not a figure of balanced variety and integration, but of spatial and temporal distancing. Unlike *Tom Jones*, which could still ignore the forces of absence in an ironic but nonetheless stabilizing celebration of manorial plenitude, *Waverley* wrestles with an irrecoverable loss.

Scott's meditation on change locates the historical origins of such loss in the political and cultural conflict between Scotland and England. In Scott's view the rebellion of 1745 was not simply the hopelessly romantic attempt of an historically backward Highland band to restore the Stuart king. It expressed, rather, a fundamental conflict between the English and Scottish nations, between their "manners and customs," as he puts it. Scott was keenly aware of such differences, even to the point of questioning whether *Tom Jones*'s portrayal of English mores "can be fully understood, or relished to the highest extent, by such natives of Scotland and Ireland, as are not habitually and intimately acquainted with the characters and manners of Old England."[3] On a military and constitutional level, the English won this conflict of national identity, and their incursions into the Highlands after 1745 initiate, in Scott's mind, Scotland's rapid transformation in the second half of the eighteenth century.

In *Waverley* the English–Scottish conflict leaves its most revealing traces in the transformation of Baron Bradwardine's Scottish manor Tully-Veolan. Scott presents in the Bradwardine manor his version of the "identification of property and government" that has occupied this study in various forms, from the continuity of self-possession, appropriation, and legislation in Defoe, to Fielding's equation of property rights and legitimate government, and Radcliffe's disenchantment of the analogy between nature, government, and property.[4] The importance of landed property for *Waverley* has been recognized by critics such as Alexander Welsh, Ian Duncan, and Judith Wilt, but they have interpreted the restoration of property in Scott's denouement as a "consolidation" or "recovery" of a landed order.[5] Such a reading might be suitable for *Tom Jones*, but I think Scott's novel tells an altogether different story, a story whose pattern Scott intimates in the image of the continuous but transformative drift of the boat ride. Under the guise of continuity, the restored Bradwardine manor enacts Scotland's incorporation into Great Britain and the end of landed property as a communal paradigm: this is the startling transformation achieved by what looks, at first sight, like a "recovery."

It has been easy to misread *Waverley*'s ending in part because it mobilizes detailed legal knowledge, drawing, in particular, on the differences between Scottish and English legal traditions.[6] Scott's familiarity with two legal traditions whose respective host cultures formed one nation, Great Britain, heightened his awareness of law as a culturally distinct body of learning. Such awareness differentiates him from a lawyer-novelist such as Fielding, who resisted the importation of detailed legal knowledge into *Tom Jones*. Fielding's resistance may have been motivated not only by his intuitive belief in the validity of the legal language of private property to describe public matters, but also by a less developed sense of legal discourse as a cultural construct, a limited body of knowledge whose details may represent or encode larger social and historical conflicts. Scott utilizes the law in this reflexive sense and displays an awareness of the cultural meaning of legal conventions that is largely absent in Fielding. By attending to the finer differences between Scottish and English law in *Waverley*, I hope to recover the transformation of the manor as the defining moment in a nationalist conflict that promotes the equation of movable and immovable property and dissolves the identification of property and right.

The previous chapter has shown that by the 1790s such identification of landed property and right had ceased to be intuitive. Thomas Paine powerfully expressed this new sense when, shortly before he left England to escape prosecution, he charged that "the custom of attaching rights to place, or in other words, to inanimate matter, instead of to the person, independently of place, is too absurd to make any part of a rational argument."[7] Even though Scott elsewhere recommends the manorial rule of the "philosophic Squire in *Tom Jones*" as the proper basis for social and moral order and rejects reason's claim to being the "exclusive and paramount court in a man's own bosom," his first novel nonetheless presents Paine's explosive charge as the outgrowth of an irreversible historical process.[8] In *Waverley* Scott uses his sharp awareness of the law as a distinct body of cultural and national knowledge to depict the dissociation of right and place as the precondition for Scotland's integration into Britain. Such dissociation destroys the traditional communal forms embodied in the manor and promotes modern communities in which material reality loses the last vestiges of the obscurity and animatedness it retained in Radcliffe. *Waverley*, as we shall see, transforms the landed estate into a simple "thing," a transformation that ushers in new modes of historical, aesthetic, and national awareness.

Landed property's imaginative and ideological hold weakened significantly in the years following the French Revolution, in part because of the exertions of novelists such as Radcliffe and theorists such as Paine or Wollstonecraft, and in part because the booming agriculture of the 1790s shifted, in Ann Bermingham's words, the "relationship between landowners and their dependents . . . from a paternalistic, quasi-feudal system of reciprocal rights and duties to an industrial employer-employee relationship, bonded only by a cash nexus."[9] In Scotland the feudal past receded with redoubled speed, and time – "sixty years since" – emerged forcefully as an independent reality, the abstract link to past practices that no longer reproduced themselves in the present. Scott's originality, recently accorded well-deserved scrutiny, seems to me not so much that he "invented" the historical novel – a claim that is, at any rate, too broad to withstand careful analysis – but rather that, in writing an historical novel, he thematized the conditions that make such an undertaking possible in the first place.[10] *Waverley* is an historical novel in the rather specific sense that it presents an extensive reflection on its own historical conditions of possibility. In my reading that reflection is anchored in the transformation of Tully-Veolan, the manorial estate of Baron Bradwardine.

The fate of the manor as *Waverley* depicts it – its irrecoverable transformation in time – is directly related to the formal possibilities of the novel. For Scott, who believed that "description and narration . . . form the essence of the novel," new possibilities of narrative and descriptive figuration were opened up by the ascendance of time over space.[11] Radcliffe's concern with spatial epistemologies led to the dominance of description over narrative, and even though time emerges as the measure of space in her picturesque scenes, it is still tied to the materiality of the landscape. In Scott the irredeemable temporal transformation of landed property finally breaks the dominance of the spatial, and he is able to integrate descriptive passages into an overall narrative movement. *Robinson Crusoe*'s transformation of a South American island prefigured this integrated relation of narrative and description, but it is in *Waverley* that it structures an entire novel and comes to bear on British soil, within the context of common law. It is nonetheless no accident that the two novels in this study that thematize British colonialism should integrate narrative and description in this manner. By exploring common law through natural law, and by contrasting English and Scottish law, *Robinson Crusoe* and *Waverley* are able to expose processes of colonial appropriation that remain inaccessible from within the tradition of English common law. The description of material reality in these texts can thus join a narrative movement and become transformative.

Scott describes Tully-Veolan at three strategic points in *Waverley*'s narrative: before the Jacobite uprising of 1745, after its defeat, and after Baron Bradwardine is pardoned for his participation in the rebellion and regains possession of his forfeited estate. Three distinct descriptive scenes shape *Waverley*'s narrative rhythm. The first description of the Bradwardine manor opens with the emblems of the Bradwardine family, a sign of ancestral right that recurs in the two subsequent depictions of Tully-Veolan:

In the centre of the exterior barrier was the upper gate of the avenue, opening under an archway, battlemented on the top, and adorned with two large weather-beaten mutilated masses of upright stone, which, if the tradition of the hamlet could be trusted, had once represented, at least had been once designed to represent, two rampant bears, the supporters of the family of Bradwardine. (I:105–106)

Under the surface of this unassuming passage one can decipher, I believe, outlines of the traditionalist community that is overturned in the course of *Waverley*'s events. The important point of the description is that, to an outsider, merely "mutilated masses of upright stone" are visible. Only the local villagers, immersed in the traditions of this particular region, know that these masses of stone are really bears, emblems of the hereditary power of their lord. No one is concerned, it seems, about the illegibility of these signs of power or about the uncertain knowledge surrounding them. Indeed, the passage suggests that knowledge of authority is not tied to the public recognition of some clearly visible and coherent representation. Authority is here a lived relation, something that is "known" through the continuity of local custom. As is characteristic of a manorial order, practice is embedded in a localized context of time and space.

Beyond this already familiar embedding function of the manor, Scott's description plays on a second, closely related register. The passage turns on a curious disjunction between the "visible" and the "knowable": what is visible (the unshapely mass of stones) by no means defines what can be known (that they are emblems of landed power). Such disjunction goes directly against the epistemological tendencies of natural law in *Robinson Crusoe* that I explored. There the occupation of land occurred independent of established communal practice and rested precisely on the conjunction of the visible and the knowable. Heraldic emblems of the sort that adorn the Bradwardine manor would be useless on Crusoe's island, where the clearly visible sign of cultivation is supposed to be the universally recognizable signifier of exclusive possession. The bears of Bradwardine embody a different configuration of persons and things, one based on customary continuity, and it is this traditionalist order that English soldiers attack when they move into Scotland and lay Tully-Veolan to waste.

In Scott's second descriptive scene, Waverley returns to Tully-Veolan's "upper gate" after a long absence:

A single glance announced that great changes had taken place. One half of the gate, entirely broken down, and split up for firewood, lay in piles ready to be taken away; the other swung uselessly about upon its loosened hinges. The battlements above the gate were broken and thrown down, and the carved Bears, which were said to have done sentinel's duty upon the top for centuries, now hurled from their posts, lay among the rubbish ... The accessaries of ancient distinction, to which the Baron, in the pride of his heart, had attached so much importance and veneration, were treated with peculiar contumely. (III:222–224)

This violent disfiguring of Scottish landed property by English soldiers betrays its true target in the care taken to destroy those emblems of ancestral right which embody Tully-Veolan's traditionalist order. Notwithstanding its own rootedness in common law, England appears here in the role of a colonial power subjugating one of its rebellious subject states. This, at any rate, is how Scott characterized England's intervention into Scottish property relations after the '45. When he commented in 1808 on England's bill for the abolition of Scotland's heritable jurisdictions in 1747, he was highly critical and exclaimed that Scotland should "not be regarded as an infant colony." England had been wrong to assume "the insolent air of a conqueror, imposing his laws and customs on a colony which the fate of battle has laid at his feet."[12] The scene of destruction at Tully-Veolan has to be read with this notion of England as insolent conqueror in mind. Scott's excitability over the English intervention is here fueled by his perception of England as a colonial power, and this perception is underwritten by the cultural and national valences acquired by English and Scottish legal traditions in the eighteenth century.

I

Despite considerable similarities in the construction of legitimacy, Scottish and English legal traditions differ markedly in the central area of common law – property law. I wish to emphasize two basic aspects of this difference. The first has to do with concepts of landholding and title.

Landholding in eighteenth-century Scotland was based on the notion of *dominium directum*, which gave the Scottish lord a much stronger title to his land than his English counterpart, who enjoyed, strictly speaking, only a nominal title to an interest in land. The fiction of central ownership of all land by the king established itself early in England and gave rise to what legal historians call "universal derivative tenure," a concept we have already encountered in Chapter Two under the name of *nulle terre sans seigneur*.[13] According to this notion, an English lord never has absolute interest in his property; his interest is always relative and in principle revocable.[14] Derivative tenure facilitated alienability at a comparatively early point in English history. An English vassal in the eighteenth century, for instance, did not have to appeal to his landlord in order to alienate his land. In Scotland *dominium directum* prescribes such an appeal. C. F. Kolbert and N. A. M. Mackay consider this "the greatest of all differences between the conveyancing systems of England and Scotland for eight hundred years" and argue that it indicates the comparative strength of feudal concepts in Scotland.[15]

The prominence of feudal concepts in eighteenth-century Scotland is further evinced by the fact that as late as 1685 the Scottish parliament passed a law that encouraged dynastic landholding. The "Act Concerning Tailzies" strengthened the Scottish landholder's right to keep his property unalterably within the same family. It allowed for the entailment of land in strict familial perpetuity. The slightest alteration of the property – for example, the indebting of the land – immediately dispossessed the current holder and turned the property over to the next in line. A comparable law (and a comparable reverence for dynastic landholding) did not exist in eighteenth-century England.[16] A related element that will become important later on is the fact that until 1747 Scotland retained a territorial system of jurisdiction, an association of land and right that had lost much of its practical social functions in England's more centralized jurisdiction, even while it remained critical to the theoretical construction of political community.[17]

The second aspect of the difference between Scottish and English legal traditions concerns the union of England and Scotland. The union of the crowns in 1603 had prompted several schemes for a legal unification of the two countries, but these plans met with increasing criticism on both sides of the border. The prospect of a complete fusion with England led Scottish lawyers to emphasize the unique national properties of their law; *The Institutions of the Law of Scotland* (1693) by James Dalrymple, Viscount Stair, was the most influential early work that testified to this new nationalist dimension of Scottish law.[18] The contested Treaty of Union of 1707 amplified this trend. As the Treaty strictly protected Scottish independence only in the areas of education, church policy, and jurisprudence, Scottish law and its traditions became an important register for national sentiment in the eighteenth century. Scottish lawyers, in the words of Paul Henderson Scott, "felt themselves to be in a very particular sense the chief upholders of Scottish identity and tradition."[19] It is worth emphasizing in this respect that, at least until the late eighteenth century, the landed classes dominated the Scottish legal profession.[20] Since Scottish common law was fundamentally concerned with real property, not only Scottish law, but, more specifically, Scottish concepts of title and ownership acquired a distinctly national significance.

I do not mean to suggest that English legal discourse in the eighteenth century did not center on real property. We have already seen that the opposite is the case. My point here is to emphasize a crucial and frequently overlooked difference in the two legal traditions and the attitudes to land and title that they register. The tension between England and Scotland in this area emerges in exemplary fashion in a letter Lord Chancellor Hardwicke wrote to Henry Home, Lord Kames, in 1757: "As to the general mischief of your strict entails, and the evil consequences of locking up the land of a country *extra commercium*, I have long been convinced of them, and rejoice to find a person of your knowledge and experience in the law and constitution of Scotland in the same way of thinking."[21] It is to the same difference between England and Scotland that Kames refers in 1777 when he states, following more his wishes than reality, that "even in Scotland . . . land is now restored to commerce, and is bought and sold like any other merchandise."[22]

Yet Kames is an unusual figure in the legal scene of eighteenth-century Scotland. It is no coincidence, for example, that Jeremy Bentham's early critique of William Blackstone's *Commentaries on the Laws of England* (1765– 1769) refers approvingly to Kames's *Historical Law Tracts* (1758).[23] Kames's book was intended to further the legal union of England and Scotland, a circumstance that led Scott's law professor Baron Hume to view Kames skeptically, as a censor of the law who did not promote a national Scottish law.[24] Indeed, for Scott and most Scottish lawyers the transformation of land into merchandise would have been nothing less than a catastrophe. The majority of eighteenth-century lawyers adhered to the property paradigm that ruled their discourse and they would have agreed with Edmund Burke, who in 1790 had expressed himself forcefully against the instability caused by a commodification of landed property. "By this kind of operation," Burke had warned, "that species of property becomes (as it were) volatized; it assumes an unnatural and monstrous activity."[25]

Yet despite Scott's closeness to Burke's position on landed property, the "volatization" of landed property through its immersion into the real estate market and its consequent unmooring from a century-old Scots entail (thus clearing the way for English possession), is precisely the process we can observe in the case of the Bradwardine property in *Waverley*. And we can now also explain why property can function as such a significant register of political and cultural change in the novel. In the nationalist atmosphere of eighteenth-century Scottish legal discourse, property and the peculiarly Scottish modes of landholding, conveyancing, and succession became important defining features for an indigenous legal tradition and a feeling of Scottish independence among the landed classes.[26] Many proprietors held their lands by a title established long before the contested union, in the days of political independence, and maintained strong emotional and legal ties to a Scottish past untainted by English influence. Given the fact that landed property focused such national and historical meanings, any modification of Scottish property relations immediately became, from the perspective of the Scottish landed classes, an issue with the most far-ranging implications. Scott's stress on the English intervention into Scottish property finds here its motivation. The English attack on Tully-Veolan is more than a retaliation for the rebellion against Hanover. Its focus on the ancestral emblems of the Bradwardine family indicates that Scotland's remaining cultural and national independence is under attack, and a recognition that this independence is tied to the Scottish property tradition.

II

However clear Scott's position on English–Scottish relations may have seemed so far, things become far more complicated once we reach the third description of Tully-Veolan, at the end of *Waverley*. Having last seen his estate in the state of destruction described earlier, the pardoned rebel Baron Bradwardine finally returns to his forfeited manor. This is what he finds:

The marks of devastation, unless to an eye intimately acquainted with the spot, were already totally obliterated ... Indeed, when he entered the court, ... all seemed as much as possible restored to the state in which he had left it, when he assumed arms some months before. The pigeon-house was replenished; the fountain played with its usual activity, and not only the Bear who predominated over its bason, but all the other Bears whatsoever were replaced upon their stations, and renewed or repaired with so much care, that they bore no tokens of the violence which had so lately descended upon them. While these minutiae had been so heedfully attended to, it is scarce necessary to add, that the house itself had been thoroughly repaired, as well as the gardens, with the strictest attention to maintain the original character of both, and to remove, as far as possible, all appearance of the ravage they had sustained. The Baron gazed in silent wonder. (III:345–348)

At first sight this passage appears to contradict what I have argued about *Waverley*'s irredeemable transformation of property. Everything seems to be just as it was before the rebellion, signs of which, along with the destruction wrought by English soldiers, have been so thoroughly effaced that one might question whether it has had any effect at all. Yet Scott is a little too eager to convey this impression, too insistent that the marks of the past have been "totally obliterated," that the "original character" of Tully-Veolan has been respected with the "strictest attention," and that all "minutiae" have been "heedfully attended to." These strains indicate that this passage presents not so much a recovery of the past as a fantasy of total restoration. The meticulously restored Bradwardine manor promotes a fiction of inviolate return struggling to annul the historical change that divides the beginning from the end of Scott's novel. The deep ambivalence of Scott's backward glance – at once recognizing and disbelieving the pastness of the past – recurs here in the revelatory attempt to disguise the transformation of Tully-Veolan. The most obvious clue to what is really happening in *Waverley*'s denouement lies in the English promotion of the disguise: after the soldiers' vandalism it is two Englishmen, Waverley and his friend Colonel Talbot, who are remarkably keen to engage in what will turn out to be a rather fateful restoration. Before anything can be restored, however, the Bradwardine property has to go through the neutralizing process of a sale that breaks the old hereditary order of Tully-Veolan.

After the forfeiture of Baron Bradwardine's possessions, the next heir in line, Malcolm Bradwardine, inherits the estate. Frustrated by his tenants' resistance to their new lord, Malcolm decides to sell his inheritance. He is able to do so despite the limitations usually imposed by an entailment because he is "the last institute in this entail" (III:235). This sale is the turning point in the transformation of the Bradwardine estate. Malcolm's decision to "alienat[e] the family inheritance" (3:288) successfully translates heritable property into monetary terms and releases property from the familial perpetuity so respected under Scottish law. The fourteenth-century feudal charter from Robert the First under which Tully-Veolan had been in the Bradwardine family's uninterrupted possession is void once the estate has found a new owner (III:36–37). Baron Bradwardine's greatest fear, that the family estate could "pass from the lineage that should have possessed it in *saecula saeculorum*" (i.e. permanently), is realized (III:235).

The complicated arrangements for the now necessary reacquisition indicate the sensitivity surrounding it. The full account Scott's text gives of the sale reads as follows: the money ultimately exchanged for Tully-Veolan comes from Waverley's English friend Talbot, a devoted Hanoverian. The latter buys land from Everard Waverley, Edward Waverley's uncle, who, in turn, gives the money to Edward, who then makes it over to his wife-to-be, Rose Bradwardine, the Baron's daughter. A prenuptial contract ensures that this endowment is irrevocable. From Rose the money finally goes to Malcolm in exchange for the estate. The ostensible purpose of the protracted path that the money is forced to take is to give Baron Bradwardine the impression that he is under no "pecuniary obligation" (III:354) and that the estate has not been reacquired through forces outside the family. It is regained instead from inside, through Rose Bradwardine, whose marriage does not affect her ownership of the money. More to the point, these complex arrangements effectively conceal the (for a Jacobite and Scotsman) compromising circumstance that the money used to possess his ancestral home comes from a devoted Hanoverian Englishman. With remarkable playfulness Scott reminds us of the source of reacquisition through a practical joke. When the Baron returns to his estate, he is initially greeted by Colonel Talbot and his wife, who pose, for a brief period, as the new owners of Tully-Veolan. This supposedly harmless (and, in terms of plot, entirely unmotivated) prank signals that *Waverley*'s restoration of property does not effect a simple return of possession into Scottish hands (III:344). When Talbot finally assures the Baron that "your family estate is your own once more in full property, and at your absolute disposal" (III:352–353), the suggested identicalness of the present terms of ownership with the previous ones is misleading. That the Baron has to "*acquire* the estate of his fathers" (III:357; my italics) signals the rupture of continuous ownership and of a century-old plan of inheritance. The upshot of these developments is that, owing to the reentailment that Baron Bradwardine arranges at the end, Tully-Veolan will ultimately, after the Baron's death, belong to the English Waverley family (III:356).

The same neutralizing process affects a piece of movable property that is intimately connected to the Bradwardines. The cup of the "Blessed Bear of Bradwardine," ancient heirloom of the family, is the one item that has apparently been lost during the ravages of the English soldiers. Yet at the very moment when the Baron notices the loss of this much-cherished family possession, Talbot marvelously places it in front of him. The cup, Talbot explains, had fallen into the hands of an Englishwoman, who, "having been originally the helpmate of a pawnbroker, had found opportunity, during the late unpleasant scenes in Scotland, to trade a little in her old line." Talbot is not unaware of the stain that his recovery of the cup has created when he expresses his hope that the cup's "value has not been diminished by having been restored through my means" (III:363). The cup's entrance into the market and its reacquisition by Talbot precisely mirrors the process undergone by the estate as a whole. It is the precision with which Scott here aligns movable and immovable properties that is historically and culturally significant. For this close parallel indicates that the distinction between land and things has been erased. In this way Scott's text leaves behind an earlier phase in the history of objectification during which movables continued to bear the imprint of immovable characteristics and immovables could not be fully mobilized. That the sanctity of Scottish things and institutions suddenly depends on English interference, on the "*Diva Pecunia* of the Southron," as the narrator has Baron Bradwardine observe (III:345), suggests that for Scott the equation between movable and immovable property is also a result of Scotland's absorption into a more commercial Britain. Scotland's creeping integration finds its deepest and politically most important expression in the reentailment that becomes necessary after the sale of Tully-Veolan.

The legal procedure followed in the reentailment is based on what Scottish lawyers call "a charter of resignation *in favorem*" (III:356).[27] As we have seen, the comparative strength of feudal custom in eighteenth-century Scotland and its particular practice of landholding prescribed application to the feudal lord for any change in the terms of owner-ship. Earlier in the novel, while the insurgents were still hopeful, Baron Bradwardine had identified the exiled Stuart king as his feudal lord, and we find him, at this point, eager to perform his feu-duty as determined by the fourteenth-century charter (III:5–15, 36–38). Yet the Stuart title and therefore the relationship enacted by the feu-duty are fundamentally shaken after the defeat of the Jacobite rebellion. The legal procedure of the reentailment brings this development full circle. Reentailing his in-heritance, Baron Bradwardine literally resigns his fee to the Hanoverian succession "*in favorem*," that is, "for the express purpose of its re-grant to the disponce as a *new vassal*" (my italics).[28] The reentailment thus implies not only the expiration of the original Bradwardine tailzie from the fourteenth century and the eventual surrender of the Bradwardine lands to an English family, but also the recognition of Stuart right as defeasible.

This sense is dramatized by the fact that Robert the First granted the original Bradwardine charter. As Scott knew, and as an act of the Scottish parliament in 1650 shows, Robert the First occupied a privileged position in Scottish history.[29] In its "Act in Favour of Sir James Balfoure," the Scottish parliament acknowledges Balfoure for the production "of the great Charter whairby umquile King Robert the Bruce entailed the Crown of Scotland (faileand of his airis maill) to the race of the Stewarts."[30] The legitimacy of the Bradwardine title originates, as it were, with the entailment favoring the Stuarts and is cut off from its ancient continuity precisely at the historical juncture when the interrup-tion of the Stuart line receives its final confirmation. The entailed crown of the Stuarts and the entailed estate of the Bradwardines are equally ancient and lose their hold together. The regranting of Bradwardine's feudal charter through the Hanoverian king mirrors the failed resistance against the Glorious Revolution at Culloden.

The sale of the Bradwardine manor, the creation of a Hanoverian entail, and the fact of eventual English ownership effectively remove the

Bradwardine estate from a century-old code of inheritance (the original entailment), Stuart legitimacy, Scottish history, and, ultimately, Scottish ownership. The wide contextual range of the Scottish property relation is thus curtailed, appropriated, and integrated into the constitutional order of Britain. But *Waverley*'s transformation of property does not end here. As Scott notes in his final chapter, the British parliament abolished the heritable (or territorial) jurisdictions of the Lowland lords in 1747 and Baron Bradwardine loses his proudly asserted right to "imprison, try, and execute" his vassals in cases of delinquency (III:365; I:130). The abolition of these jurisdictions in the aftermath of the '45 completes the decontextualization of Scottish property that I have been tracing. It breaks the customary link between law and land, between right and place, that underpins the manorial order, and opens the way for a homogenization of national territory.

III

As I noted with regard to Radcliffe's Marquis Mazzini, territorial jurisdictions are strictly related to the property to which they are attached. In accordance with such feudal thinking, the Treaty of Union protected Scotland's territorial jurisdictions by considering them "rights of property" (6 Anne, c. 11).[31] Their abolition by the British parliament in 1747 violated the Treaty's protection of the Scottish legal constitution and altered Scottish property relations.

The issue of territorial jurisdiction in Scott's novel shifts the emphasis from the differences to the similarities between English and Scottish common law. Within the framework of *Waverley*'s historical narrative, the abolition of these jurisdictions becomes symbolic of the conflict between two models of national community, one based on a uniform code of law that constructs the national territory as an abstract, homogeneous sphere, and the other based on a customary law, rooted in the particularities of place, and a national territory that is heterogeneous. The existence of territorial jurisdictions in Scotland signified for Scott the persistence of premodern communal forms – characterized by the unity of right and place – that were threatened by the modernizing British. The similarities between English and Scottish common law with regard to the customary grounds of legitimacy, however, allowed Scott to mount an effective critique of British legislative interventions by using arguments that are germane to the English legal tradition. Scottish national and cultural independence, in fact, had been defined by Scottish lawyers throughout the eighteenth-century by emphasizing the traditional sanctity of Scottish customs in a manner entirely compatible with English legal precepts.

Viscount Stair articulated this emphasis in 1693 when he stated that "every nation, under the name of law understand their ancient and uncontroverted customs time out of mind." "We [the Scottish people]," he continued, "are ruled in the first place by our ancient and immemorial customs, which may be called our common law."[32] This understanding is reiterated throughout the eighteenth century, among others by Baron Hume, Scott's law professor, and John Erskine, whose *The Principles of the Law of Scotland* served Scott as a legal textbook.[33] Hume praises, for instance, the customary authority of "the *Lex non scripta*, the unwritten, customary or common law," established on the basis of usage "time out of mind," and dismisses the merely declaratory power of "the *Lex scripta*, the written or statutory law." Refusing "allegiance to the Civil Law, as having dominion over us," Hume emphasizes that the "special rules according to which our own customs deviate from [the Civil Law] must ... be well understood by the lawyer, before he undertake the important trust of defending the rights, which his fellow-citizens, by the tenure of those customs, hold and enjoy."[34]

Scott himself comments on the customary authority of such a national law when he observes:

No [legal] system of great antiquity is ever theoretically perfect. The greater part of its excellencies have been produced by circumstances, some of them altogether accidental, others arising from causes which cannot be traced, and many of them incapable of being distinctly perceived ... An establishment like this, it is obviously not easy to borrow. It is only in its natural soil, where it has long been planted, that the tree can be expected to flourish; there only are to be found those peculiarities which have contributed to its beauty and vigour.[35]

The source of the law's legitimacy is here again identified (albeit not word for word) as "time out of mind." The fact that the historical origins of the law escape rational inquiry and even rational design serves only to fortify the law's legitimacy as a lived relation whose comprehensiveness exceeds the grasp of any contemporary analysis. The uniqueness of the Scottish constitution and the identity of the Scottish nation, Scott suggests, rest on the organic relation between the legal system (the "tree") and the nation (the "soil"). So deeply rooted, in fact, is Scottish law in the land that the distinction between culture and nature disappears.

Scott quotes approvingly the English lawyer Matthew Hale on this point: "[the people's] ancient laws and customs have been twisted and woven into them as part of their nature."[36] Under such conditions the moment of legal institutionalization is shrouded in invisibility. In the ideology of the common law, right and place form an inextricable unity because legitimacy finds its deepest root in local custom.

Scott's view of legal authority coincides in this respect with Blackstone's. Conceptually more explicit, Blackstone assigns the authority of law/custom to a realm of "higher antiquity than memory or history can reach: nothing being more difficult than to ascertain the precise beginning and first spring of an antient and long established custom."[37] Erskine's *The Principles* employs the same construction when stating that Scottish customary law "derives its force from the tacit consent of King and People, which consent is presumed from the ancient custom of the community ... No precise time can be fixed for constituting this sort of law."[38] For Blackstone, Scott, and Erskine, the epistemological inaccessibility of the common law's origin ensures its indivisibility from local custom and hence its legitimacy and national significance. But while the legitimacy and preeminence of the national law of Scotland rest on its rootedness in custom, these customs themselves naturally vary substantially. Any legal system that founds its legitimacy on an organic relation of right and place promotes regional variance, even within national units.[39] This is why Scott rejects the (utilitarian) "principle of 'uniformity of laws'"[40] and criticizes the Code Napoleon for its "very symmetry and theoretical consistency," characteristics that can never match a legal system that "has grown up with a nation."[41] No wonder Scott thought that the abolition of a customary, regional, and asymmetrical legal expedient such as the heritable jurisdictions constituted "the most extensive alteration in the law of Scotland" and was calculated to "subvert several fundamental principles of our law."[42] The heritable jurisdictions embodied the regional connection between the law and the land that is at the base of the traditionalist national community.

From a modern perspective, then, national identity and legitimacy in eighteenth-century common law are contradictorily grounded in a finally irreconcilable variety of regional customs. In the legal ideology of the common law that Scottish lawyers drew on, the nation does not translate into a single, unified culture of shared customs. Since the law's legitimacy hinges on local custom, the nation cannot be defined along the lines of a single cultural boundary.[43] The regional tie of eighteenth-century common law – so powerfully exemplified by the heritable jurisdictions – cannot accommodate anything like the homogeneous space of the modern nation state. The national territory constructed by an identification of right with place is essentially discontinuous, patchy, and marked by a proliferation of semipermeable local boundaries. Strong cultural contrast, linguistic diversity, regional rule, and relative permeability are, in fact, the principal characteristics of the topography drawn in *Waverley*. This discontinuous territorial model is incompatible with the modern concept of the nation in which, to quote Benedict Anderson, "state sovereignty is fully, flatly, and evenly operative over each square centimetre of a legally demarcated territory."[44]

The territory Anderson describes here, however, *is* compatible with a concept of legal legitimacy that transcends the regional root of common law. In Jeremy Bentham's utilitarian approach to law, for example, the tie between right and place is dissolved. As Bentham states in his critique of Blackstone:

With respect then to such actions in particular as are among the objects of the Law, to point out to a man the *utility* of them or the mischievousness, is the only way to make him see *clearly* that property of them which every man is in search of; the only way, in short, to give him *satisfaction* ... Governed in this manner by a principle that is recognized by all men, the same arrangement that would serve for the jurisprudence of any one country, would serve with little variation for that of any other.[45]

Bentham presupposes here a national space that is merely the empty homogeneous container for a rational and uniform legislation. We can pinpoint the implication of the passage by saying that to the extent that the law is not a manifestation of custom and regional difference, a national territory can emerge that serves as the neutral receptacle for a rational, uniformly applicable code of law. This means, however, that the law ceases to be territorial and is detached from landed property, history, and local custom. As a result, the authorization of law as the historically condensed and nationally specific expression of a people and their customs is disabled. The law's authority, in Bentham's model, is founded not on the epistemological inaccessibility of legal origins, but on the rational faculty of man. As Bentham's language shows, legitimacy can be achieved only through equal and unlimited visibility: it is essential that every individual "see *clearly* that property [of those actions regulated by the law] which every man is in search of." Utility, the transparent self-interest of the rational individual, not custom, the accumulated usage of past generations, determines the legitimacy of the law. The utilitarian relocation of legitimacy undercuts the territorial diversity stipulated by a law based on local custom and provides the conceptual means to homogenize the national space.

As his critique of the administrative changes in postrevolutionary France shows, Scott was clearly aware of the connection between a uniform system of legislation and a homogenized national space:

When . . . the whole system of provinces, districts, and feudal jurisdictions, great and small, had fallen at the word of the Abbé Siêyes, like an enchanted castle at the dissolution of a spell, and their various laws, whether written or consuetudinary, were buried in the ruins, all France, now united into one single and integral nation, lay open to receive any legislative code which the National Assembly might dictate.[46]

The figure of the disenchanted castle in this passage resonates with its use in Burke's *Reflections on the Revolution in France,* but its most immediate function here is not to embody a cumulative logic. Although Scott uses the castle metaphor elsewhere in a rather Blackstonean fashion to characterize the Scottish constitution, the castle's architectural heterogeneity serves in this passage as a figure for a discontinuous, uneven national territory whose legal constitution is determined by the strictly local association of land and law. Burke himself had characterized the French attempt at rationalizing its national space as a "carte blanche" approach that destroyed the "old bounds of provinces and jurisdictions, ecclesiastical and secular, and . . . all ancient combinations of things."[47] If we turn Scott's metaphor around, the "combination" of right and place is to him "enchanting" because it resists the visibility and uniformity that Bentham presents as the only reasonable basis for law.

The disaggregation of landed property, law, and custom; the relocation of legitimacy; and the concomitant homogenization of national space in the utilitarian legal model clarify what is at stake in *Waverley's* transformation of property. With every one of its carefully concealed actions, the English intervention into Scottish property relations disembeds property from its "ancient combinations." In the process property is unlocked not only from a fourteenth-century entail, Scottish ownership, Scottish history, and the Stuart line, but also from a system of heritable jurisdiction whose validity rested in the common law's logic of legitimacy. In eighteenth-century Scottish legal thought, this logic, as we have seen, took on particular national connotations. Yet by the end of *Waverley,* the juridico-national order that had joined Scots law and land has been brought to the point of dissolution. Scottish property and territory are disenchanted and enter the dominion of Britain, thus preparing for the homogenized space of the modern nation state.

IV

Scott's initial success in presenting Tully-Veolan as "enchanted" (I:116) has a good deal to do with the split between visibility and knowledge embodied by the Bears of Bradwardine. If the legitimacy of law depends on customs "time out of mind," a certain degree of obscurity or invisibility is indispensable. Like the Gothic castle, the Bears of Bradwardine make no sense to those who rely only on their sight – to those who, like Bentham, consider universal visibility as the crucial criterion of legality. Bentham as well as Paine considered the law to be an "unembodied system" (as Scott once described the utilitarian vision), a transparent code of written and theoretically consistent rules whose legitimacy rests on explicit contractual recognition.[48] Their argument against the equation of law with custom strikes at the common law's dependence on an inaccessible and invisible origin. The common law's foundational paradox – that, even though the origin of law is inaccessible, it still constitutes the basis of all legal knowledge – is put under pressure by a claim for the strict congruence between knowing and seeing. Paine's argument against what I want to call Burke's (but also Blackstone's) "constitutional sublime" strives to erase the difference between the knowable and the visible by rendering these terms tautological. Not only does Paine insist throughout *The Rights of Man* (1792) on the ideological nature of a legitimacy based on obscure or invisible origins, he also conceives of government as a transparent order in which what you can see has to be congruent with what you can know.[49] "Government in a well constituted republic," he states, "requires no belief from man beyond what his reason can give. He sees the *rationale* of the whole system, its origin and its operation; and as it is best supported when best understood, the human faculties act with boldness."[50] In this passage the congruence between what can be "seen" and what can be "understood" ensures transparency and legitimacy. This is confirmed by Paine's explicit association, elsewhere in *The Rights*, of reason with an act of seeing.[51] Only to the extent that seeing makes instantly grasping a government's "origin and operation" possible is a republic "well-constituted." But that constitution would be immediately threatened if a knowledge emerged that could not be reached by seeing (and thus by reason): it would be threatened if "belief" played a role in the establishment of legitimacy – the kind of belief that an intangible source of legitimacy requires.

This is Paine's argument against the British constitution and its common law defender, Burke.[52] The British constitution – that "invisible quiddity," as Bentham once called it – has for Paine an obscure reality-status because it remains merely "ideal."[53] "A constitution," he explains, "is not a thing in name only, but in fact. It has not an ideal, but a real existence; and wherever it cannot be produced in a visible form, there is none."[54] The enforcing of a congruence between reality and visibility that is here brought to bear on the "invisible" British constitution and its model of legitimacy could not be clearer. Only when to see and to know are epistemologically identical operations can legitimacy be shown to have a basis in reality. Within this constitutional logic the Bears of Bradwardine have no place. The split between seeing and knowing dramatized by their unshapely mass represents a social formation in which authority and legitimacy remain invisible because they are embedded in the lived relation of local custom. Yet even before the bears are "hurled" from their place by English soldiers, Scott discloses that his descriptive practice belongs to a different social formation, one in which landed property has lost most of its communal functions. In fact, it is only by acting from within this modern social formation that Scott is able to present such an economical sketch of a traditionalist social order. Scott's initial presentation of Tully-Veolan has a customary order for its object, and his descriptive strategy reveals that the combination of property, land, and law has lost its hold. The emphasis on figures of obscurity like the unshapely masses of the bears cannot conceal the fact that, ultimately, *Waverley*'s description presents the Bradwardine manor as an eminently visible object.

Scott's opening gesture in describing Tully-Veolan presents the landed estate as an object of knowledge, an historical artifact whose shape is being explored by the approaching Englishman Waverley. "A Scottish Manor-House Sixty Years Since": with this chapter title and the opening sentence – "it was about noon when Captain Waverley entered the straggling village" – Scott sets in motion a gradual and methodical process of investigation. Unlike Fielding, Scott does not present property in the form of a prospect. Fielding's overwhelming presentation of variety, extent, and undulation is broken up by Waverley's exploration of the estate in deliberate and clearly marked stages, which move us slowly from village to park, house, court, and garden. The proximate panorama of Paradise Hall is parceled out into the successive phases of Waverley's journey, and it is this movement that ultimately holds together the different sites of Scott's extensive description. This method allows Scott to focus on regional particularities such as Scottish vegetation and the political economy of the Scottish village without becoming completely absorbed in detail. Waverley's journey endows the description with a moving perspectival center that ensures an overall directedness and supports the kind of systematic inquiry into social life that Anthony Giddens stresses as an important trait of modernity.[55] Radcliffe's central descriptive device, the frame, is not needed to stabilize the close observance of detail. Instead, the successive stages of Waverley's journey, its temporality, break down and scrutinize Tully-Veolan's material extension.

This linkage of description to a narrative movement replicates what I observed earlier about the narrative integration of Tully-Veolan's different descriptive scenes. Just as the different states of the Bradwardine manor are linked by the narrative progression of Scott's tale of the Jacobite rebellion, so are the different parts of the Bradwardine property connected in Waverley's journey. In Scott's initial description of Tully-Veolan, time punctures space doubly: the landed estate is not only located on a precise point of an open-ended temporal line ("sixty years since"), but its material aspects emerge successively, through the investigative progress of Waverley's journey. The "crowding" that was so essential to Fielding's rendition of the manor's embedded order is here broken down into the temporal succession of different sites. Time is no longer tied to appearance; it becomes the container of material reality, the abstract medium through which the landed order of Tully-Veolan, along with its immemorial bears, is seen.

Given my emphasis on the interrelation of time, space, and practice, it should not surprise us that space, too, is separated from the materiality of things. Tully-Veolan's orderly distribution into the different parts of village, park, house, court, and garden not only suggests a general divisibility of the manor, but conjures an abstract space that exists independently of these physical parts. This sense of space as an independent reality is created in the following descriptive passage:

The southern side of the house, clothed with fruit-trees, and having many evergreens trained upon its walls, extended its irregular yet venerable front, along a terrace, partly paved, partly gravelled, partly bordered with flowers and choice shrubs. This elevation descended by three several flights of steps, placed in its center and at the extremities, into what might be called the garden proper, and was fenced along the top by a stone parapet with a heavy ballustrade, ornamented from space to space with huge grotesque figures of animals seated

upon their haunches, among which the favourite bear was repeatedly introduced. Placed in the middle of the terrace, between a sashed-door opening
from the house and the central flight of steps, a huge animal of the same species
supported on his head and fore paws a sun-dial of large circumference, inscribed
with more diagrams than Edward's mathematics enabled him to decipher.

The garden, which seemed to be kept with great accuracy and abounded in
fruit-trees, exhibited a profusion of flowers and evergreens, cut into grotesque
forms. It was laid out in terraces, which descended rank by rank from the western
wall to a large brook, which had a tranquil and smooth appearance, where it
served as a boundary to the garden. (I:113–115)

This passage exemplifies what I consider the crucial trait of Scott's descriptive production of space: the juxtaposition of outline and intricacy.
Scott is clearly concerned with naming and positioning the general architectural elements of his scene, yet he is consistently trying to complicate
the outline he creates. Thus the southern side of the house is "clothed
with fruit-trees, and having many evergreens trained upon its walls," the
terrace that runs parallel to this side is "partly paved, partly gravelled,
partly bordered," and the balustrade that "fenced along" the terrace is
ornamented with "huge grotesque figures." The term "grotesque" recurs
soon after to enliven a neatly terraced garden, kept with "great accuracy." One has the impression, indeed, that the basic elements of this
description – southern side of the house, terrace, ballustrade, western
wall – are dressed up so as to look less vacant than they really are.

The most symptomatic sentence in this respect is the one that places
an indecipherable sun-dial in the shape of a bear "in the middle of
the terrace, between a sashed-door opening from the house and the
central flight of steps." That the indecipherable becomes topical here
indicates Scott's desire to present the manor as something that is not
easily grasped, something that eludes the inquisitive gaze. Yet the carefully circumstantial positioning of the indecipherable reveals a contrary
impulse and effectively disenchants the seemingly obscure by assigning
precise limits. From the perspective of this reading, even the mutilated
masses that guard Tully-Veolan's gate appear in a different light. Although they symbolize a customary order, the bears' separation of the
knowable from the visible occurs within a methodically articulated topography whose illegible aspects are decorative rather than substantial.
The visibility of Scott's descriptive scene is maintained by a closely articulated relationality that deepens our sense of space as an independent reality. A series of spatial directions quietly pervades everything,
ranging from "southern side," "western wall," "boundary to the garden,"

to "center," "extremities," "top," "along," "middle," "between," "central." Perhaps even more than the stress on architectural elements, these directions bring to life a sense of space as a homogeneous sphere within which everything can be located. If the methodical distribution of the different parts of the manor suggested a space that exists independently of the concrete particular, the careful interrelation of these parts creates the illusion of a detachable grid within which things occupy a place.

The picturesque elements that Scott interjects into his description have ultimately no life of their own. The "grotesque" forms and figures resemble hangings on a wall and have lost the last vestiges of animatedness that they possessed in Radcliffe. Scott criticized Radcliffe's descriptive practice for not "communicating any absolute precise or individual image to the reader," charging that Radcliffe's "warm and somewhat exuberant imagination" left a "haze over her landscape." The animated picturesque scenes of Radcliffe's landscape are for Scott insufficiently pictorial. His own descriptive practice, indeed, does not, as he observed of Radcliffe's, "leave the task of tracing a distinct and accurate outline to the imagination of the painter."[56] In Scott background and foreground, ground and figure, space and appearance, are clearly separated. Things can now be viewed as purely aesthetic phenomena, distanced from the human and the social by being inserted into a homogenized, abstract space in which they appear as such, with their own set of independent relations, constituting a world of their own. This sense of the landed estate as a collection of related objects that exist apart from the human is strikingly evoked in Scott's initial presentation of the manor as a deserted place. With the exception of the village, the methodical description of the manor's material reality is uninterrupted by the presence of inhabitants. Park, house, court, and garden seem empty and are offered up as objects for undisturbed aesthetic consumption. Having lost the residual life they still possessed in Radcliffe, and being released into the abstract space of their own relationality, things now stand apart in their order and can become the objects of a detached and historically informed aesthetic sense that is purged of the "excesses" of Radcliffe's "warm and somewhat exuberant imagination."

Adumbrating the eventual narrative disembedding of property, Scott's initial description of Tully-Veolan thus already undercuts the regional association of property and land. The heterogeneous national territory of Scotland is quietly inserted into the homogeneous space of the modern nation state. Its ambassador is Waverley, whose gradual approach and unfamiliarity with Scotland brings a British perspective to bear on Tully-Veolan. The inquisitive segmentation and methodical representation this approach brings with it dispels property's primary relation to land. By stimulating a perception of space as a homogeneous sphere, Scott's description turns the Scottish landed estate into a foreground whose objective shape emerges against the neutralizing background of an abstract spatial relationality. In Scott's landscape the common law's conception of territory as fundamentally connected, via custom and inheritance, to those who occupy it, becomes topical, a visible foreground that no longer shapes the scene. The novelist's description forges an alliance between the visible and the knowable that makes possible the thematization of the split between these two categories in the symbol of the bears.

Considered from an epistemological perspective, Tully-Veolan's carefully articulated grid of spatial relations resembles a homogeneous conceptual space predicated on the assumption that, in principle, the rational mind can examine everything and integrate it into a network of clearly defined relations. If, as Scott remarks in his critique of the Code Napoleon, "the Code of France may be compared to a warehouse built with much attention to architectural uniformity ... while the Common Law of England resembles the vaults of some huge Gothic building, dark ... and ill arranged," then the spatial segmentation of Tully-Veolan is ultimately more indebted to the "carte blanche" of the warehouse than the dark irregularity of the Gothic building.[57] As Scott takes us from village to park, house, court, and garden, a sense of spatial exactitude is imparted that allows us to draw a mental map of the landscape in which nothing is dark or approximate. Although the depiction occasionally gives the idea of a heterogeneous conceptual space that keeps certain areas inaccessible to human inquiry and thus recalls the epistemology of the common law, these ideas always appear as such within a carefully defined larger homogeneous space. The indecipherable sun-dial is not permitted to spread its confusions beyond the precisely designated spot it is assigned.

While the common law's construction of legitimacy relies on the assumption that not everything that can be known is visible, *Waverley's* description of landed property sponsors an epistemology that equates the knowable with the visible. The secret of the manor, that which cannot be seen – the ancestral past locked up in its material persistence and the community-creating patterns of heredity, custom, and allegiance – is already under pressure in Scott's initial descriptive production of a space and time that exist independently of property. The resultant visibility of property is explicitly thematized in the final depiction of Tully-Veolan, where Scott suggests that the rise of the modern nation state, dependent as it is on the disembedding of landed property, also promotes new modes of seeing and feeling.

v

Baron Bradwardine's final return to his temporarily forfeited estate silences this otherwise loquacious proprietor. As he approaches the avenue that Waverley had earlier passed along, the Baron falls "into a deep study . . . and was only startled from it by observing that the battlements were replaced, the ruins cleared away, and (most wonderful of all) that the two great stone Bears, those mutilated Dagons of his idolatry, had resumed their posts over the gateway" (III:343). Further on in this momentous return, the Baron gazes "in silent wonder" at "heedfully attended to" minutiae. Even later, the Baron falls into "a deep reverie" when he learns that, contrary to his initial assumption, this estate is not Colonel Talbot's but his own (III:355). This emphasis on silence and seeing marks the final chapter throughout, and I want to suggest that the Baron's mute gaze at his restored estate has something in common with Scott's own perplexed look upstream. The emphasis on the visual in both Scott's boat-ride metaphor and in his novel's denouement is itself expressive of an altered relation to the past.

The Baron's return initiates an extended act of visual comparison between the present and the past look of things. So meticulous has Waverley's restoration been that only "an eye intimately acquainted with the spot" could discover any change at all. The Baron's gaze and Scott's description of the restored estate replay, indeed, the process of restoration, which engendered an equally intense scrutiny of past and present appearances. Trying to assimilate property to its past image, such comparative scrutiny privileges the visual and insulates the past from the present as it turns the former into an object of study and reproduction. By producing an imitation, Waverley's meticulous reconstruction transforms Tully-Veolan into a visual artifact. If such visibility already undergirds the initial description of the Bradwardine estate, it is at the end that Scott's novel exposes the complicity between its own descriptive strategy and the museumizing activities of the English. The purification of Tully-Veolan here reaches its completion: under the concentrated gaze of Waverley's restorative fantasy, the Bradwardine estate turns into a representation of its former existence. From participating in a fading but still functional dynastic tradition, Scottish property comes to stand for that tradition and its communal forms. Already disembedded from its social, political, and national contexts, the Bradwardine manor becomes a museum of Scottish history.

This is nowhere more evident than in the "one addition" that Waverley makes to the interior of the Bradwardine mansion:

It was a large and spirited painting, representing Fergus Mac-Ivor and Waverley in their Highland dress, the scene a wild, rocky, and mountainous pass, down which the clan were descending in the back-ground. It was taken from a spirited sketch, drawn while they were in Edinburgh by a young man of high genius, and had been painted on a full length scale by an eminent London artist. Raeburn himself, (whose Highland Chiefs do all but walk out of the canvas) could not have done more justice to the subject. (III:359)

This passage extends the visualization of the past that informs Scott's conclusion as a whole. Reproducing a tension that is integral to *Waverley*'s poetics, the painting arrests the Scottish past in pictorial stasis, but also evokes it powerfully – it is done on a "full length scale" and its fig-ures, rebellious Highland Jacobites, seem poised to walk back into the present. Still, all remains under English control. In a familiar pattern Scottish things pass through English hands and return transformed – clearly visible and stripped of their native power. The image of Scottish independence, sketched in Scotland at the height of the '45, is ultimately painted by an Englishman on behalf of another Englishman, Waverley, who reintroduces the painting into Scotland. Though it strives to be more than that, the painting remains a framed artifact, suspended from the walls of a building that itself has undergone an English reimaging.

Baron Bradwardine's response to this painting mirrors his response to the restoration of all his movable and immovable belongings: he cries. The Baron is not usually lachrymose, but in Scott's ending he is thor-oughly sentimentalized. He not only gazes and dreams, but repeatedly takes "long snuff[s]" (III:344, 349) and sheds tears (III:346, 359, 363). This reaction cannot simply be attributed to the comic tone of the ending. The Baron's sentimentalism goes deeper and needs to be considered in relation to Tully-Veolan's strange new visibility. It indicates that *Waverley*'s transformation of property also opens up an affective relation between persons and things. The Baron's tears are the product of *Waverley*'s com-modification of property. Tully-Veolan's destruction and forfeiture, its neutralizing passage through the real-estate market, and its subsequent restoration produce the distance between owner and thing requisite for the projection of feeling on to material reality. Tully-Veolan's visibility is at once the effect of its commodification and the cause for its availability as an object of affection. In fantastically condensed form, Scott's ending thus contains a history of sensibility in which reification, visual arrest, and emotional display are identified as the combined effects of the breakdown of manorial forms of community. In this way, too, Scott's novel erases the difference between movable and immovable property. What the snuffboxes and miniatures in the novel of sensibility achieved is here extended to the once indivisible and unwieldy manor, which has turned itself into the small and highly visible estate that Adam Smith recommended as the preferable object of modern commercial sympathy.[58]

Disembedded from its participation in the past, from its concrete organization of national and political community, the Bradwardine manor finally turns into a thing. On the market its exchangeability for other things becomes its socially relevant feature, and what before were esoteric relations of permanent attachment between persons and things are now exoteric relations between things.[59] The sale separates the order of persons from the order of things, and the distance between them is the driving force behind the Baron's lachrymose lingering over the details of restoration. His tears pronounce the end of all Jacobite hopes and the death of the possessive community's incorporating and participatory modes. From now on, things are liberated from their direct involvement with person, community, and state, and lie ready to receive the tender antiquarian gaze of the bourgeois – not of "Baron Bradwardine," as the new (and old) owner of Tully-Veolan is careful to note, but of "Mr. Bradwardine" (III:346). At the end of *Waverley*, property is no longer the center of a legitimizing nexus whose grasp extends beyond its material presence into the domains of local government, history, and state. On the contrary, that material presence itself has now become the limit of property's definition. Its form is now a shiny exterior that imposes a strict dividing line between its material identity and everything that surrounds it. The Bradwardine mansion can no longer be reached, except by the idealizing mechanism of projection, and the Baron's tears mourn this loss of a more tactile relationship. Immovable and movable property are now equals, fully objectified in a rational time-space.

Not surprisingly, Scott is not entirely comfortable with this state of affairs, and he leaves open the possibility of reading the Baron's tears as tears of recognition, as an acknowledgment that what he sees on his return is, in fact, his estate "as he had left it when he assumed arms some months before" (III:347). This is an important aspect of Scott's complicated denouement and needs to be taken seriously. But with characteristic doubleness, Scott places a large signpost over his last chapter that reveals the conceit and acknowledges the reality of the change Tully-Veolan undergoes. The chapter title bluntly declares that, in spite of the meticulous restoration, Tully-Veolan has no connection to its earlier existence: "This is no mine ain house, I ken by the bigging o't" (III:342; "This is not my own house, I recognize by the building of it"). Scott's gaze backwards, like the Baron's, remains irreducibly ambivalent. Clouded by tears, it acknowledges the fundamental difference between past and present as well as its own dependence on that difference, yet desires to see things as they once were.

Waverley's narrative and descriptive disembedding of the manor suggests that Scott's Burkean traditionalism is compromised by his own realization that the "ancient combination of things" is lost not only in France or England, but also – and perhaps especially – in Scotland. A defender of traditionalist ways of community by political inclination, Scott bids goodbye to "ancient combination[s]" in a novel that appears to rescue old ways from disappearance. Whatever Scott's longings may be, the transformation of national and political community in *Waverley*'s depiction of property winds up by affirming as historical reality the legal epistemology of Bentham and Paine. Like them, Scott in the end realized that the decline of landed property as a communal paradigm was at the base of new forms of personal, political, and national identity. The enchanting disenchantment of Tully-Veolan that Scott delivers at the end of *Waverley* articulates these new forms through a layer of eloquent dissimulations.

Conclusion

Communal forms – the changing configuration of persons and things and its influence on the broad relationship between time, space, and practice – have been a key element in my argument. They have brought a unified perspective to my analyses and have resisted, as far as that is possible, the individualized, privatized, and reified outlook of modern capitalism. Their resolute stress on relationships has clarified that no exclusive focus on either persons or things can do justice to the social function of literature, and that, in order to recognize literature as a "symbolic meditation on the destiny of community," we have to acknowledge the unity of human and material spheres.[1] The recovery of such unity, indeed, has been one of the leitmotifs of this study as it has moved from a literalist reinterpretation of Locke's "mixing" metaphor to the contextualizing powers of the mercantile fetish, and from the Gothic castle as the ineluctable ground of political community to the sentimental and picturesque production of affective distance. In these cases and in others, the emphasis on communal form has ensured that the close analysis of property in a variety of texts could reveal social, economic, epistemological, and psychological limits to community.

The most important aspect of such unity on the level of literary form has been the relationship between narrative and description. Much vilified as an agent and embodiment of reification, description has been shown to be a relational and predictive mode that intersects human and material spheres. Descriptions have been a central focus of analysis here because the communal imagination finds in them a significant forum to rewrite the material world and its relationship to the human. Precisely because it is a relational and predictive mode, however, the descriptive cannot be rigorously distinguished from the world of narrative, whose distributional functions represent the relationship between human and material spheres on a different, but related, level. The historical pattern that has emerged in this study cuts against Gerard Genette's suggestion of an earlier separation of description from narrative and a subsequent subordination by which description turns itself into a useful contributor to an overarching narrative enterprise. Within the same time period that underlies Genette's sketch, I have found that, initially, narrative and description are closely aligned, with description articulating narrative patterns and narrative assuming descriptive functions. In fact, it may very well be that the closeness of this alignment with narrative is one of the reasons why eighteenth-century fiction has not been recognized as significantly engaged with the descriptive. While it should be evident at this point that the link between description and narrative is central to the course of eighteenth-century prose fiction in Britain, a highly detailed statement about the development of that link remains difficult. What this study has been able to do, however, is to draw out a general pattern: it now seems clear that an initial alignment of narrative and descriptive functions is followed first by a gradual differentiation (brought about in part by an increased emphasis on pictorial elements and the decline of circulation as an economic and fictional paradigm), and then a more complex integration of narrative and description in the historical novel (which appears itself as an aspect of the increased economic and fictional emphasis on production and reproduction in early nineteenth-century Britain).[2]

This broad outline – initial connection, subsequent differentiation, and reconnection on a more complex and diffuse level – is, of course, familiar. It underlies Bruno Latour's account of modernization as much as it does Anthony Giddens's or Michel Foucault's. The emphasis in this study has been predominantly on the first and second phases and the prolonged struggle of the novel – that prototypically modern genre – to refigure the possessive culture of eighteenth-century Britain. What I have been arguing for is not a revision of the basic pattern of modernization, but a conceptual and chronological adjustment that responds to the particular circumstances of eighteenth-century Britain. The tenacity with which British institutions of property cling to the actual and ideological construction of community is to my mind the best explanation available for both the extent and the profundity of the novel's attempt to differentiate between persons and things. If a genre as closely associated with the process of modernization as the novel repeats, with considerable insistence throughout the eighteenth century, scenarios of how objects constitute subjects, and how subjects fail to differentiate themselves from the material world, Latour's and Foucault's arguments about the enthronement of the subject come under considerable pressure, at least as regards Britain. If the most modern economy of eighteenth-century Europe arises, somewhat paradoxically, out of the powerful persistence of a patrician society, a similar paradox would seem to govern an important aspect of British literary production. Here, too, one of the most modern and influential genres, the novel, seems to grow out of a complex engagement with the forces of the old society – with forms of community that emphasize tangible, concrete links between persons and things.

That these concrete links are eventually broken up and transformed into ideal relationships may suggest a fundamental change. The term "community," indeed, may seem inappropriate for the distancing of persons and things toward the end of the eighteenth century. But discarding the category of communal form to approach these new relationships would be unwise. After all, Marx's commodity fetish, according to the materialist reading I have been pursuing, was meant to recover the tangible mixture of persons and things that breathed beneath the alien materiality of the reified object. A powerful continuity links Locke's conception of property as arising out of a "mixture" of persons and things and Marx's sense of a "Stoffwechsel" (literally, an "exchange of matter") between human and material spheres. While each socio-economic formation produces its own distinct types of fetishism, the fetish remains the most useful general symbol we have to represent this inescapable entanglement with the material world. No break, revolution, or rupture can separate us from the fundamental continuity and essential community of our life in and through things.

Our entanglement with things has also manifested itself on a level that I have not been able to develop properly here, but to which I wish to draw attention. I believe that, in the end, our inability to distinguish rigorously between narrative and description is directly related to our inability – despite and because of the extensive reifications we have experienced under older and newer forms of capitalism – to distinguish rigorously between persons and things. I realize this is a provocative statement that I cannot substantiate here, but this book has at least been able to suggest a basic similarity between the way the novel figures things and the way it figures persons. The transformative powers of the mercantile commodity, for instance, mirror the transformations of Defoe's protagonists as they traverse uneven social and economic spaces, and Defoe's penchant for descriptive enumeration seems to be related to his narrative structures, whose effortless expandability and collective character recall the image of the list. Similar statements could be made about *Tom Jones*'s nontransformative circulation of persons and things and the embedding figurations of the undulating line (the list and the line might be viewed as the irreducible relational figures that underlie the construction of community – of persons and things – in Defoe and Fielding).

Perhaps the most dramatic instance of such similarity between persons and things is the shift effected by sentimental texts, whose framings begin to transfigure the permeable, "flat" persons and things of mercantile capitalism into the closed, "round" equivalents of a more advanced capitalist mode with its familiar play of absence and presence, distance and depth, lively feeling and deadening fixation.[3] In this way even the distancing of persons and things achieved by the novel ends up confirming the essential relatedness of the human and the material. The anthropologist Igor Kopytoff might be right when he states, extending an insight by Emile Durkheim, that "societies constrain [material and human] worlds simultaneously and in the same way, constructing objects as they construct people."[4] Such a conception underlines not only the unity of human and material spheres that I have been concerned with throughout, but also the overlaps and continuities between "premodern" and "modern" person-thing communities in the period I have been investigating. In this sense the slogan "we have never been modern" has indeed particular applicability to eighteenth-century Britain.

Notes

INTRODUCTION

1. Lukács, *Geschichte und Klassenbewußtsein*, 372 (my translation).
2. Ibid., 262. Jameson, for example, compares the "relatively natural precapitalist relationship to objects and our own" in *Marxism and Form*, 394. Goldmann articulates closely related distinctions in *Recherche Dialectique*, 64–106 (the phrase "*économie naturelle*" can be found on page 72) and in *Towards a Sociology of the Novel*, 1–18. The most vivid example for Adorno's tendency to contrast synthetic unity and depraved fragmentation as characteristics of cultural artifacts that resist or yield to capitalist reification can be found in his "Über den Fetischcharakter in der Musik," 18, 23, 28–29, 32. As Peter Bürger has shown, such idealizing tendencies can even be found in Adorno's late aesthetic. See Bürger's analysis of Adorno's defense of aesthetic "Schein" in his *Zur Kritik der Idealistischen Ästhetik*, 59–77.
3. Baudrillard's work of the late 1960s/early 1970s offers a stirring critique of the Marxist reliance on idealized contrasts between, for instance, use value/exchange value, quality/quantity. Often, however, that critique spins out of control because Baudrillard is too interested in replacing a materialist with a semiological approach. See, for example, *The Mirror of Production* and *For a Critique of the Political Economy of the Sign*.
4. Pocock's argument on civic humanism's escape from materialism can be found in *Virtue, Commerce, and History*, 43–44.
5. Pocock himself indicates that classical republicanism complemented actually existing British traditions of landed property. See *Virtue, Commerce, and History*, 107.
6. I confine myself here to three massive volumes that document the extensive new research in this area: *Consumption and the World of Goods*, ed. Brewer and Porter; *Early Modern Conceptions of Property*, ed. Brewer and Staves; and *The Consumption of Culture*, ed. Bermingham and Brewer.
7. Interestingly enough, Jameson suggests that the best available theoretical model to explain the "intensities" that mark the "waning of affect" in postmodern culture are "older theories of the sublime" – theories, in other words, that assumed new cultural importance in the eighteenth century: *Postmodernism*, 6; more generally, 1–55.

8. See, for example, Haraway, "A Cyborg Manifesto: Science, Technology, and Socialist-Feminism in the Late Twentieth Century," *Simians, Cyborgs, and Women: The Reinvention of Nature*, 149–182, and Latour, *We Have Never Been Modern*.
9. Paine, *Letter Addressed to the Addressers on the Late Proclamation* (1792), reproduced in *The Thomas Paine Reader*, ed. Foot and Kramnick, 380.
10. Latour, *We Have Never Been Modern*, 82.

I COMMUNAL FORM AND THE TRANSITIONAL CULTURE OF THE EIGHTEENTH-CENTURY NOVEL

1. This point is made extensively by McNally, *Political Economy and the Rise of Capitalism*, 1–15.
2. For a useful summary of basic economic changes in the second half of the eighteenth century, see Perkin, *Origins of Modern English Society*, 1–16. The most extensive study of property's influence on Britain's public life is Langford's *Public Life and the Propertied Englishman*.
3. On Smith's reliance on landed property and agriculture, see McNally, *Political Economy and the Rise of Capitalism*, 209–258. Smith's recognition of commodities as central indicators of stages of development is emphasized in Buck-Morss, "Envisioning Capital," especially 450–457.
4. I am alluding here to McKendrick, *The Birth of a Consumer Culture*.
5. On the role of Chancery in commercial law, see Lieberman, *The Province of Legislation Determined*, 99–122.
6. On the transition from property to contract as a dominant legal paradigm, see Atiyah, *The Rise and Fall of Freedom of Contract*, 91–112. Horwitz has argued for this transition in the American context in *The Transformation of American Law*.
7. On eighteenth-century anxieties over the future-oriented mentalities engendered by the stockmarket, see Pocock, *Virtue, Commerce, and History*, 112–113.
8. On the equity of redemption, see Sugarman and Warrington, "Land, Law, Citizenship, and the Invention of Englishness," 111–143. See also Langford, *Public Life and the Propertied Englishman*, 145 ff.
9. I take these numbers from Hay's excellent "Property, Authority, and the Criminal Law," 18.
10. On the Black Act, see E. P. Thompson, *Whigs and Hunters*.
11. Langford, *Public Life and the Propertied Englishman*, vii.
12. On women's property, see Staves, *Married Women's Separate Property in England*, and Erickson, *Women and Property in Early Modern England*.
13. Dickinson, *Liberty and Property*, 41–48.
14. See Nenner's argument on the Glorious Revolution as a triumph of private property and common law, *By Colour of Law*, especially 155–197. On the increasing use of property terms in seventeenth-century political debates, see Schlatter, *Private Property*, 11. On the rise of common law in the seventeenth century, see Levack, *The Civil Lawyers in England*, 122–158.

15. Maitland, *The Constitutional History of England*, 538.
16. Gellner, *Nations and Nationalism*, 4.
17. Paine attacks the insufficient differentiation between society and government as early as 1776 in *Common Sense*. See *The Thomas Paine Reader*, 66.
18. In this assessment I follow, among others, Finer, *Comparative Government*; R. J. Smith, *The Gothic Bequest*; Langford, *Public Life and the Propertied Englishman*; and Clark, *The Language of Liberty*.
19. Nairn, *The Break-Up of Britain*, 19.
20. See McNally, *Political Economy and the Rise of Capitalism*, xv, and Neale, *Class in English History*, 94, 99. Williams captures the process of transitionalism in terms that are congenial to this study in *The Country and the City*, 35.
21. Benedict Anderson, *Imagined Communities*, 4.
22. For Anderson's discussion of the "old-fashioned novel" (which turns out to be the nineteenth-century novel), see ibid., 22–32.
23. The initial publication, in 1976, of Lefebvre's *The Production of Space* marks the resurgence of space as a historical and cultural category. For a history of this resurgence, see Soja, *Postmodern Geographies*.
24. Giddens, *The Consequences of Modernity*, 105, 53.
25. Studies of the country house poem include Kelsall, *The Great Good Place*; McClung, *The Country House in English Renaissance Poetry*; and Kenny, *The Country-House Ethos in English Literature*.
26. Carter expands on a remark by Edward Coke: *Lex Custumaria*, A3v.
27. Thompson himself concedes that manorial holdings were socially and economically not dominant. See "The Grid of Inheritance," in his *Persons and Polemics*, 263–300.
28. See Jessel, *The Law of the Manor*, 405–415. Blount's *Fragmenta Antiquitatis: Ancient Tenures of Land and Jocular Customs of some Mannors* (1679) has to be counted as another sign of the manor's increasing legal visibility, as has Carter's *Lex Custumaria*.
29. Coke, *The Compleate Copy-Holder*, 8. Subsequent page references will appear in parentheses in the text.
30. See ibid., 5–6, 14, 65, 68 for the attempt to equate copyhold and freehold.
31. Blount, *Fragmenta Antiquitatis*, 160.
32. Carter, *Lex Custumaria*, 37, and Hale, *The History of the Common Law of England*, 144.
33. Blackstone, *Commentaries on the Laws of England*, I:76–77.
34. On custom in relation to time and tradition, see Pocock, *Politics, Language, and Time*, 233–273, and *Virtue, Commerce, and History*, 93–95.
35. See Langford, *Public Life and the Propertied Englishman*, 156–166.
36. Holdsworth, *A History of English Law*, X:426.
37. Defoe, *The Original Power of the Collective Body of the People of England Examined and Asserted*, 19.
38. Ibid., 20.
39. Schmitt, *Der Nomos der Erde*, 36–40.
40. Thompson, *Customs in Common*, 9.

41. Ibid., 43.
42. Hale, *The History of the Common Law of England*, 40.
43. Wasserman, *The Subtler Language*; Barrell, *The Idea of Landscape and the Sense of Place*; Turner, *The Politics of Landscape*; and Janowitz, *England's Ruins*.
44. A few critics have focused on eighteenth-century prose description, but Wall ("Details of Space"), Trickett (" 'Curious Eye' "), and Anne Williams ("Description and Tableau in the Eighteenth-Century British Sentimental Novel") have not made convincing claims for the importance of prose description. They either make description, in a familiar move, the servant of narrative (Wall, 405) or disclaim that novelistic description matters before the end of the century (Trickett, 250). Williams offers the puzzling claim that prose description in sentimental novels "is visual or graphic and denies the power of words" (469).
45. Lukács, *Writer and Critic and Other Essays*, 127.
46. Lukács, *Geschichte und Klassenbewußtsein*, 264. Translation adapted from Rodney Livingstone: Lukács, *History and Class Consciousness*, 90.
47. Beaujour, "Some Paradoxes of Description," 48, 27–59.
48. Barthes, "The Reality Effect," 136.
49. Ibid., 140.
50. Jameson, "The Realist Floor-Plan," 375.
51. Jameson calls "Describe or Narrate?" "one of Lukács's finest essays": *Marxism and Form*, 196. See also his remarks on the same essay in ibid., 200–202.
52. Jameson, "The Realist Floor-Plan," 375.
53. Lopes, *Foregrounded Description*, 6, 4.
54. Ibid., 6, 145–146.
55. Genette, *Figures of Literary Discourse*, 128.
56. Ibid., 134.
57. Ibid.
58. Ibid., 133, 136. See also Mitchell's discussion of Genette's argument: *Picture Theory*, 183–213.
59. Mitchell, *Picture Theory*, 154.
60. Cohen, *The Art of Discrimination*, 131.
61. Samuel Johnson, *Life of Savage*, 53. Johnson's critique of Thomson's *Seasons* follows similar lines. See *Lives of the English Poets*, III:299–300.
62. De Bossu, *Monsieur Bossu's Treatise of the Epick Poem*, II:246.
63. Ibid., 251.
64. Barthes, "The Reality Effect," 135.
65. De Bossu, *Treatise of the Epick Poem*, II:246.
66. Barthes, "The Reality Effect," 135.
67. See Mitchell's discussion of Whitman, *Homer and the Heroic Tradition*, Atchity, *Homer's Iliad: The Shield of Memory*, and Blanchard, "In the World of the Seven Cubit Spear" in his *Picture Theory*, 176–181.
68. See Bartsch, *Decoding the Ancient Novel*.
69. Trickett, " 'Curious Eye,' " 250.

70. Mitchell makes this comment (using Genette's conceptual categories) in a footnote: *Picture Theory*, 191.

2 *TERRA NULLIUS*, CANNIBALISM, AND THE NATURAL LAW OF APPROPRIATION

1. Ryan, *Property and Political Theory*, 7.
2. On the Norman origins of universal possession, see McNeil, *Common Law Aboriginal Title*, 80–86.
3. Blackstone, *Commentaries on the Laws of England*, II:258.
4. Ibid., II:258–262. On the marginal position of occupation in English legal practice, see also McNeil, *Common Law Aboriginal Title*, 73–74.
5. See Blackstone, *Commentaries on the Laws of England*, I:104.
6. Grisel emphasizes that the appropriation of the western hemisphere was conceptualized by backgrounding established national practice and foregrounding divine and natural law: "The Beginnings of International Law and General Public Law Doctrine," 305–325.
7. I disagree with Bartlett's dismissal of *terra nullius* as a critical category in the ruling: *The Mabo Decision*, ix, 41, 82–83, 142. My thanks to James Chandler for suggesting a discussion of the Mabo case.
8. For the centrality of occupation in justifying British colonial land claims, see Pagden's *Lords of All the World*, 63–103. Arneil has argued that Locke needs to be included in the British deployment of occupation: *John Locke and America*, 9, 118–131.
9. *The Journals of Captain James Cook*, vol. 1, ed. J. C. Beaglehole (Cambridge: Cambridge University Press, 1968), 397, quoted in Frost, "New South Wales as *Terra Nullius*," 520.
10. Vattel's work was quickly translated into English as *The Law of Nations* (1759). For a discussion of Vattel's significance, see Pagden, *Lords of All the World*, 78–79, and Green and Dickason, *The Law of Nations and the New World*, 73–75.
11. See Roberts-Wray's discussion of the distinction between territorial and proprietary title in *Commonwealth and Colonial Law*, 625–632.
12. In addition to Pagden's *Lords of All the World* (63–103) and Arneil's *Locke and America* (118–131), see for examination of the English way of colonial landtakings Seed's insightful *Ceremonies of Possession in Europe's Conquest of the New World*, 16–41.
13. Bartlett, *The Mabo Decision*, 64.
14. Ibid., 144.
15. Such precedent stretches back as far as 1832, when Chief Justice John Marshall, preferring conquest, dismissed occupation as establishing title to American land (*Worcester* v. *The State of Georgia* [1832]).
16. The gradual acceptance of *terra nullius* in the second half of the eighteenth century has been traced by Frost, "New South Wales as *Terra Nullius*," 513–518.

17. Gentili, *De Jure Belli*, translated by John C. Rolfe (Washington: Carnegie Classics, 1933), 80–81, quoted in Green and Dickason, *The Law of Nations and the New World*, 49.

18. For a detailed discussion of the medieval assumption that nature abhors a vacuum, see Grant, *Much Ado About Nothing*, 67–102.

19. Defoe, *Robinson Crusoe*, 166. Subsequent page references will appear in parentheses in the text.

20. For a reading of this passage that redeems its apparent conventionalism, see Richetti, *Defoe's Narratives*, 52–53.

21. Crusoe's fear of being devoured figures prominently, for instance, in Frank H. Ellis, *Twentieth-Century Interpretations of* Robinson Crusoe, 1–19; Homer Obed Brown, "The Displaced Self in the Novels of Daniel Defoe"; Zimmerman, *Defoe and the Novel*, 20–47; Pearlman, "*Robinson Crusoe* and the Cannibals"; Hulme, *Colonial Encounters*, 175–222; Gliserman, "*Robinson Crusoe*: The Vicissitudes of Greed," 197–231; Armstrong, "The Myth of Cronus"; and Markman Ellis, "Crusoe, Cannibalism, and Empire."

22. For arguments on the theological coherence of Crusoe's behavior, see Hunter, *The Reluctant Pilgrim*; Starr, *Defoe and Spiritual Autobiography*; and McKeon, *The Origins of the English Novel*, 315–337. McKeon argues that religious and economic coherence are joined on Crusoe's island. To make his case he has to downplay the "panic over the footprint" as a quickly recuperated "backsliding" (ibid., 318). Richetti recognizes the footprint's significance, but this is in tension with his overall emphasis on Crusoe's increasing self-mastery: *Defoe's Narratives*, 51. The classic reading of Crusoe as "modern economic man" is Watt's; see *The Rise of the Novel*, 60–93.

23. See footnote 21. Psychoanalytic readings are presented by Pearlman, "*Robinson Crusoe* and the Cannibals"; Armstrong, "The Myth of Cronus"; and Gliserman, "*Robinson Crusoe*: The Vicissitudes of Greed." Zimmerman touches on a central concern of this chapter when he remarks that the fear of being devoured constitutes a "reversal of the desire to accumulate": *Defoe and the Novel*, 32.

24. Hulme, *Colonial Encounters*, 176, 194–200.

25. Armstrong, "The Myth of Cronus," 208–213; Richetti, *Defoe's Narratives*, 49; and Zimmerman, *Defoe and the Novel*, 32.

26. I substantiate and complicate Richetti's suggestion that the cannibals are "full-fledged embodiments of [Crusoe's] anti-type": *Defoe's Narratives*, 51.

27. Hume, *A Treatise of Human Nature*, 506.

28. Textor, *Synopsis Juris Gentium* (Washington: Carnegie Classics, 1916), 66, quoted in Green and Dickason, *The Law of Nations and the New World*, 65; Bynkershoek, *Quaestionum Juris Publici*, translated by Tanney Frank (Washington: Carnegie Classics, 1930), 66, quoted ibid., 65; Gentili, *De Jure Belli*, 307, quoted ibid., 49. See also Pufendorf: "it is the customary thing that occupancy of movables be effected by the hands, of land by the feet": *De Jure Naturae Et Gentium Libri Octo*, II:577.

29. See McNeil's discussion of allegiance and royal authorization: *Common Law Aboriginal Title*, 116–117, 134–160. See also Roberts-Wray, *Commonwealth and Colonial Law*, 99–116.
30. Defoe, *The Farther Adventures of Robinson Crusoe*, 201.
31. Symcox, "The Battle of the Atlantic, 1500–1700," 267.
32. See Pagden's *Lords of All the World* (63–103); Seed's *Ceremonies of Possession*, (16–41); and Arneil's *Locke and America* (118–131).
33. Backscheider's attempt to relate Locke's treatise and Defoe's poem on a verbal level is unconvincing: "The Verse Essay, John Locke, and Defoe's *Jure Divino*."
34. Defoe, *Jure Divino*, IX:2–3.
35. Ibid., IV:1.
36. I strongly disagree with McKeon's suggestion that "long possession" plays a role in Crusoe's claim to the island: *The Origins of the English Novel*, 334.
37. Defoe, *Jure Divino*, IV:2.
38. Wood, *An Institute of the Laws of England*, 216–217.
39. Coke, *The Compleate Copy-Holder*, 52–53.
40. For Vitoria and the response of Spanish Thomism to the conquest, see Pagden, "Dispossessing the Barbarian," 79–98. See also Pagden's more extensive treatment of the Spanish tradition in *The Fall of Natural Man*. The following studies have informed my thinking on natural law: Tuck, *Natural Rights Theories*; Buckle, *Natural Law and the Theory of Property*; and Haakoonssen, *Natural Law and Moral Philosophy*.
41. For the relationship of natural law to seventeenth-century dissenters, see Gleissner, "The Levellers and Natural Law." Defoe quotes from the Latin edition of Grotius's *De Jure Belli Ac Pacis Libri Tres* in *Jure Divino* (III:26), he very likely owned Pufendorf's *Law of Nature and Nations* in the English edition of 1703 (see Aitken, "Defoe's Library," 706), and he refers to Locke, for example, in *Review* 108, 10 September 1706.
42. Grotius, *De Jure Belli Ac Pacis Libri Tres*, II:206, 191–192. For references to islands in Grotius, see ibid., II:92, 116, 192, 298, 301.
43. Ibid., II:190–191.
44. Ibid., II:220.
45. Locke, *Two Treatises of Government*, 292.
46. See Macpherson's discussion of this passage from Locke, *The Political Theory of Possessive Individualism*, 202.
47. Defoe, *Jure Divino* V:18; *The Complete English Tradesman in Familiar Letters* (London, 1727) I:ii, 29–30, quoted in James Thompson, *Models of Value*, 129.
48. "Then view the small Extent of Native Power,/And how unqualify'd their Subjects to devour"; "Despotick Governments are self-made things;/'Twas all usurp'd, 'twas all Tyrannic Power,/Which made great families the Small Devour"; (when Subjects) "Prompt him to exercise Tyrannick Power,/And tell him they're the Men he may Devour" (*Jure Divino*, II:3, II:20, IV:24). Examples could be multiplied; see also *Jure Divino* I:5, V:1.
49. Defoe, ibid., I:6.

50. See Defoe's preface to *Jure Divino* for his rejection of a commonwealth (I:iv).
51. Defoe, *The Original Power of the Collective Body of the People of England Examined and Asserted*, 18, 19.
52. Ibid., 19.
53. Ibid.
54. Ibid., dedication.
55. Ibid., 20.
56. Locke, *Two Treatises of Government*, 323.
57. Defoe, *The Original Power of the Collective Body of the People of England Examined and Asserted*, 5, 6, 13, 15.
58. Defoe follows a long tradition of natural law thought that Tuck, in *Natural Rights Theories*, traces back to the Middle Ages when rights were first viewed as something that we "possess."
59. Defoe, *Jure Divino*, VI:19.
60. The phrase "preservation of property" comes from Locke, *Two Treatises of Government*, 360. See also the following closely related passage from *Jure Divino* in which the sphere of one's own is irreducible to property or self: "I never found a Man so void of Sense,/As freely to abandon Self-defence;/Basely from Sense of Loyalty and Law,/Shou'd from his juster Liberties withdraw;/That to a Tyrant should his Life Subject,/And not his injur'd Property protect./That, blest with Power, should all that Power lay down,/And die a Victim to that god the Crown" (IV:14).
61. Defoe, ibid., II:3, I:5.
62. Locke, *Two Treatises on Government*, 298.
63. For an instructive account that places Locke's thinking on property and the sphere of one's own in the context of natural law, see Buckle, *Natural Law and the Theory of Property*, 125–191.
64. Locke, *Two Treatises of Government*, ed. Laslett, 287–288. In his introduction to *Two Treatises*, Laslett points out that Richard Baxter's writings are another channel that transmitted this line of thought. One might add, at least with respect to the notion of a possessive self, radical English Protestant writings from the period of the Civil War, a tradition Macpherson and Tuck have illuminated: *Political Theory of Possessive Individualism*, 107–160, and *Natural Rights Theories*, 143–156.
65. I argue here against Novak's contention that Locke's model of appropriation plays no role in the acquisition of the island: *Defoe and the Nature of Man*, 51. When Novak recommends Grotius's account of occupation, he overlooks significant continuities between Grotius and Locke. As Tuck contends, Locke's treatise needs to be seen as an extension of the Grotian account of property: *Natural Rights Theories*, 169–173.
66. Pufendorf, *De Jure Naturae Et Gentium Libri Octo*, II:16.
67. The only account I know that emphasizes the corporal tie between self and property in Locke is Olivecrona's "Locke's Theory of Appropriation."
68. The passage I refer to is in Locke, *An Essay Concerning Human Understanding*, 451.

69. Sir John Fortescue, *De Natura Legis Naturae* (London, 1869), II:32, quoted in Schlatter, *Private Property*, 73.
70. Grotius, *De Jure Belli*, II:505. On the issue of war as punishment and Pufendorf's attack on Grotius, see Arneil, "John Locke, Natural Law, and Colonialism," 587–603.
71. Arneil, ibid., 592–594.
72. For Gentili's legitimation of dispossession, see his *De Jure Belli*, 122, quoted in Green and Dickason, *The Law of Nations and the New World*, 49.
73. Pagden, "Dispossessing the Barbarian," 90–96.
74. Quoted in Honour, *The New Golden Land*, 12.
75. Hobbes, *Leviathan*, 80 (I:14:4).
76. Grotius, *De Jure Belli*, II:506.
77. Locke, *Two Treatises*, 275, 274.
78. See Locke's statement on despotical power: *Two Treatises*, 382–384.
79. "The whole country was my own meer property so that I had an undoubted right of dominion . . . I was absolute lord and lawgiver" (240–241).
80. The classic account of cannibalism's mythic nature is Arens, *The Man-Eating Myth*. See also Obeyesekere, who emphasizes in " 'British Cannibals' " the "dialogical nature of cannibalistic discourse" (630), and Boucher, *Cannibal Encounters*. Arens's account has not gone unchallenged. See, for example, the contributions in *The Ethnography of Cannibalism*, ed. Paula Brown and Donald Tuzin, and White's *Prehistoric Cannibalism at Mancos*.
81. Locke, *Two Treatises of Government*, 291.
82. Ibid., 286.
83. Ibid., 287, 293.

3 HENRY FIELDING AND THE COMMON LAW OF PLENITUDE

1. On *Robinson Crusoe*'s association with romance, see Fielding's remarks in *The Jacobite's Journal*, 27 February 1748, reprinted in *The Jacobite's Journal and Related Writings*, 178.
2. Fielding, *Joseph Andrews*, 183.
3. Ibid., 25.
4. McKeon, *The Origins of the English Novel*, 405–406.
5. Ibid., 392.
6. For McKeon's insistence on the novel's revolutionary newness, see ibid., 267–270.
7. Fielding's critique of natural law finds a direct local expression in the story of Sophia's bird. See Fielding, *Tom Jones*, 160–165. Subsequent page references will appear in parentheses in the text.
8. "The Practice of the People made the Name,/For Practices and Customs are the same," Daniel Defoe, *Jure Divino*, IV:3. For the two preceding quotations in the text, see ibid., I:ii–iv and IV:3.

9. Christopher Hill, *The World Turned Upside Down. Radical Ideas During the English Revolution* (New York: Viking, 1972), 126, quoted in McKeon, *The Origins of the English Novel*, 191.

10. For a discussion of the relation between natural law and the seventeenth-century dissenting tradition, see Gleissner, "The Levellers and Natural Law: The Putney Debates of 1647."

11. I am not the first to notice the relationship between *Tom Jones*'s two hill scenes: see Miller, "The Digressive Tales in Fielding's *Tom Jones* and the Perspective of Romance."

12. Locke, *An Essay Concerning Human Understanding*, 408.

13. Harris, *Three Treatises*, 65. See also Dryden's *An Essay of Dramatick Poesy* (1668) for a general discussion of familiarity as something that is conducive to artistic unity: *John Dryden*, 95.

14. See Hatfield, *Henry Fielding and the Language of Irony*, 7–54.

15. Fielding, *The History of the Adventures of Joseph Andrews and his Friend Mr. Abraham Adams and An Apology for the Life of Mrs. Shamela Andrews*, 310.

16. The concern over the hierarchy of different media is indicated in Harris's title – *Three Treatises; the First Concerning Art; the Second Concerning Music, Painting and Poetry; the Third Concerning Happiness* – which highlights a comparative approach to music, painting and poetry. See also the comparison of poetry and painting in *Three Treatises*, 79.

17. Battestin speculates that Fielding may have derived the name for Allworthy's estate from this regional nickname: *Henry Fielding: A Life*, 3. Clifton outlines the revolutionary traditions of Somerset in *The Last Popular Rebellion*, 37–76.

18. That Fielding took the Jacobite rebellion seriously is indicated by his rapid publication of three substantial pamphlets within two weeks of October 1745 (*A Serious Address to the People of Great Britain, The History of the Present Rebellion*, and *A Dialogue between the Devil, the Pope, and the Pretender*).

19. Pocock provides an account of liberalism in *Virtue, Commerce, and History*, 51–73.

20. Fielding is careful to stress that Tom cannot see what happens downhill and responds only to a sound: "Jones listened a Moment, and then ... ran, or rather slid, down the Hill, and without least Apprehension for his own Safety, made directly to the thicket whence the Sound had issued" (495).

21. On Smith's divided self, see Mullan, *Sentiment and Sociability*, 48–50. For Mandeville's insistence on a separation between spectator and agent, see, for example, *Fable of the Bees, or, Private Vices, Public Virtues*, I:56.

22. Coley, "General Introduction," Fielding, *The Jacobite's Journal*, xxvii.

23. Cobbett, *The Parliamentary History of England*, V:12.

24. *The Scots Statutes Revised*, 4. (The reference identifies the legislation as being the eleventh act in the sixth year of Queen Anne's reign.)

25. Fielding, *The Jacobite's Journal*, 51.

26. Cobbett, *The Parliamentary History*, V:34.

27. Ibid., V:52.

28. See, generally, Pocock, *The Machiavellian Moment*.

29. Fielding, *The Jacobite's Journal*, 50–51.
30. For an account of the decline of the court baron that is sensitive to its remarkable longevity, see Webb and Webb, *English Local Government*, II:116–126.
31. These two decisions are Partridge's expulsion from the neighborhood after he has been found guilty of fathering a bastard (98–103) and the sending of Molly Seagrim to a house of correction for being with illegitimate child (192–193). On "double justice," see Webb and Webb, *English Local Government*, I:392–396.
32. This occurs twice with particular emphasis: when Partridge is tried (98) and when Molly Seagrim is tried (192).
33. Act 22 and 23 Car. II, c 25 stated: "Bee it enacted . . . that all Lords of Manours . . . may . . . authorize one or more . . . Game-keepers . . . who may take and seize all such Guns, Bowes . . ." For the constable's association with the manor, see Hainsworth, *Stewards, Lords and People*, 193. See also Webb and Webb, *English Local Government*, II:4: "the whole force of police that then [in the late seventeenth century] existed owed its appointment neither to the parish nor the county, but to Manorial Courts or Municipal Corporations." See in this respect also the scene where Tom encounters the constable who is charged to deliver Molly Seagrim to jail, which illustrates the paternalist relationship between manorial lord and constable (*Tom Jones*, 192).
34. As Charles Gray pointed out in 1751, the commission of the peace allowed landowners "to keep their own parish under their own government; and to prevent other persons from exercising authority there": *Considerations on Several Proposals Lately Made for the Better Maintenance of the Poor* (London, 1751), 25, quoted in Webb and Webb, *English Local Government*, I:346.
35. Webb and Webb, ibid., II:31–50, shows the extent to which new jurisdictional institutions in the eighteenth century casually coexisted with more ancient courts and forms of authority.
36. Fielding, *An Enquiry*, 69–70.
37. Fielding's concern with the mobility of persons may very well have been influenced by Dalton's *The Country Justice*, which makes this a prominent concern (4). Fielding quotes from Dalton in *An Enquiry*, 85.
38. Fielding, *An Enquiry*, 136. Holdsworth defines frankpledge as "a system of compulsory collective bail fixed for individuals, not after the arrest for crime, but as a safeguard in anticipation of it": *A History of English Law*, I:13. The Webbs remark that "though any 'View of Frankpledge' or enrolment in tithings had long since been obsolete, the roll of inhabitants was, in 1689, still supposed to be called over" for the gathering of the manorial leet court: *English Local Government*, II:22.
39. Fielding, *An Enquiry*, 133.
40. Landau, *The Justices of the Peace*, 9.
41. Berman, *Law and Revolution*, 322. See also Berman's overview of the history of manorial law in Europe, 316–333.
42. Locke, *Two Treatises of Government*, 268.

43. Landau points to the mid-century as the period when the older patriarchal and local justice begins to be supplanted by a more neutral, nationally minded administrator of justice: *The Justices of the Peace*, 339–342.
44. See Webb and Webb, *English Local Government*, II:18.
45. Fielding, *The Jacobite's Journal*, 9–10.
46. Ibid., 11.
47. Ibid., 12.
48. Ibid., 13. During the debate over the Bill of Rights, Sir George Treby, in defending the "entail upon the persons named" (Mary, William, and Anne), asserts that "this bill leaves the descent of the Succession to the common law, and no otherwise": Cobbett, *The Parliamentary History of England*, V:249–250. Other references to the succession as an entail can be found in the speeches by Mr. Ettrick (250); Henry Herbert (251); Sir Henry Capel (251); and Thomas Herbert, Earl of Pembroke (103). The general importance of common law and property for the succession is emphasized by Sir Henry Goodrick (252); Sir Christopher Musgrave (39); and Sir Gilbert Dolben (47). See Nenner's *By Colour of Law* on how the common law and its focus on property comes to dominate constitutional politics in the late seventeenth century. See also Landon, *The Triumph of the Lawyers*.
49. For Locke's use of the term "trust," see *Two Treatises of Government*, 367. Laslett's introduction usefully clarifies Locke's reliance on the term.
50. My argument here challenges Brown's and Battestin's suggestion that Fielding relies on Lockean ideas in explaining the title of the Protestant succession. See Brown's "Tom Jones: The Bastard of History," and Battestin's footnote in *Tom Jones*, ed. Fredson Bowers, 77–78.
51. *The Champion: or, Evening Advertiser* 153 (4 November 1740). The close similarities in argument between the *Dialogue* and the *Address* confirm the attribution of the latter to Fielding. See Cleary, "The Case for Fielding's Authorship of *An Address to the Electors of Great Britain* (1740) Re-opened," and Battestin, *Henry Fielding: A Life* (698), who both argue for Fielding's authorship.
52. Wood, *An Institute of the Laws of England*, 255. The sale catalogue of Fielding's library notes that Wood's *Institutes* were "interleaved with MSS. Notes of Mr. Fielding": *Sale Catalogues of Libraries of Eminent Persons*, vol. VII, ed. Amory, 148.
53. Wood, *An Institute of the Laws of England*, 257.
54. See Holdsworth, *A History of English Law*, VII:312.
55. Blackstone, *Commentaries on the Laws of England*, II:175.
56. One *locus classicus* of such concerns is Thomas Sprat's *The History of the Royal Society* (1667).
57. Dryden, *An Essay of Dramatick Poesy*, in *John Dryden*, 81.
58. See Battestin's comments in *Tom Jones*, 42, footnote 1.
59. This nexus between description, gift exchange, and literary art was familiar to Fielding from texts such as Virgil's third Eclogue, in which two singers compete for the possession of an elaborately described object (Fielding

refs to this Eclogue, for example, in *The Champion* 5 [27 November 1739], reprinted in Fielding, *The Criticism of Henry Fielding*, 61–65). Given Fielding's occasional references to Theocritus, one suspects that he would also have been familiar with this tradition through his *Idylls*. See Mitchell's discussion of ekphrasis, which elaborates on the relationship between description and exchange: *Picture Theory*, 151–165.

60. Malinowski, *Argonauts of the Western Pacific*, and Mauss, *The Gift*. For a critique of Malinowski and Mauss and an argument that adjusts the idealized distance between "modern" and "primitive" commerce, see Thomas, *Entangled Objects*, 9–22.

61. James Thompson, *Models of Value*, 133.

62. *The Spectator*, ed. Bond, III:541.

63. *Old England* (27 May 1749), reproduced in *Henry Fielding: The Critical Heritage*, ed. Paulson, 167.

64. The anonymous author of *An Examen of the History of Tom Jones, A Foundling* (1750) comments on the tendency toward exhaustiveness: "Nor do I perceive the Use of so particular a Description . . . with *Hills, Groves, Lawns, Springs, Lakes, Plains, Rivers, Woods, Seas, Abbeys, – Hills, Lawns, Wood*, and *Water* again, *in infinitum*": *The Critical Heritage*, 194–195.

65. For a brief history of the ha-ha, see Hussey, *English Gardens and Landscapes*, 35–36.

66. Walpole, *The History of the Modern Taste in Gardening* (1771), reproduced in Chase, *Horace Walpole: Gardenist*, 25.

67. I have in mind here the following lines of Fielding's description: "The left Hand Scene presented a View of a fine Park, composed of very unequal Ground, and agreeably varied with all the Diversity that Hills, Lawns, Wood and Water, laid out with admirable Taste, but owing less to Art than to Nature, could give."

68. The most wide-ranging account of space as a historical phenomenon is Lefebvre's *The Production of Space*, but compare the more specific histories of Neil Smith, *Uneven Development*, and Sack, *Human Territoriality*. For a history of the rediscovery of space as a historical category see Soja, *Postmodern Geographies*.

69. Hume, *A Treatise of Human Nature*, 39–40. For a discussion of Locke's and Hume's ideas of space, see Yolton, *Thinking Matter*, 64–90.

70. Locke, *An Essay Concerning Human Understanding*, 180.

71. Ibid., 198, 199.

72. See Locke, *An Essay Concerning Human Understanding*, 179, for his insistence on separating the idea of space from that of the body.

73. Although the *Analysis of Beauty* was published in 1753, Hogarth discussed his favorite aesthetic principle as early as 1745, when he published a frontispiece that was adorned by a serpentine line on a painter's pallet, with the words "THE LINE OF BEAUTY" under it: *Analysis of Beauty*, x.

74. Hogarth, *Analysis of Beauty*, 25, 38–39.

75. Hume, *A Treatise of Human Nature*, 11.

76. See here again Hume's discussion, in which he points out that the "quality" of resemblance "alone is to the fancy a sufficient bond and association": ibid., 11.

77. An active construction of sight is common in the eighteenth century. Addison, for example, described sight as "a more delicate, diffusive kind of Touch" (*The Spectator*, 3:536) and Hogarth relied on the notion of a "ray" emanating from the eye to conceive of vision: *Analysis of Beauty*, 25–26.

78. I am drawing here on Baudrillard's description of nineteenth-century commodities in *The System of Objects*, 27–28.

79. See footnote 64.

80. Fielding, *The Criticism of Henry Fielding*, 197. Fielding owned nine editions and translations of Lucian. Mace has recently argued against Lucian's importance to Fielding; her argument does not affect the claim I am advancing here. See Mace, *Henry Fielding's Novels and the Classical Tradition*, 54–57.

81. Doody has recently offered a revaluation of this usage in *The True Story of the Novel*.

82. Graham Anderson, *Philostratus* (London: Croom Helm, 1986), 259, quoted in Bartsch, *Decoding the Ancient Novel*, 14.

83. *The Works of Lucian*, I:63–71.

84. Ibid., III:479–481.

85. E. C. Harlan, "The Description of Paintings as a Literary Device and its Application in Achilles Tatius," Ph.D. dissertation, Columbia University, quoted in Bartsch, *Decoding the Ancient Novel*, 29.

86. Savage, *The Bastard*, lines 13–20 (I quote from Savage, *The Poetical Works of Richard Savage*, 87–92).

87. For an extended account of the cultural construction of bastardy in eighteenth-century Britain, see my "Illegitimacy and Social Observation: The Bastard in the Eighteenth-Century Novel," *ELH* 69 (2002), 133–166.

88. Amory, *Law and the Structure of Fielding's Novels*, 298; Brown, "Tom Jones: The Bastard of History," 210; and Hunter, *Occasional Form*, 184–185.

89. On this, see also Defoe's comments on Taunton, which closely link Monmouth and William III: *A Tour through the Whole Island of Great Britain*, 252.

90. I argue here against Stevenson's enterprising linkage between Tom and the pretender Bonnie Prince Charlie, which he constructs, among other things, by capitalizing on the supposed disjunction between the bastard motif and the Whig succession: "*Tom Jones* and the Stuarts," especially 579–584.

91. Richardson to Astrea and Minerva Hill, 4 August 1749, in *Henry Fielding: The Critical Heritage*, 174.

92. Richardson to Thomas Edwards, 21 February 1752, in ibid., 334; Defoe, *The True-Born Englishman*, line 172 (I quote from *Poems on Affairs of State*, ed. Ellis et al., 259–310).

93. Defoe, *Roxana*, 115–116.

94. See Kramnick's discussion of mixed government in *Bolingbroke and his Circle*, 137–152.
95. One of the lawyers complaining about the potential injustice done to right heirs is Brydall. See his *Lex Spuriorum*, 27.
96. Blackstone, *Commentaries on the Laws of England*, II:295.
97. Ibid., II:242.
98. Ibid., I:128 (Blackstone's italics). The evidence I am presenting here challenges Brown's suggestion that the connection between Tom's and the crown's title is to be seen in the fact that both hold their estates by trust: "Tom Jones: The Bastard of History," 211.

4 COMMODITY FETISHISM IN HETEROGENEOUS SPACES

1. Pocock, *Virtue, Commerce, and History*, 109.
2. Defoe, *The Complete English Tradesman*, I:245.
3. See, for example, Dijkstra's *Defoe and Economics*, 13.
4. Defoe also, for example, vigorously defended the integral role landed property played in the legitimation of government, but did so in the context of an argument asserting the "people's rights": see my discussion in Chapter Two. I quote from Pocock, *The Machiavellian Moment*, 448.
5. See, for example, Flint's observation that "object narratives typically display a capricious mobility of animate and inanimate forms that disrupts any coherent sense of social order": "Speaking Objects," 215. See also Douglas, who contends that "ever-widening, ever-quickening, systems of trade and exchange threatened traditional order and hierarchy": "Britannia's Rule and the It-Narrator," 71. Building on Barrell's *English Literature in History*, Lynch's recent *The Economy of Character* modifies this emphasis. Yet her claim that the prominence of circulation in eighteenth-century narratives serves to neutralize social space essentializes circulation because it does not include a specific account of its relationship to social ground. In her argument, as in Flint's and Douglas's, circulation is a disembodied and disembodying force.
6. Dijkstra, *Defoe and Economics*, 13.
7. Laura Brown, *Alexander Pope*, 6–23; Bunn, "The Aesthetics of British Mercantilism," 303–323; Flint, "Speaking Objects"; Mackie, *Market à la Mode*, 50–54; Nicholson, *Writing and the Rise of Finance*, xii, 32–35; and James Thompson, *Models of Value*, 145–147.
8. My translation: "Die eigentlich bürgerlich ökonomische Sphäre der damaligen Zeit war die Sphäre der Waarencirkulation. Vom Gesichtspunkt dieser elementarischen Sphäre aus beurtheilten sie daher den ganzen verwickelten Process der bürgerlichen Produktion," Marx, *Zur Kritik der Politischen Ökonomie* (1859), reproduced in *Karl Marx Friedrich Engels Gesamtausgabe, Zweite Abteilung, Band 2*, 218.
9. Marx, *Zur Kritik der Politischen Ökonomie*, 217–219.
10. Defoe, *Robinson Crusoe*, 72–73.

11. See Goody's remarks on the etymology of the word 'list': *The Domestication of the Savage Mind*, 80.

12. The fear that description isolates and reifies once it is disconnected from human presence is evident in Adam Smith, *Lectures on Rhetoric and Belles Lettres*, 67–72, and Home, Lord Kames, *Elements of Criticism*, 30–31. Lukács and Jameson vent their concerns about description's reifying tendencies in, respectively, "Narrate or Describe?," in *Writer and Critic and Other Essays*, 110–148, and "The Realist Floor-Plan," 373–383 (see my discussion in Chapter One).

13. On the history of lists and their early uses, see Goody's discussion in *The Domestication of the Savage Mind*, 74–112.

14. Watt's *The Rise of the Novel* emphasizes Crusoe's accounting habits (63–64). Vickers argues for the influence of the new science on Defoe's prose in *Robinson Crusoe* in *Defoe and the New Science*, 122–131. The call for a primitive syntax is famously made by Thomas Sprat, who, significantly for my context, links such prose to the "disposition of merchants": see his *The History of the Royal Society* (1667), reprinted in *Critical Essays of the Seventeenth Century*, ed. Spingarn, 118. McKeon has stressed the ascendance of "quantitative demands for full and faithful detail" in seventeenth- and eighteenth-century writings: *The Origins of the English Novel*, 90–128.

15. Laura Brown has pointed to mercantile lists in an analysis of Alexander Pope's listing rhetoric: *Alexander Pope*, 11–13. The discussion that follows significantly expands Brown's suggestion.

16. The classic study on Defoe and economic ideas is Novak's *Economics and the Fiction of Daniel Defoe*. Despite two chapters on *Robinson Crusoe*, Novak's study fails to establish a specific link between Defoe's mercantilist ideas and his first novel. Dijkstra's *Defoe and Economics*, as we have already seen, simplifies Defoe's economic beliefs. Trotter's *Circulation* has the merit of fully appreciating the importance of circulation in Defoe's economic thought, but does not recognize this concern in Defoe's fiction.

17. For use of the terms "enumerated commodities" and "enumeration" with respect to mercantile policy, see, for example, Adam Smith, *An Inquiry into the Nature and Causes of the Wealth of Nations*, 89–92, and Hume, "Of the Balance of Trade," in *Essays Moral, Political, and Literary*, 310.

18. See the act in *Seventeenth-Century Economic Documents*, ed. Thirsk and Cooper, 520.

19. The quotation is from a 1696 letter of custom-house officials to the Treasury: ibid., 566–567). See also Schumpeter's comments on exchange control, which describe the practice of enumeration (*History of Economic Analysis*, 342), and Appleby's remark that "the balance of trade theory prompted the demand for accurate trade figures": *Economic Thought and Ideology in Seventeenth-Century England*, 80.

20. Defoe, *The Complete English Tradesman*, I:19. Defoe refers, for example, to goods controlled by the Navigation Act and to their listing in "Custom-house Books" in *A Plan of the English Commerce*, 209, 218.

21. Praising British improvements in manufacture, Defoe states that "it is not many Years since the best Scissars, the best Knives, and the best Razors were made in France" (*A Plan*, 218) and claims that this situation has largely changed, later on repeating a similar list of items (*A Plan*, 226). When Crusoe finds things on the ship, this list is echoed as follows: "two or three razors, and one pair of large sizzers, with some ten or a dozen of good knives and forks": *Robinson Crusoe*, 75.

22. See Heckscher, *Mercantilism*, II:25–26; and Pribram, *A History of Economic Reasoning*, 75.

23. Defoe, *Review* I:366, quoted in Earle, *The World of Defoe*, 138. See also, on the mercantilist assumption of limited wealth, Pribram, *A History of Economic Reasoning*, 46.

24. Defoe, *A Plan*, xii, 98, 99.

25. Heckscher, *Mercantilism*, II:57.

26. Defoe, *A Plan*, 192.

27. Ibid., 193.

28. Earle, *The World of Defoe*, 109.

29. Ibid., 126, 117. For Defoe's intense appreciation of circulation, see also *The Complete English Tradesman*, I:254–268.

30. Defoe, *Review* IX:101, quoted in Earle, *The World of Defoe*, 151. Tribe explores the logic of mercantile circulation thought-provokingly and remarks that mercantilists "did not seek . . . an origin" for circulation: Tribe, *Land, Labour and Economic Discourse*, 85.

31. Defoe, *A Plan*, 51, 10.

32. Ibid., 33, 63, 51.

33. My translation: "[die Waare ist] voller metaphysischer Spitzfindigkeit und theologischer Mucken," Marx, *Das Kapital: Kritik der Politischen Ökonomie* (1867), reproduced in *Karl Marx Friedrich Engels Gesamtausgabe, Zweite Abteilung, Band 5*, 44.

34. The most extreme example of economic historians' difficulty with appreciating mercantile theories is probably Hutchinson's *Before Adam Smith*, which considers every preceding theory as a flawed anticipation of the first real economist. One important exception to this tendency is Meek; see his *Studies in the Labour Theory of Value*, *The Economics of Physiocracy* and *Smith, Marx, and After*. Apart from Meek and Heckscher, I have found the following books helpful: Pribram, *A History of Economic Reasoning*; Appleby, *Economic Thought and Ideology in Seventeenth-Century England*; Schumpeter, *History of Economic Analysis*; Tribe, *Land, Labour and Economic Discourse*; *Revisions in Mercantilism*, ed. Coleman; and Foucault, *The Order of Things*, especially 217–303.

35. Heckscher, *Mercantilism*, II:208, 217.

36. Defoe, *Robinson Crusoe*, 67. Subsequent page references will appear in parentheses in the text.

37. The rationalization of Crusoe's work on the ship occurs in Defoe, *The Farther Adventures of Robinson Crusoe*, 118–119.

38. "Alle Beziehungen zwischen Robinson und den Dingen . . . sind . . . einfach und durchsichtig," Marx, *Das Kapital*, 45.
39. My reading of the ship episode goes against Richetti's claim that it evidences a "clear-eyed co-operation with circumstances": *Defoe's Narratives*, 39.
40. See my extensive discussion of *terra nullius* in Chapter Two.
41. I allude here to Schmitt's definition of the Greek term *nomos* as the unity of "*Ortung*" (location) and "*Ordnung*" (order): *Der Nomos der Erde*, 36–40.
42. On the territorializing function of the fetish, see William Pietz, "The Problem of the Fetish," 15.
43. Ibid., 10.
44. On the European perception of the "primitive" appreciation of Western commodities, see Thomas, *Entangled Objects*, 83–100.
45. Defoe, *A Plan*, 103. On Defoe's economic ideas about domestic circulation and international trade, see Earle, *The World of Defoe*, 107–110, 117–118, 130. See also Defoe's statements on London's centrality in *The Complete Tradesman*, I:254–269, II:63–82.
46. Quotation from the title page of *Robinson Crusoe*'s first edition. On the largely unexplored and deeply unfamiliar zone that Crusoe finds himself in, see Defoe's comment that about those "Countrys and Kingdoms bordering on both sides of the River Oroonoko" "Fame tells us strange Stories" (quoted from Defoe's contribution to *Atlas Maritimus & Commercialis*, 313). In "Prices in Europe from 1450 to 1750," Braudel and Spooner show the dependence of the mercantile economy on uneven price levels even within Europe (*The Cambridge Economic History of Europe*, VI:378–486).
47. Jameson, "The Ideology of the Text," in *The Ideologies of Theory*, I:52. See also Thompson's use of this passage: *Models of Value*, 8–9.
48. Defoe, *A Plan*, 110.
49. Defoe, *Captain Singleton*, 27.
50. Sack, *Human Territoriality*, 48.
51. On these personal business helpers, see Thompson, *Models of Value*, 102–103, and Hulme, *Colonial Encounters*, 212–213.
52. See the suggestions by Braudel and Spooner, who sketch the rise and decline of mercantile capitalism as a movement from exploitation of regional differences to a leveling of difference through overexploitation: "Prices in Europe," 395.
53. *A Young Squire of the Seventeenth Century: from the Papers (A.D. 1676–86) of Christopher Jeaffreson* (London, 1878), 190–193, reproduced in *Seventeenth-Century Economic Documents*, ed. Thirsk and Cooper, 545–546.
54. Defoe, *A Plan*, 103.
55. Hume, "Of Interest," *Essays Moral, Political, and Literary*, 300.
56. I quote from Marx's *Excerpt Notes of 1844*, reproduced in *Karl Marx: Selected Writings*, 43.
57. In *Iconology* Mitchell distinguishes between modern and ancient fetishism: 190–196.

58. On the eighteenth-century debate about the fetish in "primitive" religions and how it influenced Marx, see Pietz, "Fetishism and Materialism," 133–143.
59. Marx, *Zur Kritik der Politischen Ökonomie*, 115.
60. On Marx's appreciation of the materialist implications of the fetish, see Pietz, "Fetishism and Materialism," 142.
61. Thomas, *Entangled Objects*, 83–124.
62. Pietz, "The Problem of the Fetish," 15.
63. I disagree with McKeon's reading of *Robinson Crusoe* as a text that naturalizes desire: *The Origins of the English Novel*, 315–338.
64. Marx describes the gradual development of general equivalence in *Zur Kritik der Politischen Ökonomie*, 129.
65. Richardson, *Pamela*, 31. Subsequent page references will appear in the text.
66. As Lamb has reminded us recently, such connections between the representational practices of domestic and colonial spheres did not go unnoticed. John Hawkesworth, for instance, defends the "relation of little circumstances" in his colonial travel narrative by referring to Pamela's descriptive practice: Lamb, "Minute Particulars," 289.
67. See Opie and Opie, *The Classic Fairy Tales*, 117–127.
68. Douglas, "Britannia's Rule and the It-Narrator," 66, footnote.
69. See Bond's note to *Tatler* 143 in *The Tatler*, ed. Bond, 2:317. I owe this reference to Mackie's *Market à la Mode*, 75.
70. The affiliation of object narrative and "secret" history was well-established by the 1730s. *The Secret History of an Old Shoe* (London, 1734), for example, presents a political satire that draws on the conventions of the object narrative to generate interest, but fails to offer an actual object narrative or even an object narrator. Even in 1760 the narrator of *The Adventures of a Black Coat* (London, 1760) still feels the need to differentiate him/herself from tales of political intrigue: *The Adventures of a Black Coat*, xi.
71. The reference to *Rape* can be found on page 45; the reference to *Pamela* occurs indirectly through a character named Slip-Slop after the servant in Fielding's *Joseph Andrews*, which, of course, begins as a parody of *Pamela*.
72. Anon., *The History and Adventures of a Lady's Slippers and Shoes*, 5–6, 39–40.
73. In addition to the following quotation, see *Lady's Slippers*, 7, 12, 22, 42, 43, 54.
74. Ibid., 46–47.
75. Pope, *Rape of the Lock*, I:120–144, in *The Poems of Alexander Pope*, 222.
76. Ibid., V: 87–96.
77. Fielding, *The History of the Adventures of Joseph Andrews and his Friend Mr. Abraham Adams and An Apology for the Life of Mrs. Shamela Andrews*, 307.
78. For references to Shamela's wearing the clothes of her mistress, see ibid., 308, 315, 330. Fielding's parody of inventorial poetics can be found in ibid., 327. Fielding warned elsewhere against the verbal display of upper-class wealth outside the proper spheres: see *The Champion* 42, Tuesday, 19 February 1739.

79. The two women who wear their betters' clothes in *Tom Jones* are Jenny Jones and Molly Seagrim: Fielding, *Tom Jones*, 49, 176–184. For the other objects, see *Tom Jones*, 920, 145, 546, 631, 621.
80. Ibid., 621.
81. Thompson, *Models of Value*, 134.
82. Richardson, *Pamela*, 80.
83. Fielding, *Tom Jones*, 546.
84. Ibid., 548, 551.
85. Ibid., 207.
86. Ibid., 643.
87. Smith, *Wealth of Nations*, I:437. Subsequent page references appear in the text.
88. Hirschman suggests that Smith's depiction of the feudal lord's folly results from his excessive attachment to the rule of unintended consequences: *The Passions and the Interests*, 105. I am arguing here that such excess is, rather, connected to Smith's polemic against the mercantile commodity.
89. Smith, *The Theory of Moral Sentiments*, 182–183.
90. These "mean and malignant expediences" include the "primitive" identification of money and wealth, the "absurd" concept of the balance of trade, the "useless" institution of custom-house books, and the misguided view of trade as an international competition for limited wealth: *Wealth of Nations*, I:450–451, 499, 513, 519.
91. See ibid., I:403, 405, II:155.
92. Sutherland, "Adam Smith's Master Narrative," 101.
93. I should note here that Smith distinguishes these two commodities by reserving the term "frivolous" to mercantile, and "trifling" to manufactured, commodities. This appears to reflect a conscious decision, as in 1763 Smith was still using the term "frivolous" with regard to the pin: Smith, *Lectures on Jurisprudence*, 341.
94. See Smith, *Lectures on Rhetoric and Belles Lettres*, 68.
95. On the complicated history of Quesnay's tableau, see Meek, *The Economics of Physiocracy*, 265–272.
96. Quesnay's letter is reproduced in Meek, *The Economics of Physiocracy*, 117. Ross suggests that Smith was "emulating what Quesnay had achieved in the *Tableau Economique*": *The Life of Adam Smith*, 237. Smith draws attention to the tableau in *Wealth of Nations*: II:193, 200. For a discussion of visibility in eighteenth-century political economy and beyond, see Buck-Morss, "Envisioning Capital."
97. Smith, *Lectures on Rhetoric and Belles Lettres*, 67–74.
98. Ibid., 72.
99. Smith, *The Theory of Moral Sentiments*, 12.
100. Ibid., 18, 21.
101. Ibid., 26, 27.
102. Sterne, *A Sentimental Journey*, 51, 33.
103. Ibid., 33–35.

104. Markman Ellis in his *The Politics of Sensibility*, 152–155, misleadingly associates mercantile circulation with sensibility and misses the critique of circulation in both Sterne and Mackenzie.
105. Mackenzie, *The Man of Feeling*, 7–9.
106. Ibid., 125.
107. Ibid., 17–18.
108. Ibid., 121–122.
109. Sterne, *A Sentimental Journey*, 97.
110. References to the act of gazing and the "fixed eye": Mackenzie, *The Man of Feeling*, 105, 107, 110, 114, 130, 131.
111. Mackenzie, *The Man of Feeling*, 5. Sterne is equally interested in the fragmentary in this sense in the episode of the waste paper that turns out to be a fragment of a sixteenth-century manuscript: *Sentimental Journey*, 125–129.
112. Benedict, "Literary Miscellanies," 407–430.
113. For Fried's discussion of Diderot's tableau, see *Absorption and Theatricality*, 71–105.
114. Ibid., 118–136.
115. Mackenzie, *The Man of Feeling*, 130–132.
116. Lamb, "Language and Hartleian Associationism," 297.
117. Mackenzie, *The Man of Feeling*, 46.
118. Sterne, *A Sentimental Journey*, 44.
119. Ibid., 45.
120. See Benedict, *Framing Feeling*, 1–19.
121. Mullan, *Sentiment and Sociability*, 135.

5 ANN RADCLIFFE AND THE POLITICAL ECONOMY OF GOTHIC SPACE

1. Ghent, *The English Novel*, 80; Hilles, "Art and Artifice in *Tom Jones*"; Battestin, *The Providence of Wit*, 149; and Hunter, *Occasional Form*, 169.
2. I refer here to Hogarth's commendation of the accretional and unplanned nature of Gothic architecture in *Analysis of Beauty*, 45. Twentieth-century critics have not been unaware of the compatibility between Gothic architecture and the English landscape garden: see Lovejoy's 1932 "The First Gothic Revival and the Return to Nature."
3. Holland and Sherman, "Gothic Possibilities," 289.
4. Johnson, *Equivocal Beings*, 76. Psychological readings of the Gothic castle can be found in Holland and Sherman, "Gothic Possibilities," 279–295; Kahane, "The Gothic Mirror"; Wolff, "The Radcliffian Gothic Novel"; and Masse, "Gothic Repetition."
5. Durant, "Ann Radcliffe and the Conservative Gothic," and Paulson, *Representations of Revolution*, 215–247. London's "Ann Radcliffe in Context" argues that "Radcliffe's conservatism is clearly similar in order and

intensity to Burke's" (10). Benedict aligns Radcliffe's texts with the conservative critique of sensibility after the French Revolution in *Framing Feeling*, 172, 194.

6. Johnson, *Equivocal Beings*, 92, and Miles, *Ann Radcliffe*.
7. In addition to Johnson (*Equivocal Beings*, 92) and Miles (*Ann Radcliffe*, 15, 127), Cottom's reading of Radcliffe's landscapes is similarly invested in positioning Radcliffe on the boundary between distinct political and aesthetic positions: *The Civilized Imagination*, 46–50.
8. *Gazetteer and New Daily Advertiser*, Saturday, 1 January 1791. For further evidence on the initial reaction to Burke's *Reflections on the Revolution in France*, see McCalman, "Mad Lord George and Madame La Motte," 343–346.
9. Cobbett's *The Parliamentary History of England*, vol. XIX, quoted in O'Brien, *The Great Melody*, 487.
10. Butler, introduction to *Burke, Paine, Godwin and the Revolution Controversy*, 10.
11. On the historical and political context of Radcliffe's early novels, compare Miles's discussion in *Ann Radcliffe*, 57–73.
12. Radcliffe, *The Romance of the Forest*, 269.
13. I am extending Johnson's more general point on this footnote as "intensifying the political resonance" of Radcliffe's novel: *Equivocal Beings*, 76–77.
14. Radcliffe, *A Journey Made in the Summer of 1794*, 319–320.
15. Ibid., 291.
16. Miles, *Ann Radcliffe*, 62.
17. Radcliffe, *A Journey*, 369.
18. Durant, "Ann Radcliffe and the Conservative Gothic," 525.
19. See Guest's argument on the late eighteenth-century association of the Gothic with "a fondness for the traditions of the past": "The Wanton Muse," 120.
20. *Monthly Review* 8 (1792), 82.
21. See, for example, the review of *The Castles of Athlin and Dunbayne* in *Critical Review* (September 1789), Samuel Taylor Coleridge's remarks on *The Mysteries of Udolpho* in *Critical Review* (August 1794), and the "Sketch of the Progress of Novel-Writing" in the *British Review* (1820), all reproduced in *The Critical Response to Ann Radcliffe*, ed. Rogers, 1, 18, 107.
22. Readers were divided over Radcliffe's descriptions, but their testimony clearly shows how central description was in the reception of Radcliffe's work. Horace Walpole, William Hazlitt, Anna Seward, Thomas Green, Joseph Farrington, and numerous anonymous readers registered their awareness of Radcliffe's descriptive prowess. Norton's *Mistress of Udolpho*, 103–123, collects important evidence on the centrality of description in the response to Radcliffe.
23. Sedgwick's unexamined assumption that Piranesi's *Carceri* are relevant to the Gothic novel critically weakens her argument on space: *The Coherence of Gothic Conventions*, 9–37. See also Fred Botting's "Power in the Darkness," whose reliance on the figure of the labyrinth becomes questionable when

it is linked to Bentham's panopticon (269). For Scott's comments on the descriptive in Radcliffe, see Scott, *On Novelists and Fiction*, 103.

24. Radcliffe herself reflects on the powers of description in *A Journey*, 136, 419. Wollstonecraft, *A Vindication of the Rights of Men*, 7.

25. Radcliffe, *A Sicilian Romance*, 5. Subsequent page references will appear in parentheses in the text.

26. See for example, Cottom, *The Civilized Imagination*, 46–50; Miles, *Ann Radcliffe*, 15, 127.

27. See Radcliffe, *A Sicilian Romance*, 69, where this characterization of Mazzini's power is repeated.

28. Holdsworth, *A History of English Law*, X:426. See Chapter Three for my discussion of heritable jurisdictions.

29. William Radcliffe edited and translated a number of works that dealt with questions of political economy. These include Baron Holberg, *An Introduction to Universal History* (London, 1787); Karl Ivanovich Hablitz, *The Natural History of East Tartary* (London, 1789); and I. F. Henry Drevon, *A Journey through Sweden* (Dublin, 1790). On William's career, see Arnaud, "William Radcliffe, Journaliste."

30. Holberg, *An Introduction to Universal History*, footnote on 271.

31. Burke's *Reflections* was published on 1 November 1790. Radcliffe's *A Sicilian Romance* was first reviewed in September 1790 (*Monthly Review* 3).

32. The *Gazetteer* had already called attention to the term "prejudice" in its New Year editorial for Friday, 1 January 1790. Three weeks before William took on the editorship, and after the publication of the *Reflections*, the newspaper attacked Burke's text by highlighting the role the term prejudice played in it (Saturday, 1 January 1791).

33. Mackintosh, *Vindiciae Gallicae*, 345–346.

34. See my discussion in Chapter Three.

35. Radcliffe, *A Journey*, 106.

36. I owe this reference to Miles, *Ann Radcliffe*, 69.

37. Mackintosh, *Vindiciae Gallicae*, 49, 198–199.

38. Ibid., 197, xiii.

39. Radcliffe discovers Swiss scenery in her *A Journey* during a tour of England (484). The English pleasure ground in France appears in *The Romance of the Forest*, 164ff. Chandler makes his point about anachronism and anatopism in *England in 1819*, 109.

40. Holdsworth, *A History of English Law*, X:426. See also Maitland, *The Constitutional History of England*, 538.

41. On the perception of eighteenth-century Britain as rooted in landed property and feudal tradition, see my discussion in Chapter One.

42. Kliger, *The Goths in England*, 33–34. On Gothic revival architecture in England, see McCarthy's chapter "Political Buildings" in *The Origins of the Gothic Revival*, 27–31, and Germann, *Gothic Revival in Europe and Britain*, 53–73.

43. See Clarke's discussion of Stowe and the Temple of Liberty in "Grecian Taste and Gothic Virtue."

44. *The Gentleman's Magazine* 9 (1739) (reprint of an essay from the opposition journal *Common Sense*).
45. One recent text that works with the castle metaphor is Clery's *The Rise of Supernatural Fiction*, 124–128.
46. See Blackstone's introduction, "Elements of Architecture [ca. 1743–1747]," MS 333.
47. Ibid., 36, 58.
48. Blackstone to Seymour Richmond, 28 January 1745.
49. Blackstone expresses this hope in "The Lawyer's Farewell to his Muse," reproduced in Lockmiller, *Sir William Blackstone*, 191–195.
50. Blackstone, *Commentaries on the Laws of England*, III:268.
51. The Gothic vogue is first ridiculed in *The World* (1753–1756) and Richard Owen Cambridge's *Scribleriad* (1751). See Allen's discussion in *Tides in English Taste*, II:91–99. Blackstone expresses his wish to propagate knowledge of the law among landed gentlemen in *Commentaries*, I:7.
52. Maitland, *The Constitutional History of England*, 538.
53. Blackstone, *Commentaries*, III:267, 268.
54. Ibid., III:268.
55. Ibid., III:267, 268.
56. Ibid., III:265–266.
57. Wollstonecraft, *A Vindication of the Rights of Men*, 12.
58. Burke praised Blackstone in 1767 for having "cleared the law of England from the rubbish in which it was buried; and now shows it to the public, in a clear, concise, and intelligible form": *Annual Register* 1767, quoted in Warden, *The Life of Blackstone*, 268.
59. Burke, *Reflections*, 50.
60. Ibid., 29–30.
61. Burke emphasizes the importance of "ground," for example, in *Reflections*, 70, 72, 77.
62. Schmitt, *Der Nomos der Erde*, 40 (my translation).
63. Ibid., 36.
64. Wollstonecraft, *A Vindication of the Rights of Men*, 19.
65. Ibid., 11, 42.
66. See *Vindiciae Gallicae*, 115–116, for another prominent example of Mackintosh's use of architectural imagery to characterize the old regime. See pages 111–114 for his contrasting use of "machine" and "mechanism."
67. Mackintosh, ibid., 60.
68. Ibid., 361, 304–305.
69. More, *Village Politics: Addressed to all the Mechanics, Journeymen, and Day Labourers, in Great Britain* (Canterbury, 1793), reproduced in Butler (ed.), *Burke, Paine, Godwin and the Revolution Controversy*, 181.
70. Williams, "To Dr. Moore," 75.
71. Samuel Horsley, *A Sermon, Preached Before the Lords Spiritual and Temporal, in the Abbey Church of St. Peter, Westminster, on . . . January 30, 1793*, excerpted in Butler (ed.), *Burke, Paine, Godwin and the Revolution Controversy*, 143.

72. Bentham, *A Fragment on Government*, 20.
73. See *A Sicilian Romance*, 151, for the temporary suspension of pursuit through landscape description.
74. Radcliffe, *The Romance of the Forest*, 236. Subsequent page references will appear in parentheses in the text. Natural and cultural spaces are again confusingly interrelated (15, 21) and past and present are closely intertwined (20).
75. Price, *An Essay on the Picturesque*, 198–199. For Price's critique of extent, see *A Letter to H. Repton*, 100–101.
76. Price's remark on Hogarth appears in the 1798 edition of *An Essay* and is quoted in Paulson, *Hogarth: His Life, Art, and Times*, II:498.
77. Price, *A Letter*, 88.
78. Burke, *A Philosophical Inquiry*, 115.
79. Price, *A Letter*, 88. The same tendency toward greater perceptual complexity is evident in Price's preference of "sudden" over "gradual variation": *An Essay*, 76–77.
80. Knight, *The Landscape* (1794), quoted in Malins, *English Landscaping and Literature*, 148.
81. Price, *An Essay*, 5. References to framed views can be found throughout Price's writings (see, for example, *An Essay*, 207; *A Letter*, 78). See also Andrews's discussion of picturesque framing: *The Search for the Picturesque*, 29–33, 67–73.
82. Leloncourt is referred to as a paradise, for example, on page 277 of *The Romance of the Forest*. The reference to the English landscape garden is to be found ibid., 164–167.
83. Price, *An Essay*, 112.
84. Ibid., 18.
85. Examples of landscapes that are subject to continual temporal change can be found in Radcliffe, *The Romance of the Forest*, 22, 74–75, 83, 100, 229, 236.
86. Johnson, *Equivocal Beings*, 87.

6 SCOTTISH LAW AND *WAVERLEY*'S MUSEUM OF PROPERTY

1. Scott, *On Novelists and Fiction*, 52, 53.
2. Scott, *Waverley*, III:365–366. Subsequent page references will appear in parentheses in the text.
3. Scott, *On Novelists and Fiction*, 46.
4. Holdsworth, *A History of English Law*, X:426.
5. Welsh, *The Hero of the Waverley Novels*, 63–86; Duncan, *Modern Romance and Transformations of the Novel*, 103–104; and Wilt, *Secret Leaves*, 26–37. See also Hart, "Scott's Endings."
6. An important early essay that addresses Scottish law as a key to *Waverley* is Marshall, "Sir Walter Scott and Scot's Law."

7. Paine, "Letter Addressed to the Addressers on the late Proclamation" (1792), in *The Thomas Paine Reader*, 380.
8. Scott, *On Novelists and Fiction*, 144.
9. Bermingham, *Landscape and Ideology*, 74.
10. The most substantial case against Scott's originality has been made in Trumpener's excellent "National Character, Nationalist Plots."
11. Scott, *On Novelists and Fiction*, 49.
12. Scott, "View of the Changes," 183–184; 192.
13. See Kolbert and Mackay, *History of Scots and English Land Law*, 25. See also my discussion in Chapter Two.
14. Ibid., 105–112. For the lateness of the Scottish acknowledgment of central ownership, see ibid., 26–27.
15. Ibid., 240.
16. The only comparable statute in England is *De Donis Conditionalibus*, dating from 1285 and long superseded by the principle of individual ownership (ibid., 203).
17. For Scotland's comparative lateness in developing a more centralized jurisdiction, see ibid., 26–27.
18. Dalrymple, Viscount Stair, *The Institutions of the Law of Scotland*. See also Levack, "English Law, Scots Law, and the Union, 1603–1707," 105–120.
19. Paul Henderson Scott, *Walter Scott and Scotland*, 52.
20. Phillipson, *The Scottish Whigs and the Reform of the Court of Session*, 8–10.
21. Hardwicke to Kames, 12 July 1757, quoted in Home, Lord Kames, *Elucidations Respecting the Common and Statute Law of Scotland* (1777), 388.
22. Home, *Elucidations*, 334.
23. Bentham, *A Fragment on Government*, 41.
24. Home, *Historical Law Tracts*, xiii–xiv, and Hume, *Baron David Hume's Lectures*, I:15.
25. Burke, *Reflections*, 277.
26. Almost all Scottish legal scholars agree that the most important part of the indigenous Scottish law concerns the law of real property and the rules of succession. See, for example, Scott, "View of the Changes," 175; Dalrymple, *The Institutions of the Law of Scotland*, 87; Erskine, *The Principles of the Law of Scotland*, I:8; and Hume, *Baron David Hume's Lectures*, I:10–11.
27. For a detailed account of the procedure to be followed in the transfer of lands see Hume, *Baron David Hume's Lectures*, IV:275–284.
28. Kolbert and Mackay, *History of Scots and English Land Law*, 251. Underscoring the sense of resignation, Erskine describes the process as follows: "The resigner must surrender the lands to the superior by the symbol of staff and baton, which he gives on his knee to the superior": *The Principles of the Law of Scotland*, I:194. See also Hume, who speaks in this context of the "surrendery of the lands": *Baron David Hume's Lectures*, IV:277.
29. For a glowing account of Robert the Bruce's achievement for Scottish national independence, see Scott's review essay "Tyler's History of Scotland," in *The Prose Works of Sir Walter Scott*, V:180–184.

30. *The Acts of the Parliaments of Scotland, 1648–1660*, vol. VI, part ii (Edinburgh, 1823), 628, quoted in Pratt Insh, *The Scottish Jacobite Movement*, 10.

31. *The Scots Statutes Revised*, 4. (The reference identifies the legislation as being the eleventh act in the sixth year of Queen Anne's reign.)

32. Dalrymple, *The Institutions of the Law of Scotland*, 87.

33. Scott's admiration for Hume comes through in his "Memoir of the Early Life of Sir Walter Scott, Written by Himself" (1808), reprinted in Lockhart, *Memoirs of the Life of Sir Walter Scott*, vol. I, 48.

34. Hume, *Baron David Hume's Lectures*, I:11, 14, 2.

35. Scott, "View of the Changes," 185–186.

36. Ibid., 185–186.

37. Blackstone, *Commentaries on the Laws of England*, I:67.

38. Erskine, *The Principles of the Law of Scotland*, I:8.

39. See Blackstone on common law and regional difference: *Commentaries on the Laws of England*, I:64.

40. Scott, "Letters of Malachi Malagrowther on the Currency," in *The Prose Works of Sir Walter Scott*, V:304.

41. Scott, *Life of Napoleon Buonaparte*, *The Prose Works of Sir Walter Scott*, XII:326, 330. See also Scott's teacher Hume on the impossibility of theoretical consistency and uniformity of the law as well as its regional validity: *Baron David Hume's Lectures*, I:4–7.

42. Scott, "View of the Changes," 183.

43. See Gellner's definition of modern nationalism in *Nations and Nationalism*, 10–11.

44. Benedict Anderson, *Imagined Communities*, 19.

45. Bentham, *A Fragment on Government*, 26 (Bentham's italics).

46. See Scott, *Life of Napoleon Buonaparte*, *Prose Works*, XII: 318.

47. Burke, *Reflections*, 284. Burke uses the expression "carte blanche" to characterize France's attempt at rationalizing its national territory: *Reflections*, 231.

48. Scott, "View of the Changes," 184.

49. Paine, *The Rights of Man*, 58–59 (part 1), 15–17 (part 2).

50. Ibid., 74 (part 1).

51. On this association, see *The Rights of Man*, 59 (part 1).

52. On Burke's debt to the common law, see Pocock, *Politics, Language, and Time*, 202–253.

53. Bentham, *A Comment on the Commentaries*, 195.

54. Paine, *The Rights of Man*, 24 (part 1).

55. Giddens, *The Consequences of Modernity*, 53

56. Scott, *On Novelists and Fiction*, 118–119.

57. Scott, *Life of Napoleon Buonaparte*, *Prose Works*, XII: 330.

58. See my discussion of Smith in Chapter Four.

59. I paraphrase here Appadurai's definition of the "commodity situation" of things in *The Social Life of Things*, ed. Appadurai, 13.

CONCLUSION

1. Jameson, *The Political Unconscious*, 70.
2. On the increasing emphasis on production in various areas of early nineteenth-century practice, see Siskin, *The Work of Writing*, 44–53.
3. Lynch has done important work on this difference. See her *The Economy of Character*.
4. Kopytoff, "The Cultural Biography of Things," 90.

Bibliography

Adorno, Theodor, "Über den Fetischcharakter in der Musik und die Regression des Hörens," in Adorno, *Dissonanzen: Einleitung in die Musiksoziologie*, Frankfurt: Suhrkamp, 1973, 14–51.

Aitken, George, "Defoe's Library," *The Athenaeum* 1 (1895), 706.

Allen, B. Sprague, *Tides in English Taste, 1619–1800: A Background for the Study of Literature*, 2 vols., Cambridge: Harvard University Press, 1937.

Amory, Hugh (ed.), *Sale Catalogues of Libraries of Eminent Persons*, 7 vols., London: Mansell and Sotheby Parke Bernet Publications, 1973.

Law and the Structure of Fielding's Novels, Ann Arbor: University Microfilms, 1974.

Anderson, Benedict, *Imagined Communities: Reflections on the Origin and Spread of Nationalism*, revised edition, London: Verso, 1992.

Anderson, Graham, *Philostratus*, London: Croom Helm, 1986.

Andrews, Malcolm, *The Search for the Picturesque: Landscape Aesthetics and Tourism in Britain, 1760–1800*, Aldershot: Scolar Press, 1989.

Anon., *The Adventures of a Black Coat*, London, 1760.

Anon., *The History and Adventures of a Lady's Slippers and Shoes*, London, 1754.

Anon., *The Secret History of an Old Shoe*, London, 1734.

Appadurai, Arjun (ed.), *The Social Life of Things: Commodities in Cultural Perspective*, Cambridge: Cambridge University Press, 1986.

Appleby, Joyce, *Economic Thought and Ideology in Seventeenth-Century England*, Princeton: Princeton University Press, 1978.

Arens, William, *The Man-Eating Myth: Anthropology and Anthropophagy*, New York: Oxford University Press, 1979.

Armstrong, Dianne, "The Myth of Cronus: Cannibal and Sign in *Robinson Crusoe*," *Eighteenth-Century Fiction* 4 (1992), 207–230.

Arnaud, Pierre, "William Radcliffe, Journaliste," *Etudes Anglaises* 22 (1969), 231–249.

Arneil, Barbara, "John Locke, Natural Law, and Colonialism," *History of Political Thought* 13 (1990), 587–603.

John Locke and America: The Defence of English Colonialism, Oxford: Clarendon Press, 1996.

Atchity, Kenneth, *Homer's Iliad: The Shield of Memory*, Carbondale: Southern Illinois Press, 1978.

Atiyah, P. S., *The Rise and Fall of Freedom of Contract*, Oxford: Clarendon Press, 1988.

Atlas Maritimus & Commercialis: or, a General View of the World so far as Relates to Trade and Navigation, London, 1728.

Backscheider, Paula, "The Verse Essay, John Locke, and Defoe's *Jure Divino*," *ELH* 55 (1988), 99–124.

Barrell, John, *The Idea of Landscape and the Sense of Place: An Approach to the Poetry of John Clare*, Cambridge: Cambridge University Press, 1972.

English Literature in History, 1730–1780: An Equal, Wide Survey, London: Hutchinson, 1983.

Barthes, Roland, "The Reality Effect," in *Realism*, ed. Lilian Furst, London: Longman, 1992, 135–141.

Bartlett, Richard, *The Mabo Decision*, Sydney: Butterworth, 1994.

Bartsch, Shadi, *Decoding the Ancient Novel: The Reader and the Role of Description in Heliodorus and Achilles Tatius*, Princeton: Princeton University Press, 1989.

Battestin, Martin, *The Providence of Wit: Aspects of Form in Augustan Literature and the Arts*, Charlottesville: University Press of Virginia, 1989.

Henry Fielding: A Life, London: Routledge, 1993.

Baudrillard, Jean, *The Mirror of Production*, translated by Mark Poster, St. Louis: Telos Press, 1975.

For a Critique of the Political Economy of the Sign, translated by Charles Levin, St. Louis: Telos Press, 1981.

The System of Objects, translated by James Benedict, London: Verso, 1997.

Beaujour, Michel, "Some Paradoxes of Description," *Yale French Studies* 61 (1981), 27–59.

Benedict, Barbara, "Literary Miscellanies: The Cultural Mediation of Fragmented Feeling," *ELH* 57 (1990), 407–430.

Framing Feeling: Sentiment and Style in English Prose Fiction, 1745–1800, New York: AMS, 1994.

Bentham, Jeremy, *A Comment on the Commentaries and A Fragment on Government*, ed. J. H. Burns and H. L. A. Hart, London: Athlone Press, 1977.

A Fragment on Government, Cambridge: Cambridge University Press, 1990.

Berman, Harold, *Law and Revolution: The Formation of the Western Legal Tradition*, Cambridge: Harvard University Press, 1983.

Bermingham, Ann, *Landscape and Ideology: The English Rustic Tradition, 1740–1860*, Berkeley: University of California Press, 1986.

and John Brewer (eds.), *The Consumption of Culture, 1600–1800: Image, Object, Text*, London: Routledge, 1995.

Blackstone, William, "Elements of Architecture [ca. 1743–1747]," MS 333, All Souls College Library, Oxford University.

"Letter to Seymour Richmond, 28 January 1745," *Harvard Law Review* 32 (1919), 976.

Commentaries on the Laws of England, 4 vols., Chicago: University of Chicago Press, 1979.

Blanchard, Marc Eli, "In the World of the Seven Cubit Spear: The Semiotic Status of the Object in Ancient Greek Art and Literature," *Semiotica* 43 (1983), 205–244.

Blount, Thomas, *Fragmenta Antiquitatis: Ancient Tenures of Land and Jocular Customs of some Mannors. Made Public for the Diversion of Some, and Instruction of Others*, London, 1679.

Bossu, Rene de, *Monsieur Bossu's Treatise of the Epick Poem: Containing many Curious Reflections, very Useful and Necessary for the Right Understanding and Judging of the Excellencies of Homer and Vergil*, 2 vols., London, 1719.

Botting, Fred, "Power in the Darkness: Heterotopias, Literature and Gothic Labyrinths," *Genre* 26 (1993), 253–282.

Boucher, Philip P., *Cannibal Encounters: Europeans and Island Caribs, 1492–1763*, Baltimore: The Johns Hopkins University Press, 1992.

Braudel, F. P., and F. Spooner, "Prices in Europe from 1450 to 1750," in *The Cambridge Economic History of Europe*, vol. VI, ed. E. E. Rich and C. H. Wilson, Cambridge: Cambridge University Press, 1967, 378–486.

Brewer, John, and Roy Porter (eds.), *Consumption and the World of Goods*, London: Routledge, 1993.

and Susan Staves (eds.), *Early Modern Conceptions of Property*, London: Routledge, 1995.

Brown, Homer Obed, "The Displaced Self in the Novels of Daniel Defoe," *ELH* 38 (1971), 562–590.

"Tom Jones: The Bastard of History," *Boundary* 27 (1979), 201–233.

Brown, Laura, *Alexander Pope*, New York: Basil Blackwell, 1985.

Brown, Paula, and Donald Tuzin (eds)., *The Ethnography of Cannibalism*, Washington: Society for Psychological Anthropology, 1983.

Brydall, John, *Lex Spuriorum; or, the Law Relating to Bastardy*, London, 1703.

Buckle, Stephen, *Natural Law and the Theory of Property: Grotius to Hume*, Oxford: Clarendon Press, 1991.

Buck-Morss, Susan, "Envisioning Capital: Political Economy on Display," *Critical Inquiry* 21 (1995), 434–467.

Bunn, James, "The Aesthetics of British Mercantilism," *New Literary History* 11 (1980), 303–323.

Bürger, Peter, *Zur Kritik der Idealistischen Ästhetik*, Frankfurt: Suhrkamp, 1983.

Burke, Edmund, *Reflections on the Revolution in France, and on the Proceedings in Certain Societies in London Relative to that Event*, 1st edition, London, 1790.

A Philosophical Inquiry into the Origin of Our Ideas of the Sublime and Beautiful, ed. James Boulton, Notre Dame: University of Notre Dame Press, 1986.

Butler, Marilyn (ed.), *Burke, Paine, Godwin and the Revolution Controversy*, Cambridge: Cambridge University Press, 1994.

Carter, Samuel, *Lex Custumaria: or, a Treatise of Copy-Hold Estates*, London, 1696.

Chandler, James, *Wordsworth's Second Nature: A Study of the Poetry and Politics*, Chicago: University of Chicago Press, 1984.

England in 1819: The Politics of Literary Culture and the Case of Romantic Historicism, Chicago: University of Chicago Press, 1998.

Chase, Isabel Wakelin, *Horace Walpole: Gardenist,* Princeton: Princeton University Press, 1943.

Clark, J. C. D., *The Language of Liberty, 1660–1832: Political Discourse and Social Dynamics in the Anglo-American World,* Cambridge: Cambridge University Press, 1994.

Clarke, George, "Grecian Taste and Gothic Virtue: Lord Cobham's Gardening Programme and its Iconography," *Apollo* 97 (June 1973), 566–571.

Cleary, Thomas, "The Case for Fielding's Authorship of *An Address to the Electors of Great Britain* (1740) Re-opened," *Studies in Bibliography* 28 (1975), 308–318.

Clery, E. J., *The Rise of Supernatural Fiction, 1762–1800,* Cambridge: Cambridge University Press, 1995.

Clifton, Robin, *The Last Popular Rebellion: The Western Rising of 1685,* London: Maurice Temple Smith, 1984.

Cobbett, William, *The Parliamentary History of England, from the Earliest Period to the Year 1803,* 36 vols., London, 1806–1820.

Cohen, Ralph, *The Art of Discrimination: Thomson's* The Seasons *and the Language of Criticism,* London: Routledge and Kegan Paul, 1964.

Coke, Edward, *The Compleate Copy-Holder: Wherein Is Contained a Learned Discourse of the Antiquity and Nature of Manors and Copy-Holds,* London, 1641.

Coleman, D. C. (ed.), *Revisions in Mercantilism,* London: Methuen, 1969.

Copley, Stephen, and Kathryn Sutherland (eds.), *Adam Smith's* Wealth of Nations: *New Interdisciplinary Essays,* Manchester: Manchester University Press, 1995.

Cottom, Daniel, *The Civilized Imagination: A Study of Ann Radcliffe, Jane Austen and Sir Walter Scott,* Cambridge: Cambridge University Press, 1985.

Dalrymple, James, Viscount Stair, *The Institutions of the Law of Scotland: Deduced from its Originals, and Collated with the Civil, Canon and Feudal Laws, and with the Customs of Neighbouring Nations,* ed. David M. Walker, Edinburgh: University of Edinburgh and Glasgow Press, 1981.

Dalton, Michael, *The Country Justice,* London, 1697.

Defoe, Daniel, *The Original Power of the Collective Body of the People of England Examined and Asserted,* London, 1702.

Jure Divino, London, 1706.

The Farther Adventures of Robinson Crusoe: Being the Second and Last Part of His Life, London, 1719.

A Plan of the English Commerce, Oxford: Basil Blackwell, 1927.

The Complete English Tradesman in Familiar Letters, 2 vols., New York: Burt Franklin, 1970.

The Life and Strange Surprizing Adventures of Robinson Crusoe, London: Penguin, 1985.

A Tour Through the Whole Island of Great Britain, ed. Pat Rogers, London: Penguin, 1986.

Roxana, ed. David Blewett, London: Penguin, 1987.

Captain Singleton, Oxford: Oxford University Press, 1990.

Dickinson, H. T., *Liberty and Property: Political Ideology in Eighteenth-Century Britain*, New York: Holmes and Meier, 1977.

Dijkstra, Bram, *Defoe and Economics: The Fortunes of Roxana in the History of Interpretation*, London: Macmillan, 1987.

Dixon, John Hunt, and Peter Willis (eds.), *The Genius of the Place: The English Landscape Garden*, London: Paul Elek, 1979.

Doody, Margaret, *The True Story of the Novel*, London: Fontana Press, 1997.

Douglas, Aileen, "Britannia's Rule and the It-Narrator," *Eighteenth-Century Fiction* 6 (1993), 65–82.

Dryden, John, *John Dryden*, ed. Keith Walker, The Oxford Authors, Oxford: Oxford University Press, 1992.

Duncan, Ian, *Modern Romance and Transformations of the Novel: The Gothic, Scott, Dickens*, Cambridge: Cambridge University Press, 1992.

Durant, David, "Ann Radcliffe and the Conservative Gothic," *Studies in English Literature* 22 (1982), 519–530.

Earle, Peter, *The World of Defoe*, London: Weidenfeld and Nicolson, 1976.

Ellis, Frank H. et al. (eds.), *Poems on Affairs of State: Augustan Satirical Verse, 1660–1704*, 7 vols., New Haven: Yale University Press, 1963–1975.

Ellis, Frank H. (ed.), *Twentieth-Century Interpretations of* Robinson Crusoe, Englewood Cliffs: Prentice-Hall, 1969.

Ellis, Markman, "Crusoe, Cannibalism, and Empire," in *Robinson Crusoe: Myths and Metamorphoses*, ed. Lieve Spaas and Brian Simpson, New York: St. Martin's Press, 1996, 45–61.

The Politics of Sensibility: Race, Gender and Commerce in the Sentimental Novel, Cambridge: Cambridge University Press, 1996.

Erickson, Amy Louise, *Women and Property in Early Modern England*, New York: Routledge, 1995.

Erskine, John, *The Principles of the Law of Scotland*, 2 vols., Edinburgh, 1754.

Fielding, Henry, *The Criticism of Henry Fielding*, ed. Ioan Williams, London: Routledge and Kegan Paul, 1970.

Miscellanies, vol. I, ed. Henry Knight Miller, Middletown: Wesleyan University Press, 1972.

The Journal of a Voyage to Lisbon, New York: Dutton, 1973.

The History of Tom Jones, a Foundling, ed. Fredson Bowers, Middletown: Wesleyan University Press, 1975.

The Jacobite's Journal and Related Writings, ed. W. B. Coley, Middletown: Wesleyan University Press, 1975.

The History of the Adventures of Joseph Andrews, ed. R. F. Brissenden, London: Penguin, 1985.

The True Patriot and Related Writings, ed. W. B. Coley, Middletown: Wesleyan University Press, 1987.

An Enquiry into the Causes of the Late Increase of Robbers and Related Writings, ed. Malvin R. Zirker, Middletown: Wesleyan University Press, 1988.

Miscellanies, vol. II, ed. Hugh Amory, Middletown: Wesleyan University Press, 1993.

The History of the Adventures of Joseph Andrews and his Friend Mr. Abraham Adams and An Apology for the Life of Mrs. Shamela Andrews, ed. Douglas Brooks-Davies, Oxford: Oxford University Press, 1999.

Fielding, Sarah, *Familiar Letters between the Principal Characters in David Simple, and some Others*, London, 1747.

Finer, S. E., *Comparative Government*, London: Allen Lane, 1970.

Flint, Christopher, "Speaking Objects: The Circulation of Stories in Eighteenth-Century Prose Fiction," *PMLA* 113:2 (1998), 216–226.

Foucault, Michel, *The Order of Things: An Archaeology of the Human Sciences*, London: Tavistock, 1980.

Fried, Michael, *Absorption and Theatricality: Painting and Beholder in the Age of Diderot*, Berkeley: University of California Press, 1980.

Frost, Alan, "New South Wales as *Terra Nullius*: The British Denial of Aboriginal Land Rights," *Historical Studies* 19 (1981), 513–523.

Fussell, Paul, *The Rhetorical World of Augustan Humanism: Ethics and Imagery from Swift to Burke*, Oxford: Clarendon Press, 1967.

Gellner, Ernest, *Nations and Nationalism*, Ithaca: Cornell University Press, 1992.

Genette, Gerard, *Figures of Literary Discourse*, translated by Alan Sheridan, New York: Columbia University Press, 1982.

Germann, George, *Gothic Revival in Europe and Britain: Sources, Influences, and Ideas*, Cambridge, Mass.: MIT Press, 1973.

Gerrard, Christine, *The Patriot Opposition to Walpole: Politics, Poetry and National Myth, 1725–1742*, Oxford: Clarendon Press, 1994.

Ghent, Dorothy van, *The English Novel: Form and Function*, New York: Rinehart, 1953.

Giddens, Anthony, *The Consequences of Modernity*, Stanford: Stanford University Press, 1992.

Gildon, Charles, *The Golden Spy*, London, 1709.

Gleissner, Richard, "The Levellers and Natural Law: The Putney Debates of 1647," *Journal of British Studies* 20 (1980), 74–90.

Gliserman, Martin, "*Robinson Crusoe*: The Vicissitudes of Greed – Cannibalism and Capitalism: Displaced Desire: Money, Mother, Eating, and Encirclement," *American Imago* 17 (1990), 197–231.

Godwin, William, *Enquiry Concerning Political Justice and its Influence on Morals and Happiness*, 3 vols., ed. F. E. L. Priestley, Toronto: University of Toronto Press, 1946.

Goldgar, Bertrand G., *Walpole and the Wits: The Relation of Politics to Literature, 1722–1742*, Lincoln: University of Nebraska Press, 1976.

Goldmann, Lucien, *Recherche Dialectique*, Paris: Gallimard, 1959.
Towards a Sociology of the Novel, translated by Alan Sheridan, London: Tavistock, 1986.

Goody, Jack, *The Domestication of the Savage Mind*, Cambridge: Cambridge University Press, 1984.

Grant, Edward, *Much Ado About Nothing: Theories of Space and Vacuum from the Middle Ages to the Scientific Revolution*, Cambridge: Cambridge University Press, 1981.

Green, L. C., and Olive P. Dickason, *The Law of Nations and the New World*, Alberta: University of Alberta Press, 1989.

Grisel, Etienne, "The Beginnings of International Law and General Public Law Doctrine: Francisco de Vitoria's *De Indiis Prior*," in *First Images of America: The Impact of the New World on the Old*, vol. I, ed. Fredi Chiapelli, Berkeley: University of California Press, 1976, 305–325.

Grotius, Hugo, *De Jure Belli Ac Pacis Libri Tres*, 2 vols., ed. James Brown Scott and translated by Francis W. Kelsey, Oxford: Clarendon Press, 1925.

Guest, Harriet, "The Wanton Muse: Politics and Gender in Gothic Theory after 1760," in *Beyond Romanticism: New Approaches to Texts and Contexts, 1780–1832*, ed. Stephen Copley and John Whale, London: Routledge, 1992, 118–139.

Haakoonssen, Knud, *Natural Law and Moral Philosophy: From Grotius to the Scottish Enlightenment*, Cambridge: Cambridge University Press, 1996.

Hainsworth, D. R., *Stewards, Lords and People: The Estate Steward and his World in Later Stuart England*, Cambridge: Cambridge University Press, 1992.

Hale, Matthew, *The History of the Common Law of England*, ed. Charles Gray, Chicago: University of Chicago Press, 1971.

Haraway, Donna, *Simians, Cyborgs, and Women: The Reinvention of Nature*, New York: Routledge, 1991.

Harris, James, *Three Treatises; the First Concerning Art; the Second Concerning Music, Painting and Poetry; the Third Concerning Happiness*, London, 1765.

Hart, Francis R., "Scott's Endings: The Fictions of Authority," *Nineteenth-Century Fiction* 33 (1978), 48–69.

Haslag, Josef, *"Gothic" im Siebzehnten und Achtzehnten Jahrhundert*, Köln: Boehlau Verlag, 1963.

Hatfield, Glenn W., *Henry Fielding and the Language of Irony*, Chicago: University of Chicago Press, 1968.

Hay, Douglas, "Property, Authority and the Criminal Law," in *Albion's Fatal Tree: Crime and Society in Eighteenth-Century England*, ed. Douglas Hay et al., London: Penguin, 1975, 17–63.

Heckscher, Eli, *Mercantilism*, 2 vols., translated by Mendel Shapiro, London: Allen and Unwin, 1955.

Hilles, Frederick, "Art and Artifice in *Tom Jones*," in *Imagined Worlds: Essays on Some English Novels and Novelists in Honour of John Butt*, ed. Maynard Mack and Ian Gregor, London: Methuen, 1968, 91–110.

Hirschman, Albert, *The Passions and the Interests: Political Arguments for Capitalism Before its Triumph*, Princeton: Princeton University Press, 1981.

Hobbes, Thomas, *Leviathan*, ed. Edwin Curley, Indianapolis: Hackett, 1994.

Hogarth, William, *Analysis of Beauty*, London, 1753.

Holberg, *An Introduction to Universal History. Translated from the Latin of Baron Holberg; with Notes, Historical, Chronological, and Critical. By Gregory Sharpe. A New Edition, Revised, Corrected, and Improved by William Radcliffe A. B. of Oriel College, Oxford*, London, 1787.

Holdsworth, William, *A History of English Law*, 17 vols., London: Methuen, 1971.

Holland, Norman, and Leona Sherman, "Gothic Possibilities," *New Literary History* 8 (1977), 178–194.

Home, Henry, Lord Kames, *Historical Law Tracts*, Edinburgh, 1761.
   Sketches of the History of Man, 4 vols., Edinburgh, 1788.
   Elucidations Respecting the Common and Statute Law of Scotland, Edinburgh, 1800.
   Elements of Criticism, New York: Garland Publishing, 1972.

Honour, Hugh, *The New Golden Land: European Images of America from the Discoveries to the Present Time*, New York: Pantheon, 1975.

Horwitz, Morton J., *The Transformation of American Law, 1780–1860*, Cambridge: Harvard University Press, 1977.

Hulme, Peter, *Colonial Encounters: Europe and the Native Caribbean, 1492–1797*, London: Methuen, 1986.

Hume, David, *Essays Moral, Political, and Literary*, ed. Eugene F. Miller, Indianapolis: Liberty Fund, 1987.
   A Treatise of Human Nature, ed. P. H. Nidditch, Oxford: Clarendon Press, 1990.

Hume, David, *Baron Hume's Lectures, 1786–1822*, 6 vols., ed. G. Campbell and H. Paton, Edinburgh: J. Skinner, 1939–1958.

Hunter, J. Paul, *The Reluctant Pilgrim: Defoe's Emblematic Method and the Quest for Form in* Robinson Crusoe, Baltimore: The Johns Hopkins University Press, 1966.
   Occasional Form: Henry Fielding and the Chains of Circumstance, Baltimore: The Johns Hopkins University Press, 1975.

Hussey, Christopher, *English Gardens and Landscapes, 1700–1750*, London: Country Life Limited, 1967.

Hutchinson, Terence, *Before Adam Smith: The Emergence of Political Economy, 1662–1776*, Oxford: Basil Blackwell, 1988.

Jameson, Fredric, *Marxism and Form: Twentieth-Century Dialectical Theories of Literature*, Princeton: Princeton University Press, 1974.
   "The Realist Floor-Plan," in *On Signs*, ed. Marshall Blonsky, Baltimore: The Johns Hopkins University Press, 1985, 373–383.
   The Ideologies of Theory: Essays 1971–1986, 2 vols., Minneapolis: University of Minnesota Press, 1988.
   The Political Unconscious: Narrative as a Socially Symbolic Act, Ithaca: Cornell University Press, 1981.
   Postmodernism: or, the Cultural Logic of Late Capitalism, Durham: Duke University Press, 1992.

Janowitz, Anne, *England's Ruins: Poetic Purpose and the National Landscape*, Cambridge: Basil Blackwell, 1990.

Jessel, Christopher, *The Law of the Manor*, Chichester: Barry Rose Law Publishers, 1998.

Johnson, Claudia L., *Equivocal Beings: Politics, Gender, and Sentimentality in the 1790s: Wollstonecraft, Radcliffe, Burney, Austen*, Chicago: University of Chicago Press, 1995.

Johnson, Samuel, *Lives of the English Poets*, ed. George Birkbeck Hill, 3 vols., Oxford: Clarendon Press, 1905.

Life of Savage, ed. Clarence Tracy, Oxford: Clarendon Press, 1971.

Kahane, Claire, "The Gothic Mirror," in *The (M)other Tongue: Essays in Feminist Psychoanalytic Interpretation*, ed. Shirley Garner, Claire Kahane, and Madelon Sprengnether, Ithaca: Cornell University Press, 1985, 335–351.

Kelsall, Malcolm, *The Great Good Place: The Country House and English Literature*, New York: Harvester Wheatsheaf, 1993.

Kenny, Virginia, *The Country-House Ethos in English Literature 1688–1750: Themes of Personal Retreat and National Expansion*, New York: St. Martin's Press, 1984.

Kliger, Samuel, *The Goths in England: A Study in Seventeenth- and Eighteenth-Century Thought*, Cambridge: Harvard University Press, 1952.

Kolbert, C. F., and N. A. M. Mackay, *History of Scots and English Land Law*, Berkhamsted: Geographical Publications Limited, 1977.

Kopytoff, Igor, "The Cultural Biography of Things: Commoditization as Process," in *The Social Life of Things: Commodities in Cultural Perspective*, ed. Arjun Appadurai, Cambridge: Cambridge University Press, 1986, 64–91.

Kramnick, Isaac, "Augustan Politics and English Historiography: The Debate on the English Past, 1730–35," *History and Theory* 6 (1967), 33–56.

Bolingbroke and his Circle: The Politics of Nostalgia in the Age of Walpole, Ithaca: Cornell University Press, 1992.

Lamb, Jonathan, "Language and Hartleian Associationism in *A Sentimental Journey*," *Eighteenth-Century Studies* 13 (1979–1980), 285–312.

"Minute Particulars and the Representation of South Pacific Discovery," *Eighteenth-Century Studies* 28 (1995), 281–294.

Landau, Norma, *The Justices of the Peace, 1679–1760*, Berkeley: University of California Press, 1984.

Landon, Michael, *The Triumph of the Lawyers: Their Role in English Politics, 1678–1689*, University: University of Alabama Press, 1970.

Langford, Paul, *Public Life and the Propertied Englishman, 1689–1798*, Oxford: Clarendon Press, 1994.

Latour, Bruno, *We Have Never Been Modern*, Cambridge: Harvard University Press, 1995.

Lefebvre, Henri, *The Production of Space*, Oxford: Blackwell, 1992.

Levack, Brian, *The Civil Lawyers in England, 1603–1641: A Political Study*, Oxford: Clarendon Press, 1973.

"English Law, Scots Law and the Union, 1603–1707," in *Law-Making and Law-Makers in British History*, ed. Alan Harding, London: Royal Historical Society, 1980, 105–120.

Lieberman, David, *The Province of Legislation Determined: Legal Theory in Eighteenth-Century Britain*, Cambridge: Cambridge University Press, 1989.

Locke, John, *An Essay Concerning Human Understanding*, ed. Peter H. Nidditch, Oxford: Clarendon Press, 1991.

Two Treatises of Government, ed. Peter Laslett, Cambridge: Cambridge University Press, 1993.

Lockhart, John Gibson, *Memoirs of the Life of Sir Walter Scott*, 5 vols., Cambridge: Riverside Press, 1902.

Lockmiller, David, *Sir William Blackstone*, Chapel Hill: University of North Carolina Press, 1938.

London, April, "Ann Radcliffe in Context: Marking the Boundaries of *The Mysteries of Udolpho*," *Eighteenth-Century Life* 10 (1986), 35–46.

Lopes, José Manuel, *Foregrounded Description in Prose Fiction: Five Cross-Literary Studies*, Toronto: University of Toronto Press, 1995.

Lovejoy, Arthur, "The First Gothic Revival and the Return to Nature," *Modern Language Notes* 47 (1932), 419–446.

Lucian, of Samosata, *The Works of Lucian*, translated by A. M. Harmon, K. Kilburn, and M. D. Macleod, Loeb Classical Library, 8 vols., London: Heinemann, 1913–1967.

Lukács, Georg, *Geschichte und Klassenbewußtsein*, Neuwied: Luchterhand, 1968.
  Writer and Critic and Other Essays, ed. and translated by Arthur Kahn, New York: Grosset and Dunlap, 1970.
  History and Class Consciousness, translated by Rodney Livingstone, Cambridge, Mass.: MIT Press, 1971.

Lynch, Deidre, *The Economy of Character: Novels, Market Culture, and the Business of Inner Meaning*, Chicago: University of Chicago Press, 1998.

Lyttelton, George, *Letters from a Persian in England to his Friend at Ispahan*, London, 1735.

Mace, Nancy, *Henry Fielding's Novels and the Classical Tradition*, Newark: University of Delaware Press, 1996.

Mackenzie, Henry, *The Man of Feeling*, ed. Brian Vickers, London: Oxford University Press, 1967.

Mackie, Erin, *Market à la Mode: Fashion, Commodity, and Gender in* The Tatler *and* The Spectator, Baltimore: The Johns Hopkins University Press, 1997.

Mackintosh, James, *Vindiciae Gallicae: Defence of the French Revolution and its English Admirers, Third Edition, with Additions*, London, 1791.

Macpherson, C. B., *The Political Theory of Possessive Individualism: Hobbes to Locke*, Oxford: Oxford University Press, 1964.

Maitland, F. W., *The Constitutional History of England*, Cambridge: Cambridge University Press, 1963.

Malinowski, Bronislaw, *Argonauts of the Western Pacific*, London: Routledge, 1922.

Malins, Edward, *English Landscaping and Literature, 1660–1840*, London: Oxford University Press, 1966.

Mandeville, Bernard, *Fable of the Bees, or, Private Vices, Public Virtues*, 2 vols., Oxford: Clarendon Press, 1966.

Marshall, David, "Sir Walter Scott and Scot's Law," *The Scottish Law Review* 46 (1930), 303–310, 329–338, 373–381.

Marx, Karl, *Karl Marx Friedrich Engels Gesamtausgabe, Zweite Abteilung, Band 2: Ökonomische Manuskripte und Schriften, 1858–1861*, Berlin: Dietz Verlag, 1980.

Karl Marx Friedrich Engels Gesamtausgabe, Zweite Abteilung, Band 5: Das Kapital und Vorarbeiten, Berlin: Dietz Verlag, 1983.

Selected Writings, ed. Laurence H. Simon, Indianapolis: Hackett, 1994.

Masse, Michele, "Gothic Repetition: Husbands, Horrors, and Things that Go Bump in the Night," *Signs* 15 (1990), 679–709.

Mauss, Marcel, *The Gift: The Form and Reason for Exchange in Archaic Societies*, translated by W. D. Halls, New York: Norton, 1990.

McCalman, Iain, "Mad Lord George and Madame La Motte: Riot and Sexuality in the Genesis of Burke's *Reflections on the Revolution in France*," *Journal of British Studies* 35 (1996), 343–367.

McCarthy, Michael, *The Origins of the Gothic Revival*, New Haven: Yale University Press, 1987.

McClung, William, *The Country House in English Renaissance Poetry*, Berkeley: University of California Press, 1977.

McKendrick, Neil, *The Birth of a Consumer Culture: The Commercialization of Eighteenth-Century England*, London: Europa, 1982.

McKeon, Michael, *The Origins of the English Novel, 1600–1740*, Baltimore: The Johns Hopkins University Press, 1991.

McNally, David, *Political Economy and the Rise of Capitalism: A Reinterpretation*, Berkeley: University of California Press, 1990.

McNeil, Kent, *Common Law Aboriginal Title*, Oxford: Clarendon Press, 1989.

Meek, Ronald, *Studies in the Labour Theory of Value*, London: Lawrence and Wiseheart, 1956.

The Economics of Physiocracy: Essays and Translations, London: Allen and Unwin, 1962.

Smith, Marx and After: Ten Essays in the Development of Economic Thought, London: Chapman and Hall, 1977.

Miles, Robert, *Ann Radcliffe: The Great Enchantress*, Manchester: Manchester University Press, 1995.

Miller, Henry Knight, "The Digressive Tales in Fielding's *Tom Jones* and the Perspective of Romance," *Philological Quarterly* 54 (1975), 258–274.

Mitchell, W. J. T., *Iconology: Image, Text, Ideology*, Chicago: University of Chicago Press, 1987.

Picture Theory: Verbal and Visual Representation, Chicago: University of Chicago Press, 1995.

Mullan, John, *Sentiment and Sociability: The Language of Feeling in the Eighteenth Century*, Oxford: Clarendon Press, 1988.

Nairn, Tom, *The Break-Up of Britain: Crisis and Neo-Nationalism*, London: NLB, 1977.

Neale, R. S., *Class in English History*, Oxford: Oxford University Press, 1981.

Nenner, Howard, *By Colour of Law: Legal Culture and Constitutional Politics in England, 1660–1689*, Chicago: University of Chicago Press, 1977.

Nicholson, Colin, *Writing and the Rise of Finance: Capital Satires of the Early Eighteenth Century*, Cambridge: Cambridge University Press, 1994.

Norton, Rictor, *Mistress of Udolpho: The Life of Ann Radcliffe*, London: Leicester University Press, 1999.

Novak, Maximillian, *Economics and the Fiction of Daniel Defoe*, Berkeley: University of California Press, 1962.

Defoe and the Nature of Man, Oxford: Oxford University Press, 1963.

O'Brien, Conor Cruise, *The Great Melody: A Thematic Biography of Edmund Burke*, Chicago: University of Chicago Press, 1993.

Obeyesekere, Gananath, "'British Cannibals': Contemplation of an Event in the Death and Resurrection of James Cook, Explorer," *Critical Inquiry* 18 (1992), 630–654.

Olivecrona, Karl, "Locke's Theory of Appropriation," *The Philosophical Quarterly* 24 (1974), 220–234.

Opie, Iona, and Peter Opie, *The Classic Fairy Tales*, London: Oxford University Press, 1974.

Pagden, Anthony, *The Fall of Natural Man: The American Indian and the Origins of Comparative Ethnology*, Cambridge: Cambridge University Press, 1982.

"Dispossessing the Barbarian: the Language of Spanish Thomism and the Debate over the Property Rights of the American Indians," in *The Languages of Political Theory in Early-Modern Europe*, ed. Anthony Pagden, Cambridge: Cambridge University Press, 1987, 79–98.

Lords of All the World: Ideologies of Empire in Spain, Britain, and France, New Haven: Yale University Press, 1995.

Paine, Thomas, *The Rights of Man: Being an Answer to Mr. Burke's Attack on the French Revolution*, London, 1792.

The Thomas Paine Reader, ed. Michael Foot and Isaac Kramnick, London: Penguin, 1987.

Paulson, Ronald (ed.), *Henry Fielding: The Critical Heritage*, New York: Barnes and Noble, 1969.

Hogarth: His Life, Art, and Times, 2 vols., New Haven: Yale University Press, 1971.

Representations of Revolution, 1789–1820, New Haven: Yale University Press, 1983.

Pearlman, E., "*Robinson Crusoe* and the Cannibals," *Mosaic* 10: 1 (1976–1977), 39–55.

Perkin, Harold, *Origins of Modern English Society*, New York: Routledge, 1986.

Phillipson, Nicholas, *The Scottish Whigs and the Reform of the Court of Session, 1785–1830*, Edinburgh: The Stair Society, 1990.

Pietz, William, "The Problem of the Fetish," *RES* 9 (1985), 5–17.

"Fetishism and Materialism: The Limits of Theory in Marx," in *Fetishism as Cultural Discourse*, ed. Emily Apter and William Pietz, Ithaca: Cornell University Press, 1993, 119–151.

Pocock, J. G. A., *The Machiavellian Moment: Florentine Political Thought and the Atlantic Republican Tradition*, Princeton: Princeton University Press, 1975.

Politics, Language, and Time: Essays on Political Thought and History, Chicago: University of Chicago Press, 1989.

Virtue, Commerce and History: Essays on Political Thought and History, Chiefly in the Eighteenth Century, Cambridge: Cambridge University Press, 1991.

Pope, Alexander, *The Poems of Alexander Pope*, ed. John Butt, London: Routledge, 1989.

Pratt Insh, George, *The Scottish Jacobite Movement: A Study in Economic and Social Forces*, Edinburgh: The Moray Press, 1952.

Pribram, Karl, *A History of Economic Reasoning*, Baltimore: The Johns Hopkins University Press, 1983.

Price, Uvedale, *An Essay on the Picturesque*, London, 1794.

   A Letter to H. Repton, London, 1795.

Pufendorf, Samuel, *De Jure Naturae Et Gentium Libri Octo*, 2 vols., translated by C. H. Oldfather and W. A. Oldfather, Oxford: Clarendon Press, 1934.

Radcliffe, Ann, *A Journey Made in the Summer of 1794 through Holland and the Western Frontier of Germany*, Dublin, 1795.

   The Italian, ed. Frederick Garber, Oxford: Oxford University Press, 1981.

   The Romance of the Forest, ed. Chloe Chard, Oxford: Oxford University Press, 1986.

   A Sicilian Romance, ed. Alison Milbank, Oxford: Oxford University Press, 1993.

Richardson, Samuel, *Pamela or, Virtue Rewarded*, ed. T. C. Duncan Eaves and Ben Kimpel, Boston: Houghton Mifflin, 1971.

Richetti, John, *Defoe's Narratives: Situations and Structures*, Oxford: Clarendon Press, 1975.

Roberts-Wray, Kenneth, *Commonwealth and Colonial Law*, London: Stevens and Sons, 1966.

Robinson, Sidney, *Inquiry into the Picturesque*, Chicago: University of Chicago Press, 1991.

Rogers, Deborah (ed.), *The Critical Response to Ann Radcliffe*, Westport: Greenwood Press, 1994.

Ross, Ian, *The Life of Adam Smith*, Oxford: Clarendon Press, 1995.

Ryan, Alan, *Property and Political Theory*, New York: Basil Blackwell, 1984.

Sack, Robert, *Human Territoriality: Its Theory and History*, Cambridge: Cambridge University Press, 1986.

Savage, Richard, *The Poetical Works of Richard Savage*, ed. Clarence Tracy, Cambridge: Cambridge University Press, 1962.

Schlatter, Richard, *Private Property: The History of an Idea*, New Brunswick: Rutgers University Press, 1951.

Schmitt, Carl, *Der Nomos der Erde im Völkerrecht des Jus Publicum Europaeum*, Berlin: Duncker und Humblot, 1974.

Schumpeter, Joseph, *History of Economic Analysis*, ed. Elizabeth Boody Schumpeter, New York: Oxford University Press, 1976.

The Scots Statutes Revised: The Public General Statutes Affecting Scotland 1707–1900, 10 vols., Edinburgh: William Green, 1899–1902.

Scott, Paul Henderson, *Walter Scott and Scotland*, Edinburgh: William Blackwood, 1981.

Scott, Sir Walter, *Waverley: or, 'Tis Sixty Years Since*, 3 vols., Edinburgh, 1814.
  The Prose Works of Sir Walter Scott, 12 vols., Edinburgh, 1835.
  On Novelists and Fiction, ed. Ioan Williams, London: Routledge and Kegan
    Paul, 1968.
  "View of the Changes Proposed and Adopted in the Administration of Justice
    in Scotland," in *Sir Walter Scott's Edinburgh Annual Register*, ed. Kenneth Curry,
    Knoxville: University of Tennessee Press, 1977, 183–192.
  The Visionary, ed. Peter Garside, Cardiff: University College Cardiff Press,
    1984.
Sedgwick, Eve Kosofsky, *The Coherence of Gothic Conventions*, New York: Methuen,
    1986.
Seed, Patricia, *Ceremonies of Possession in Europe's Conquest of the New World, 1492–
    1640*, Cambridge: Cambridge University Press, 1995.
Siskin, Clifford, *The Work of Writing: Literature and Social Change in Britain, 1700–
    1830*, Baltimore: The Johns Hopkins University Press, 1998.
Skinner, Andrew, and Thomas Wilson (ed.), *Essays on Adam Smith*, Oxford:
    Clarendon Press, 1975.
Smith, Adam, *An Inquiry into the Nature and Causes of the Wealth of Nations*, 2 vols.,
    ed. Edwin Cannan, Chicago: University of Chicago Press, 1976.
  The Theory of Moral Sentiments, ed. D. D. Raphael and A. L. Macfie, Oxford:
    Clarendon Press, 1976.
  Lectures on Jurisprudence, ed. R. L. Meek, D. D. Raphael, and P. G. Stein, Oxford:
    Clarendon Press, 1978.
  Lectures on Rhetoric and Belles Lettres, ed. J. C. Bryce, Oxford: Clarendon Press,
    1983.
Smith, Neil, *Uneven Development: Nature, Capital and the Production of Space*, Oxford:
    Basil Blackwell, 1984.
Smith, R. J., *The Gothic Bequest: Medieval Institutions in British Thought, 1688–1863*,
    Cambridge: Cambridge University Press, 1987.
Smollett, Tobias, *The History and Adventures of an Atom*, ed. D. M. Brack, Athens,
    Ga.: University of Georgia Press, 1989.
Soja, Edward, *Postmodern Geographies: The Reassertion of Space in Critical Social Theory*,
    London: Verso, 1989.
The Spectator, 5 vols., ed. Donald Bond, Oxford: Clarendon Press, 1965.
Spingarn, J. E. (ed.), *Critical Essays of the Seventeenth Century*, 2 vols., Oxford:
    Oxford University Press, 1957.
Squire, Samuel, *An Enquiry into the Foundations of the English Constitution*, London,
    1753.
Starr, George A., *Defoe and Spiritual Autobiography*, Princeton: Princeton University
    Press, 1965.
Staves, Susan, *Married Women's Separate Property in England, 1660–1833*,
    Cambridge: Harvard University Press, 1990.
Sterne, Laurence, *A Sentimental Journey*, ed. Graham Petrie, London: Penguin,
    1986.
Stevenson, John Allen, "*Tom Jones* and the Stuarts," *ELH* 61 (1994), 571–595.

Sugarman, David, and Ronnie Warrington, "Land, Law, Citizenship and the Invention of Englishness: The Strange World of the Equity of Redemption," in *Early Modern Conceptions of Property*, ed. John Brewer and Susan Staves, London: Routledge, 1995, 111–143.

Sutherland, Kathryn, "Adam Smith's Master Narrative: Women and the *Wealth of Nations*," in *Adam Smith's* Wealth of Nations: *New Interdisciplinary Essays*, ed. Stephen Copley and Kathryn Sutherland, Manchester: Manchester University Press, 1995, 97–121.

Symcox, Geoffrey W., "The Battle of the Atlantic, 1500–1700," in *First Images of America: The Impact of the New World on the Old*, vol. I, ed. Fredi Chiapelli, Berkeley: University of California Press, 1976, 265–278.

The Tatler, 3 vols., ed. Donald Bond, Oxford: Clarendon Press, 1987.

Thirsk, Joan, and J. P. Cooper (ed.), *Seventeenth-Century Economic Documents*, Oxford: Clarendon Press, 1972.

Thomas, Nicholas, *Entangled Objects: Exchange, Material Culture, and Colonialism in the Pacific*, Cambridge: Harvard University Press, 1991.

Thompson, E. P., *Whigs and Hunters: The Origin of the Black Act*, New York: Pantheon Books, 1975.
  Customs in Common: Studies in Traditional Popular Culture, New York: New Press, 1993.
  Persons and Polemics, London: Merlin Press, 1994.

Thompson, James, *Models of Value: Eighteenth-Century Political Economy and the Novel*, Durham: Duke University Press, 1996.

Tribe, Keith, *Land, Labour and Economic Discourse*, London: Routledge, 1978.

Trickett, Rachel, " 'Curious Eye': Some Aspects of Visual Description in Eighteenth-Century Literature," in *Augustan Studies: Essays in Honor of Irvin Ehrenpreis*, ed. Douglas Lane Patey and Timothy Keegan, Newark: University of Delaware Press, 1985, 239–252.

Trotter, David, *Circulation: Defoe, Dickens and the Economies of the Novel*, London: Macmillan, 1988.

Trumpener, Katie, "National Character, Nationalist Plots: National Tale and Historical Novel in the Age of *Waverley*, 1806–1830," *ELH* 60 (1993), 685–731.

Tuck, Richard, *Natural Rights Theories: Their Origin and Development*, Cambridge: Cambridge University Press, 1979.

Turner, James, *The Politics of Landscape: Rural Scenery and Society in English Poetry, 1630–1660*, Cambridge: Harvard University Press, 1979.

Vattel, Emeric, *The Law of Nations; or, Principles of the Law of Nature*, London, 1759.

Vickers, Ilse, *Defoe and the New Science*, Cambridge: Cambridge University Press, 1996.

Wall, Cynthia, "Details of Space: Narrative Description in Early Eighteenth-Century Novels," *Eighteenth-Century Fiction* 10 (1998), 387–405.

Warden, Lewis, *The Life of Blackstone*, Charlottesville: Michie Company, 1938.

Wasserman, Earl, *The Subtler Language: Critical Readings of Neoclassic and Romantic Poems*, Baltimore: The Johns Hopkins University Press, 1959.

Watt, Ian, *The Rise of the Novel: Studies in Defoe, Richardson, and Fielding*, Berkeley: University of California Press, 1957.

Webb, Sidney, and Beatrice Webb, *English Local Government from the Revolution to the Municipal Corporations Act*, 11 vols., London: Longman, Green and Co., 1908.

Welsh, Alexander, *The Hero of the Waverley Novels*, Princeton: Princeton University Press, 1992.

White, Timothy, *Prehistoric Cannibalism at Mancos*, Princeton: Princeton University Press, 1992.

Whitman, Cedric, *Homer and the Heroic Tradition*, Cambridge: Harvard University Press, 1958.

Williams, Anne, "Description and Tableau in the Eighteenth-Century British Sentimental Novel," *Eighteenth-Century Fiction* 8 (1996), 465–484.

Williams, Helen Maria, "To Dr. Moore, In Answer to a Poetical Epistle Written by Him, in Wales, to Helen Maria Williams" (1792), in *Romantic Women Poets, 1770–1838: an Anthology*, ed. Andrew Ashfield, Manchester: Manchester University Press, 1995, 75.

Williams, Raymond, *The Country and the City*, New York: Oxford University Press, 1973.

Wilt, Judith, *Secret Leaves: The Novels of Walter Scott*, Chicago: University of Chicago Press, 1985.

Wolff, Cynthia Griffin, "The Radcliffian Gothic Novel: A Form for Feminine Sexuality," in *The Female Gothic*, ed. Juliann E. Fleenor, Montreal: Eden Press, 1983, 207–223.

Wollstonecraft, Mary, *A Vindication of the Rights of Men with A Vindication of the Rights of Woman and Hints*, ed. Sylvana Tomaselli, Cambridge: Cambridge University Press, 1995.

Wood, Thomas, *An Institute of the Laws of England: or, the Laws of England in their Natural Order, According to Common Use*, London, 1720.

Yolton, John, *Thinking Matter: Materialism in Eighteenth-Century Britain*, Minneapolis: University of Minnesota Press, 1983.

Zimmerman, Everett, *Defoe and the Novel*, Berkeley: University of California Press, 1975.

Index